# Books and Bibliophiles

## Studies in honour of Paul Auchterlonie on the Bio-Bibliography of thc Muslim World

edited by

Robert Gleave

Gibb Memorial Trust
2014

Published by

The E. J. W. Gibb Memorial Trust





ISBN Hardcover edition: 978-1-909724-40-2
ISBN Digital edition: 978-1-909724-41-9

A CIP record for this book is available from the British Library

Further details of the E. J. Gibb Memorial Trust and its publications
are available at the Trust's website

www.gibbtrust.org

Printed in Great Britain by
Short Run Press
Exeter

# Contents

1. INTRODUCTION 1
   1.1 Studies in Bio-bibliography 1
   Robert Gleave (University of Exeter)
   1.2 Paul Auchterlonie: A memoir and a partially annotated bibliography 4
   Peter Colvin (SOAS)

PART 1: TEXTS, CONTEXTS AND TRANSMISSIONS IN THE MUSLIM WORLD

2. THE WRITINGS OF JAʿFAR AL-ṢĀDIQ 14
   Ronald P. Buckley (University of Manchester)
3. THE CREEDS OF AḤMAD IBN ḤANBAL 29
   3.1 The Creeds of Aḥmad Ibn Ḥanbal 29
   Saud Al-Sarhan (King Faisal Center for Research and Islamic Studies)
   3.2 A Response to Saud Al-Sarhan's *The Creeds of Aḥmad Ibn Ḥanbal* 45
   Christopher Melchert (University of Oxford)
4. SAYYID NIʿMATULLĀH AL-JAZĀʾIRĪ AND HIS (LITERARY) ANTHOLOGIES 51
   Sajjad H. Rizvi (University of Exeter)
5. MAJLIS READINGS IN THE GOLDEN AGE OF ISLAM: TEXT AND INTERTEXT 62
   Ian Richard Netton (University of Exeter)
6. INTELLECTUAL GOLD? OXFORD'S *BOOK OF CURIOSITIES* AND ITS IMPORTANCE FOR RESEARCH ON THE MIDDLE EAST AND ISLAMIC WORLD 79
   Lesley Forbes (University of Oxford)
7. TRANSLATIONS OF NAGUIB MAHFOUZ IN ENGLISH 89
   Rasheed El-Enany (University of Exeter)

PART 2: TEXTS, CONTEXTS AND TRANSMISSIONS IN THE WEST

8. THE LURE OF THE NEAR EAST FOR EUROPEAN TRAVELLERS 96
   Derek Hopwood (University of Oxford)
9. CHARLES PELLAT AND THE *ENCYCLOPAEDIA OF ISLAM*: A PERSONAL REMINISCENCE 104
   C. Edmund Bosworth (University of Manchester)
10. ARABIC PRINTING IN SCOTLAND: AN HISTORICAL SKETCH 109
   Geoffrey Roper (University of Cambridge)

11. 'THE USUAL LEIDEN TYPES'. A COMPOSITOR'S PERSONAL ACCOUNT OF BRILL'S ARABIC PRINTING IN THE LATE 19TH AND EARLY 20TH CENTURY 119
Arnoud Vrolijk (University of Leiden)

12. L'ORGANISATION DES COLLECTIONS ORIENTALES Ã LA BIBLIOTHÈQUE NATIONALE DE FRANCE 133
Sara Yontan Musnik (Bibliothèque nationale de France)

13. SOME ARABIC TEXTBOOKS FROM KERALA 141
Jan Just Witkam (University of Leiden)

# 1

# Introduction

## 1.1 STUDIES IN BIO-BIBLIOGRAPHY

*Robert Gleave*

The studies collected in this volume come in two categories. First, there are bio-bibliographical studies of Middle Eastern and Muslim literature, in which contributors examine texts and their interrelations in a series of discrete studies. In the second section, the focus is on the advancement of the study of this literary heritage outside of the Muslim world, primarily in Western Europe. The two sections reflect, to an extent, the interests of Paul Auchterlonie, to whom we dedicate this collection of studies. He has engaged himself in the study of bio-bibliography in the Muslim world, whilst at the same time developing resources for its study by present and future generations of researchers. In addition to these activities, Paul has also made a major contribution to the development of the infrastructure of Middle East and Islamic Studies librarianship in the UK – an activity no less important than the actual development of resources for study. At this time, in the second decade of the twenty-first century, subject specialist librarians are an increasingly rare breed. Those that survive need a national and international context in which to develop their work. Peter Colvin in the second part of this introductory chapter, describes Paul's contribution to MELCOM and MELCOM International. Through his part in the development of these organisations, Paul has aided in the construction of a crucial support mechanism and pressure group for dedicated research resources for Islamic and Middle East Studies. This, as much as his day-to-day librarian work in Exeter, and his own publications in bio-bibliography, forms part of his legacy to the subject area when he retired in 2011.

In the first section, pressing intellectual questions run through the various contributions which form central concerns of the bio-bibiliographer. The first of these is the vexed question of 'authorship'; extant books, tracts or reports are attributed to particular authors, but their content, at times, seems to indicate an alternative author. This suspicion of 'attribution of authorship' primarily emerges because of a disjuncture between the literary item itself and what we know of the intellectual context of the supposed author (as is the case with Al-Sarhan's assessment of some of Aḥmad b. Ḥanbal's creeds [Chapter 3.1]). But a suspicion of attribution can also develop from our construction of a particular personality for the author, and finding that a particular work seems out of kilter with that construction. This also forms part of Al-Sarhan's methodology, which is then critically analysed by Melchert

[Chapter 3.2]; but it also creeps into Buckley's catalogue of the works attributed to Jaʿfar al-Ṣādiq [Chapter 2]. This creation of an authorial personality, against which works can be assessed and evaluated, forms the basis for Rizvi's account of the literary activity of Sayyid Niʿmatallāh al-Jazāʾirī [Chapter 3]. In both chapters, an individual's literary output is presented against the background of a developing, controlling author or compiler, whose agency creates the literary product. Both Rizvi and Buckley recognise that this creative act is not ex nihilo, but synthetic as authors collate and collect fragments and influences from their immediate context and various literary traditions. The pitfalls of relying too heavily on individual authorship are exemplified by Netton's piece, in which the literary form of the 'Arabic Symposium' found in Masʿūdī's *Murūj al-Dhahab* is understood as a continuation and adaptation of pre-Islamic (specifically Greek) literary forms, in which the description of the particular present context is controlled not only by the author's original contribution, but also by the heritage on which the author draws [Chapter 5]. In contrast to these themes, and perhaps in complement to them, Lesley Forbes presents the academic finding of the study of an authorless (or rather, anonymous) literary artefact, the *Kitāb Gharāʾib al-funūn wa-mulaḥ al-ʿuyūn* [Chapter 6]. Her record of the analysis of the provenance, dating and originality of the *Kitāb Gharāʾib al-funūn* is, one might argue, an example of how critical examination of Islamicate and Arabic literature relies on the methodologies explored in the other chapters in this first section. This piece, together with the others in this section, are examples of how bio-bibliography is reliant on the resources devised and maintained by librarians. Finally, Rasheed El-Enany, who analyses the sucecsses and failures (primarly the latter) of the translations of the novels of Mahfouz [Chapter 7]. Some translators misunderstood Mahfouz's work; others have understood the works, but produced translations which fail to entertain as reading a novel should. It is, of course, difficult to achieve both in a single translation, and few have managed it with respect to Mahfouz's voluminous production.

The second section is a little more eclectic. Here we have a set of studies which describe the processes and individuals within the development of the western study of the Islamicate world. Hopwood [Chapter 8] examines the manner in which the 'East' became a subject of study and fascination for European travellers, many of whom went on to make major contributions to the early development of what is today called 'Middle Eastern Studies'. Similarly, Bosworth [Chapter 9] recounts a personal recollection of one of the major contributors to the academic study of the Muslim world in the modern period, Charles Pellat. Pellat, to an extent, continues the tradition of the individual's contact between the European and the Middle East – that of the fusion of traveller, academic and diplomat. The excitement and exoticism engendered by these contacts with the Muslim world prompted the development of a European publishing industry in Middle Eastern literatures. For this to succeed, an infrastructure was needed. Arabic printing and publishing by western publishers ran alongside book production in the Islamic world, and is an interesting case study of how skills and techniques within the Muslim world were transferred to Western Europe through individual contacts and projects. Roper's study of Arabic printing in Scotland [Chapter 10] gives an overview of how the publishing industry sought to serve the needs of a burgeoning academic community, interested in the linguistic, literary and cultural aspects of the Muslim world.

The technical challenge of producing Arabic script was taken on by a few brave publishers in Europe, foremost amongst these was the Dutch publishing company E.J. Brill, whose experimentation with Arabic types, and production of editions of Arabic literary works, form the subject of Vrolijk's study [Chapter 11]. The final two chapters concern the central tasks of a librarian: the acquisition and cataloguing of material. Yonatan [Chapter 12] presents a history of the oriental collection in the Biblioteque Nationale de France in Paris. The history of the study of the Muslim world in western Europe is, to an extent, mirrored in the history of the collections of (primarily) Arabic, Persian and Turkish manuscripts. The assembling and organising these collections was a topic of study in itself for the early pioneers of the subject area. They were rarely simply academic 'users' of the collections; they contributed greatly to their development and organisation. This was possible in the period before the division of tasks in higher education became the norm and librarians and academics became responsible to different elements of a developing managerial structure. Jan Just Witkam [Chapter 13], himself a major contributor to bio-bibliography of the Muslim world, presents an unusual collection of Arabic works produced outside of the Arab world. The production of Muslim literature in Arabic in the non-Arab Muslim world is a neglected field of study of Islamicists, and this chapter demonstrates the rich possibilities for research in this area.

The diverse studies in this volume, then, recount the production, understanding and organisation of Muslim literature, both in the Muslim world and Western Europe. Research becomes possible when there are resources on which to draw. These resources are maintained through the dedication of librarians across the subject areas. These colleagues are rarely made the focus of attention, scholarly or otherwise, and yet the health and vitality of a subject area such as Middle Eastern and Islamic Studies depends on their engagement and endeavours. Their contribution is implicit in all Middle Eastern scholarship of the modern period. Paul Auchterlonie's colleagues in Exeter through the years owe him a special note of gratitude. Primarily through his efforts, a well-organised and accessible collection, with rich and comprehensive coverage, has been available for a constant stream of academics and researchers. We wish him, and his wife Mizzi, many happy years of retirement together.

# 1.2 PAUL AUCHTERLONIE: A MEMOIR AND A PARTIALLY ANNOTATED BIBLIOGRAPHY

*Peter Colvin*

I first met Paul Auchterlonie when we both worked in SOAS Library from 1970 to 1971. He began acquiring Arabic cataloguing skills under the exacting supervision of Geoffrey Schofield, the Assistant Librarian for the Islamic Near and Middle East Section. Paul had just graduated from Oxford where he had taken a degree in Arabic, and had by chance heard about the possibility of being a SCONUL scholarship library student at a party in his final year. The Librarian of SOAS at that time was James Pearson. Known to friends and colleagues as Jim, Pearson was enormously influential in all the areas of Asian and African librarianship. His greatest memorial is SOAS Library, which he guided through its most important era of expansion, up to the point in 1973 at which it occupied its purpose built premises. His own particular area of interest was the Middle East and he founded the indispensable reference work *Index Islamicus.*

Paul and I both left SOAS at the same time and spent 1971 to 1972 together at UCL Library School.

After gaining a diploma in Library Science Paul immediately found a job worthy of his mettle at Lancaster University, where Departments of Arabic and Islamic studies had been recently established, and he worked there from 1972–1981, setting up a collection of Arabic and Islamic books to support these subjects. In 1981 he moved to Exeter where he became the third Arabist librarian after Ian Netton and Parvine Foroughi, and he worked as the subject Librarian for Middle Eastern and Islamic Studies from then until 2007. He was Librarian in charge of the Old Library 1994–2009, and a member of the Library's Senior Management Group from 1996 to 2006. He retired from the University Library in 2011 and was then appointed as an Honorary University Fellow in the Institute of Arab and Islamic Studies, where he continued his researches into North African captivity narratives and relations between the South-West of England and the Middle East.

Paul has been an extremely effective specialist librarian in his two posts, and the extent of the appreciation of his work by his colleagues at Exeter is evident from the production of this festschrift. Researching this article threw up the fact that Paul edited the Library's newsletter, *The Line, Library and Information News at Exeter* for a number of years, unexpected further proof of his indefatigability. However, he has also has been very influential in the wider field of Middle Eastern librarianship, both in the United Kingdom and abroad. The body through which Paul has exerted his influence has mainly been MELCOM, The Middle East Libraries Committee. To give the context of his wider career, it will be necessary to give a short account of this body and its history.

## *MELCOM (Middle East Libraries Committee)*

If J. Alfred Prufrock's life was measured out in coffee spoons, the lives of many British Middle Eastern specialist librarians in the last forty years have been measured out in MELCOM meetings. MELCOM emerged from a meeting held in Cambridge on June 7th, 1967. Professor Sergeant of Cambridge University was elected as its first chair and Derek Hopwood of St Antony's was the first secretary. The latter guided MELCOM through its early years, remaining Secretary for eleven years, and then Chairman for the following eight. Hayter's report which led to the expansion of area studies in the 1970's had not yet appeared. Jim Pearson, as the Librarian of SOAS, was an important driving force behind the foundation of the body, but his work as the Librarian of SOAS and his involvement in the other area library groups coming into existence probably prevented him from becoming the Chairman, although he was an important presence during its first period. The Committee's first act was to define its area of interest as being Arab countries plus Turkey and Iran, but excluding Israel, and it was to be concerned with 'modern' studies.

In its second meeting in Durham later the same year it agreed on an area specialisation scheme for the member libraries. Another important field that it soon entered was heralded with a Conference on Middle Eastern Bibliography held in Cambridge in 1969. This was in response to a request by Monash University for a list of the works that would be required to set up an Islamic Institute, and led to the compilation of *Middle East and Islam: a bibliographical introduction.*[1]

Throughout it existence MELCOM has remained an informal organisation with no specific membership requirements beyond the wish to participate, and no membership fee, and has attempted to caste its net as wide as possible to include academics, booksellers, publishers as well as librarians in all kinds of libraries united by an interest in the area. It has remained small enough to retain something of the atmosphere of a club, with an awareness of the importance of personal contacts, and has been important in creating a feeling of solidarity and awareness among its members by its policy of holdings its meetings all over the country wherever invited.

Paul first appears in the Minutes of MELCOM at its 10th Meeting held at Manchester in November 1972 as the Arabic specialist Librarian at Lancaster University, and he committed Lancaster to collect material on Kuwait as its part of the Area specialisation scheme. Two other items of significance for the future were discussed at this meeting. One was the "possibility of holding future meetings in Europe" and "Mr Pearson suggested that at future meetings members might report on work they were undertaking".

The following two meetings were held at Lancaster University. At the first "Mr Auchterlonie reported on the initial steps that had been taken to establish a basic library to service the institutes of Arabic and Islamic studies. There were now approximately 2500 titles in the Library". The creation of BRISMES was also announced. At the second, under an item entitled Union list of Arabic periodicals "Mr Auchterlonie produced a sample of the list he was working on" and, an omen of what was to come, "Mr Auchterlonie described briefly the computerization of the circulation system at Lancaster University".

---

[1] Derek Hopwood and Diana Grimwood-Jones (eds), *Middle East and Islam: a bibliographical introduction* (Zug, 1972), revised edition Diana Grimwood-Jones (ed.), (Zug, 1979).

At the 20th Meeting in July 1978 Derek Hopwood was President and Paul Auchterlonie Acting secretary, and during the meeting Paul was elected as secretary in place of Derek Hopwood.

At the 22nd Meeting in the following year Paul reported on the Joint MELCOM-France Conference held in March in Aix of that year which he had convened. This was the first of a series of annual conferences held in the UK, Western Europe and the Middle East and North Africa that for the first few years was organised by MELCOM and a local host.

At the 36th Meeting in SOAS 1986 Paul was elected as the next Chairman and he chaired the 37th Meeting at Cambridge in December1986. At the 38th Meeting at Exeter 1987 it was announced that MELCOM International had been established to run the International Conferences which had steadily grown, and the parent body would be called MELCOM UK.

At the 43rd Meeting in SOAS in January 1990 Paul resigned from the Chair and Geoffrey Roper was voted as his successor. Paul then became treasurer. Geoffrey Roper, who had, through his own efforts, succeeded in keeping *Index islamicus* alive after taking over the editorship from Jim Pearson, had the happy idea of instituting the annual James Pearson lectures, and arranged for the family to give an annual subvention towards its costs. It was natural that it was Paul who delivered the first Pearson lecture entitled *Victorian Periodicals and the Middle East* on 5th July 2000 in Cambridge.

At the 54th Meeting at Durham in July 1995 Paul was again voted in as Chair, and as one of his first acts updated the method of communications of both MELCOM UK and MELCOM International by instituting an online discussion list called lis-middle-east. He continued as Chair until the 81st Meeting in SOAS in January 2009 when he resigned.

Along with the other long serving Secretary and Chairman, Derek Hopwood, Paul Auchterlonie has been the backbone of MELCOM throughout his professional career. He has occupied every official position in the Committee, having been Treasurer for five years from 1990–1995, Secretary for eight years from 1978–1986, and Chair for a total of eighteen years from 1986–1990, and again from 1995–2009.

He has also been prominent in the body to which MELCOM reported from 1979, and which has been entitled among other things SCONUL, the Advisory Committee on Oriental Materials. He served on the Steering Committee for the *Mapping Asia Project* from 2001–2003. He has also been a Fellow of the British Society for Middle Eastern Studies, and was the Bibliographical Book Review Editor of the Society's *Bulletin* from 1976–1980.

## PUBLICATIONS

A search of the online *Index Islamicus* produces a list of some of 63 items under Paul's name. Separate articles and books number around 20 items, which means that in addition to these, Paul has 40 or more book reviews to his credit.

The number of Paul's publications would be commendable for a university lecturer, but for a regional specialist working in the conditions of modern academic libraries it is extraordinary. Paul's career has spanned the radical and revolutionary technological changes introduced by digitisation and the World Wide Web, and the transformations that these have wrought in Libraries. The developments that come in an endless stream are almost immediately taken for granted, and the pains that led to their birth, are as quickly forgotten. When Paul first became Secretary of MELCOM in 1978, the benefits of reliable and fast Xerox machines were only beginning to be felt, and Agendas and Minutes had to be sent out in individual envelopes. In 2009 the same documents are sent out on lis-middle-east, and are picked up and broadcast around North America on the list of it sister organisation MELA on the night of the same day. Cataloguing was carried out by typing records onto slips of paper or cards, which were reproduced by a long forgotten mechanical process onto catalogue cards. Most catalogue entries are now downloaded from data bases, and since the invention of Unicode also include original scripts for most Middle Eastern languages. The process of accommodating and adjusting to these changes has created new roles for librarians that have left very little time for other activities. However these changes have come at a very great cost. Library systems which have to be updated or changed every few years are enormously expensive, as are the subscriptions to electronic journals. Libraries have become information centres, and Chief Librarians have become managers. The emphasis on scholarly specialisation and painstaking accuracy have given way to an emphasis on process rather than content, and currently the managerial re-organisation of librarians into teams, all overshadowed by the constant need to reduce costs.

As long as I have known him Paul has always been a great enthusiast, with boundless energy to pursue his interests. When he was working in SOAS he was greatly interested in films, and in those days before videos and DVDs was greatly excited by the possibilities available in London, with the National Film Theatre and several independent cinemas. He came to work on one Monday looking tired, as the result of a weekend during which he had seen five or six films in a variety of cinemas. At the same time Paul has also has the knack of turning what catches his attention into interesting articles of academic importance. Examples of this are his 2000 article ‘A Turk of the West: the Career of Sir Edgar Vincent in Egypt and the Ottoman Empire’ and his 2006 paper ‘A British Family in the Middle East: the Barkers of Aleppo, Smyrna and Alexandria as revealed by the Barker Papers’, which was based on the papers of a business man who had lived and worked in Egypt, which were presented to Exeter University Library. With regard to the latter, what sounds potentially rather dry and dull was turned into a fascinating talk that enlivened the afternoon of the third day of a MELCOM International Conference in Istanbul, where it was first presented, and is an exemplary model of the social history that can be created from a small family archive.

Paul’s first published work was the union catalogue of Arabic periodicals in UK Libraries that he compiled in cooperation with Yasin Safadi in 1977. In the days before the internet and e-mail, this involved him in much travel up and down the country extracting the information on Libraries’ holdings with considerable difficulty, and in some cases establishing the holdings himself. It also initiated a series of union catalogues that MELCOM published that eventually included Iranian and Turkic languages. Many of Paul’s publications are contributions to edited collections of works published by MELCOM, which were often also edited by him. The word editor here not only covers the thankless task of inducing contributors to send in their contributions on time, but in those days before word processors, the long winded process of checking proofs and seeing works through the press.

Paul published an important study in bibliometrics in 1986 entitled ‘The Coverage and Distribution of Modern Arabic Books in British Libraries’, which he revisited in 2005 in

'The acquisition of Arabic books by British libraries 20 years on: progress or decline?' These were studies on the successes and failures of the MELCOM Area specialisation scheme, and overall its conclusions do not make particularly cheerful reading. British government funding for Middle Eastern and Islamic studies has been somewhat wayward and capricious, rising with the periodical crises in the international situation, only to fall again when they pass. This has only partially been offset by the massive funds that oil has brought to the area, a tiny proportion of which has found itself into the coffers of some lucky universities thanks to the generosity of individual rulers. Even this tiny proportion has had an effect out of all proportion on British Universities, with professorial chairs and institutes being endowed as a result. Paul's own Library of Exeter University has benefited in this way, with its magnificent building that houses the Institute of Arab and Islamic Studies and the Arab World Documentation Unit. The Library has been able to carry on fulfilling its MELCOM role of specialist collection for the Gulf, but many other Libraries in the scheme have been unable to do so. Paul found special problems in gathering data for his two studies of Arabic book acquisition in the U.K. because of very poor bibliographical control of the massively increased output of publishing in the Arab world in the Arab World. He has created some methodological innovations, especially in the ways of estimating the percentage of academically valuable works of the total output of some Arabic countries for which there is comparatively little hard data to go on.

Towards the end of his career Paul has made a very important contribution to Islamic studies in this country, which is already bearing fruit. Terrorist bombs in London and wars in Iraq and Afghanistan have persuaded the British Government of the importance of studying Islam, and this has filtered down into funding for the digitisation of materials for such studies. In late 2007 JISC issued a call for bids for a project which would give recommendations on which materials in Islamic studies should be digitised. Paul with Ahmed Abu-Zayed and other colleagues at Exeter University formed a team which succeeded with its bid and went on to produce a report which will be a model for similar surveys in the future. Once again it was necessary to develop new methodologies which included an online survey of academics, a survey of existing databases, and a workshop of librarians and others. Its report has been issued as DigiIslam in 2008 and had been included in the bibliography under its URL. In March of 2009 JISC has issued an invitation for bids for a sizeable amount of money being made available for digitising projects, and Paul's continuing influence in Middle Eastern Librarianship in this country is assured, even when he finally begins his well earned retirement from the profession.

## PUBLICATIONS

### a) Books

1977

(with Y.H. Safadi), *Union Catalogue of Arabic Serials and Newspapers in British Libraries* (London), p. xvi, 146.

1987

*Arabic Biographical Dictionaries: a Summary Guide and Bibliography* (Durham), p. 16.

1998

*Yemen. Revised Edition. (World Bibliographical Series)* (Oxford and Santa Barbara) p. xxii, 348.

2012

*Encountering Islam: Joseph Pitts: An English Slave in 17th Century Algiers and Mecca: a critical edition, with biographical introduction and notes, of Joseph Pitts of Exeter's A Faithful Account of the Religion and Manners of the Mahometans*, 1731 London. p. xiv, 354pp., ill.

### b) Editions

1982

*Collections in British Libraries on Middle Eastern and Islamic Studies* (Durham), p. 99.

1986

*Middle East and Islam: a Bibliographical Introduction, 1977–1983* (Zug), p. vii, 244.

1990

*Introductory Guide to Middle Eastern and Islamic Bibliography* (Oxford), p. v, 84 p.

### c) Articles

1976

'British Books on Islam and the Muslim World since 1970' in *British Book News*, Summer, p. 397–405.

1977

'Recent Publications from Italy on the Middle East' in *Bulletin/British Society for Middle Eastern Studies* 4, p. 57–60.

'The Arabic serials held by the Institute of Development Studies Library (University of Sussex)' in *Bulletin/British Society for Middle Eastern Studies* 4, p. 102–111.

'Arabic Grammars' in *Arab Islamic Bibliography*, ed. D. Grimwood-Jones et al. (Hassocks, Sussex), p. 70–77.

'Middle Eastern Libraries' in *Arab Islamic Bibliography*, ed. D. Grimwood-Jones et al. (Hassocks, Sussex), p. 235–65.

1981

'A Guide to Cairo Bookshops and the Cairo International Book Fair' in *Bulletin/British Society for Middle Eastern Studies* 8, i, p. 51–9.

'British Library Collections on Islam and the Muslim World and some Problems of Acquisition' in *New Books Quarterly on Islam and the Muslim World* 1, ii, p. 29–37.

1982

'The Middle East Libraries Committee' in P. Auchterlonie (ed.), *Collections in British Libraries on Middle Eastern and Islamic studies* (1982): 19–22.

'The problems faced by Lancaster University when establishing a new library in Arabic and Islamic studies' in P. Auchterlonie (ed.), *Collections in British Libraries on Middle Eastern and Islamic studies* (1982): 81–88.

'The role of the librarian in Middle Eastern Studies' in P. Auchterlonie (ed.), *Collections in British Libraries on Middle Eastern and Islamic studies* (1982): 91–98.

1983

'Reader Instruction in Middle Eastern Studies' in *Bulletin/British Society for Middle Eastern Studies* 10, p. 153–7.

'Muslim Geographers and Travellers to Iran, 7–15th Centuries' in *Bibliographical Guide to Iran*, ed. L.P. Elwell-Sutton (Hassocks, Sussex), p. 134–42.

1986

'Some Western Views of the Arab Gulf' in *Arabia and the Gulf*, ed. I.R. Netton (London), p. 43–56.

'The Development of Arabic Studies in Britain' in *Arabic Resources*, ed. D. Burnett (London), p. 1–10.

'The Coverage and Distribution of Modern Arabic Books in British Libraries' in *Arabic Resources*, ed. D. Burnett (London), p. 121–32.

'Oriental, Islamic and Middle Eastern Studies' in *Middle East and Islam: a Bibliographical Introduction, 1977–1983*, ed. P. Auchterlonie (Zug), p. 21–26.

'Islamic law' in *Middle East and Islam: a Bibliographical Introduction, 1977–1983*, ed. P. Auchterlonie (Zug), p. 69–71.

'Islamic theology' in *Middle East and Islam: a Bibliographical Introduction, 1977–1983*, ed. P. Auchterlonie (Zug) p. 72–74.

'Iran' in *Middle East and Islam: a Bibliographical Introduction, 1977–1983*, ed. P. Auchterlonie (Zug), p. 149–154.

1990

'Bibliographies' in *Introductory Guide to Middle Eastern and Islamic Bibliography*, ed. P. Auchterlonie (Oxford), p. 1–11.

'Reference works' in *Introductory Guide to Middle Eastern and Islamic Bibliography*, ed. P. Auchterlonie (Oxford), p. 12–19.

'Encyclopedias' in *Introductory Guide to Middle Eastern and Islamic Bibliography*, ed. P. Auchterlonie (Oxford), p. 40–44.

'Biographical dictionaries' in *Introductory Guide to Middle Eastern and Islamic Bibliography*, ed. P. Auchterlonie (Oxford), p. 45–50.

2000

'A Turk of the West: the Career of Sir Edgar Vincent in Egypt and the Ottoman Empire' in *British Journal of Middle Eastern Studies* 28, p. 49–67.

2001

'From the Eastern Question to the Death of General Gordon: Representations of the Middle East in the Victorian Periodical Press, 1876–1885' in *British Journal of Middle Eastern Studies* 28, p. 5–24 (Originally given as the first James D. Pearson Memorial Lecture).

2004

'Historians and the Arabic Biographical Dictionary: Some New Approaches' in *Islamic Reflections, Arabic Musings: Studies in Honour of Professor Alan Jones*. ed. R.G. Hoyland and P.F. Kennedy (Cambridge), p. 186–200.

2005

'The Acquisition of Arabic Books by British Libraries Twenty Years on: Progress or Decline?' *Library Collections, Acquisitions and Technical Services* 29, p. 140–8.

2011

'Joseph Pitts: Exeter's first Orientalist?', *Rivista Orientale*, Vol. 91 Issue ii, 2011, p. 171–180.

2012

'English captivity narratives as sources of information in the Ottoman period1 in *Actes du Symposium international: le Livre. La Roumanie*. L'Europe. 4ème édition, 20–23 Septembre 2011 / Bibliothèque Métropolitaine de Bucarest. Tome III: Troisième section – Latinité orientale. Textes réunis et présentés par Martin Hauser, Ioana Feodorov, Nicholas V. Sekunda, Adrian George Dumitru: Editura Biblioteca Bucureştilor, Bucharest p. 138–149, 2012.

### *d) Reports*

*Review of User Requirements for Digitised Resources in Islamic Studies (commonly known as the DigiIslam Report)*. Published online by the Joint Information Systems Committee (JISC), 2008. http://projects.exeter.ac.uk.digiIslam

# PART 1

# TEXTS, CONTEXTS AND TRANSMISSIONS IN THE MUSLIM WORLD

# 2

# The Writings of Jaʿfar al-Ṣādiq

*Ronald P. Buckley*

No other Shiʿite Imam receives as much praise for their knowledge and erudition in all aspects of scientific, ethical and religious learning as does the sixth Imamī Imam Jaʿfar al-Ṣādiq (d. 148/765). The Imamī theologian al-Shaykh al-Mufīd (d. 413/1022) remarks that he was

> the cleverest, the greatest in stature, and the most venerated among the scholars and the common people. People took from him so much knowledge that men conveyed it to remote areas. He was known in all parts of the Islamic homeland. No other member of the Ahl al-Bayt was also remembered and praised by the historians and biographers as he was. Nor did the historians ever quantitatively report from anyone as they did from Abū ʿAbdallāh [al-Ṣādiq].[1]

As a result of this it is elsewhere stated that there were nine hundred men in the mosque of Kufa each of them saying "Jaʿfar b. Muḥammad [al-Ṣādiq] informed me."[2]

The present article deals with one aspect of al-Ṣādiq's alleged output, that is, the various letters, treatises and other writings attributed to him. The aim is not primarily to question this attribution, even though our comments are clearly relevant to this, but rather to provide an initial outline of the nature and scope of the corpus.

Al-Ṣādiq's prime significance within Imamī Shīʿism is as the main source of a specially Shīʿī collection of *ḥadīth* and attendant body of religio-legal norms, so much so that Imamī law is alternatively referred to as Jaʿfarī law. This is not the place to attempt to trace the development of al-Ṣādiq's status as *muḥaddith* and jurisconsult within early Shīʿī thought and his elevation to spokesman for his and subsequent generations of followers. Nonetheless, at the risk of being overly elliptical, we might remark that the circumstances which facilitated the rise of al-Ṣādiq were the contemporary florescence of concern with Islamic law and the elevation of *ḥadīth* as the vehicle for articulating that law, the accession of the Abbasids instead of the expected Shīʿī regime and the resulting disillusionment of many Shiʿite sympathisers which led to zealous efforts to define a specifically Shīʿī body of law and

---

[1] Shaykh al-Mufid, *Kitāb al-Irshād: The Book of Guidance into the Twelve Imams* (translated by I.K.A. Howard: New York, 1981), p. 270.

[2] ʿUmar b. Muḥammad al-Kashshī, *Akhbār Maʿrifat al-Rijāl* (Mashhad, 1970), p. 447. See also al-Najāshī, *Kitāb al-Rijāl* (Tehran, n.d.), p. 31.

doctrine in contradistinction to that of the rulers. There are doubtless a number of contributory factors as to why, amongst all the other members of the family of ʿAlī b. Abī Ṭālib, it fell to al-Ṣādiq to be the mouthpiece of Shīʿī elaborations. These perhaps include the usurpation of the line of Muḥammad b. al-Ḥanafiyya by the Abbasids who claimed that Muḥammad's son Abū Hāshim had passed the Imamate on to them, the decimation of the line of al-Ḥasan b. ʿAlī by the Abbasid caliph al-Manṣūr during the revolt of Muḥammad al-Nafs al-Zakiyya, and the supporters of Zayd b. ʿAlī following their own particular path. Perhaps the most crucial factor, however, was that upon the accession of the Abbasids al-Ṣādiq was the only member of the family to concern himself with the elaboration of law and doctrine. Moreover, al-Ṣādiq's father Muḥammad al-Bāqir also appears to have had a reputation as a legal scholar and source of *ḥadīth*, this prestige perhaps being inherited by his son al-Ṣādiq.

Although at the time there was no generally agreed doctrine on the nature of the Imam and dissenting voices were raised to deny him any infallibility, nevertheless, the major bodies of opinion within early Shīʿī thought eventually concurred on this point, and every aspect of doctrine and law subsequently had to have the Imam's stamp of approval. The Imam *par excellence* was al-Ṣādiq and his status as authority was subsequently raised to a sublime degree. As noted above, al-Ṣādiq's significance lies particularly in his contributions to Shīʿī legal and doctrinal *ḥadīth*. This may be seen in that the four canonical collections of Shīʿī *ḥadīth* reveal an overwhelming preponderance of traditions on the authority of al-Ṣādiq. For example, in Ibn Bābūya's (d. 381/991) *Man lā yaḥḍuruhu al-faqīh* al-Ṣādiq is the authority for some 65% of the traditions concerning *ʿibādāt*, such as regards the *ḥajj*, the *ʿumra*, ablutions and prayer, and also for traditions relating to legal subjects, such as sales, the purchase of slaves, silent partnership, reclamation of lands, guarantees, *ḥudūd*, bloodmoney, judges, witnesses and so on. This may be compared with the percentage of traditions narrated by other Shiʿite authorities: the Prophet (7%), ʿAlī b. Abī Ṭālib (5%), Muḥammad al-Bāqir (15%) and ʿAlī al-Riḍā (5%), with al-Ḥasan b. ʿAlī, ʿAlī b. al-Ḥusayn and Mūsā b. Jaʿfar supplying the majority of the remainder.

There are, however, doubts regarding al-Ṣādiq's contribution in this field. These are partly fuelled by an examination of his place within Sunni *ḥadīth* collections and the nature of his traditions within that corpus. Al-Ṣādiq appears very infrequently as a transmitter of these traditions with the six canonical Sunnī works recording a total of only some eighty or ninety separate *ḥadīth* which feature him as an authority. In the light of the relatively small number of Sunnī traditions which feature al-Ṣādiq as relater, it might be argued that he was not a great repository of *ḥadīth*, at least that which purported to come from the Prophet, as had this been the case his name would surely appear more regularly among the many tens of thousands of traditions within the Sunnī collections. This conclusion is further corroborated by the *Muwaṭṭaʾ* of Mālik b. Anas (d. 179/795). Mālik was a contemporary of al-Ṣādiq and furthermore was a fellow Medinan. He was therefore able to meet with him and to receive from him any *ḥadīth* that were in his possession. However, the *Muwaṭṭaʾ* contains only ten traditions on the authority of al-Ṣādiq.

A further consideration which leads to some uncertainty about the authenticity of many of the Shīʿī traditions attributed to al-Ṣādiq is the fact that within Sunnī collections there is nothing in his *ḥadīth* of a strictly legal nature, such as sales, debts, manumission, legacies, contracts and so on. The Sunnī traditions on al-Sadiq's authority largely pertain to Islamic ritual; half of them relate to the pilgrimage, followed by prayer and ablutions and a miscellany of others including general ethical pronouncements. Indeed, of the ten traditions in Mālik's *Muwaṭṭa'*, six concern the pilgrimage. This is in stark contrast with the nature of Jaʿfarī *ḥadīth* in the Shīʿī compilations which, as mentioned above, account for the bulk of strictly legal traditions.

It might appear then, that al-Ṣādiq was not the transmitter of many of the Shīʿī traditions ascribed to him, but rather his name was appropriated as validating authority. This desire, or necessity, to cite al-Ṣādiq as authority is well illustrated in a long account provided by Imamī biographer al-Kashshī (d. c. 340/951) in his *Akhbār Maʿrifat al-Rijāl.* He relates that a group of *ḥadīth* collectors from Basra travelled to al-Ṣādiq in Medina to hear *ḥadīth* from him. When they arrived they recited some traditions on the authority of al-Ṣādiq in his presence but without, however, being aware of his identity. All the traditions were false, and when al-Ṣādiq asks them if they would doubt the *ḥadīth* if the originator (i.e. himself) were to tell them that it was fabricated, they reply that they would not.[3]

The position which al-Ṣādiq attained as validator of Shīʿī *ḥadīth* was translated into a role as legitimizing authority for a multitude of conflicting doctrinal statements and opinion. Thus, the heresiographer al-Shahrastānī (d. 548/1153) states that after al-Ṣādiq "the Shīʿa split up into groups, each wanting to spread their doctrines among their followers, so they ascribed them to al-Ṣādiq and connected them with him,"[4] the Imamī Shīʿī heresiographer al-Nawbakhtī (d. c. 310/929) relates that the extremist Shīʿī sect the Nāwūsiyya cite *ḥadīth* supporting their position from al-Ṣādiq,[5] and the Sunnī theologian and heresiographer ʿAbd al-Qāhir al-Baghdādī (d.429/1037) reports that a certain ʿAbd al-Karīm b. Abī al-ʿAwja was a Shiʿite sympathiser who

> had invented numerous traditions bearing *sanads* with which he deceived those who had no knowledge of deciding between false and true... It is he who led the Rawafid to abandon the inauguration of the fast of Ramadan with the coming of the new moon by means of a calculation which he provided for them. He ascribed this calculation to Jaʿfar al-Ṣādiq.[6]

The Andalusian Ibn Ḥazm (d.456/1064) relates a similar anecdote:

> It is said that when the Rawāfiḍ saw al-Jāḥiẓ writing many books and writing for every group, they said to him: "Write a book for us". He replied: "I don't see that you have any vagueness for me to put in order and deal with". So they said: "Then show us something we can adhere to". He said: "I don't see that you have any method except when you want to say something and claim it you say that it is what Jaʿfar al-Ṣādiq said. I can't see that you have anything else to rely on apart from this". So they adhered to their ignorance and stupidity in this disgraceful act which he led them to, and every time they wanted to invent an innovation and fabricate a lie they attributed it to Jaʿfar al-Ṣādiq.[7]

---

[3] al-Kashshī, *Akhbār Maʿrifat al-Rijāl*, pp. 393–7.

[4] Muhammad ibn Abd al-Karim al-Shahrastānī, *Muslim Sects and Divisions* (translated by A.K. Kazi and J.G. Flynn: London, 1984), p. 166.

[5] Al-Ḥasan b. Mūsā al-Nawbakhtī, *Firaq al-Shīʿa* (Istanbul, 1931), p. 57.

[6] Ibn Ṭāhir al-Baghdādī, *al-Fark Bain al-Firak Part II* (translated by Abraham S. Halkin: Philadelphia, 1978) vol. 2, p. 95.

[7] I. Friedlander (trans.), 'The Heterodoxies of the Shiites in the Presentation of Ibn Ḥazm', *Journal*

## AL-ṢĀDIQ AS AUTHOR

Once the notion of the ultimate authority of the Imam was established, all doctrine was to be based on his authority. Given the status of al-Ṣādiq in Shīʿī thought, it is no surprise that a great number of treatises and other writings are also attributed to him and carry his sanction.

Before proceeding to outline the nature of these works it is interesting to note that a number of Muslim scholars have expressed doubts concerning the attribution of at least some of them. Thus, Ibn al-Nadīm (d. 380/990) remarks that although it is alleged that al-Ṣādiq wrote *al-Ihlīlaja* (Myrobalan) this is disputed.[8] Ibn Kathīr also remarks:

> It is clear that the *Knowledge of Rhapsodomancy* (*rajaz*) and *Predications by the movements of the eye* and the *Twitching of the limbs* ascribed to Jaʿfar al-Ṣādiq should in fact be ascribed to Jaʿfar b. Muʿashshir. They make a mistake in ascribing it to al-Ṣādiq.[9]

Elsewhere, Muḥsin al-Amīn quotes Aḥmad b. ʿAlī al-Najāshī (d. 450/1058), the writer of the *Kitāb al-Rijāl*, as saying that he has only seen one work by al-Ṣādiq, this being called *Risāla ʿAbd allāh al-Najāshī*.[10] Amīn says, however, that this may be taken to mean this was the only work produced by al-Ṣādiq himself, and that the other writings are collections of his sayings compiled by those who related from him.[11] Amīn also mentions a number of scholars who consider that the *Miṣbāḥ al-Sharīʿa* is incorrectly attributed to al-Ṣādiq. For example, al-Majlisī says in his introduction to the *Biḥār al-Anwār* that its style and content is unlike that of the Imams.[12]

## THE WORKS

As to the nature of the writings attributed to al-Ṣādiq, he is said to have authored numerous letters and short tracts many of which are scattered in works of *tārīkh* and *ḥadīth*. A number of these are listed by Muhṣin al-Amīn in his *Aʿyān al-Shīʿa*.[13] For example, he mentions a letter written by al-Ṣādiq to his companions, his advice to ʿAbd allāh b. Jandab, his advice to Abū Jaʿfar Muḥammad b. Nuʿmān al-Aḥwal, his description of the love due to the family of the Prophet, his epistle against the Ṣūfīs, a large compilation of letters narrated to the alchemist Jābir b. Ḥayyān al-Kūfī and a treatise called *Taqsīm al-Ruʾyā* (The Categorisation of Dreams) which Amīn considers was a later compilation of al-Ṣādiq's thoughts on the subject.[14]

---

*of the American Oriental Society* 29 (1908) pp. 104–5.

[8] Ibn al-Nadīm, *The Fihrist*, (translated by B. Dodge, Chicago: 1997) p. 744. Also quoted in Ramaḍān Lāwand, *al-Imām al-Ṣādiq: ʿIlm wa ʿAqīda* (Beirut, 1960), p. 112.

[9] ʿImād al-Dīn Ibn Kathīr, *al-Bidāya wa al-Nihāya* (Beirut, 1966) vol. 1, p. 51.

[10] The *risāla* is available online on a number of web pages. See, for example, the website of the Imam al-Shīrāzī, viewed 3 April 2011, <http://www.alshirazi.com/compilations/patg/alsabeel/part3/2.htm>.

[11] Muḥsin al-Amīn, *Aʿyān al-Shīʿa*, (Beirut, 1980) vol. 4, p. 52.

[12] Ibid., vol. 4, p. 53.

[13] Ibid., vol. 4, pp. 52–6.

[14] This is perhaps identical to the collection of sayings attributed to al-Ṣādiq which comprise the

Among other works attributed to al-Ṣādiq there is an omen (*faʾl*) at the end of a manuscript of a Qurʾān copied in the 12th century AH,[15] and a request for a blessing (*istikhāra*, i.e. a prayer to God to ask for help in a choice that one has made) also ascribed to al-Ṣādiq at the end of another manuscript of the Qurʾān written in 915/1509.[16] Indeed, al-Ṣādiq is reputed to have made copies of the Qurʾān with his own hand. One of these is in the Topkapi library in Istanbul, although the entry in the catalogue remarks that the attribution is false as the manuscript dates from the 6th century AH (12th century CE).[17] Similarly, the Dār al-Kutub al-Ẓāhiriyya in Damascus has a handwritten copy of the Qurʾān also said to have been done by the Imam.[18]

A number of the more substantial works allegedly composed by al-Ṣādiq or transcriptions of his words are listed in Fuat Sezgin's *Geschichte des Arabischen Schrifttums*.[19] These are still extant in one form or another. Although the list cannot be claimed to be exhaustive, it provides a good illustration of the scope of the literature attributed to al-Ṣādiq and the problems involved in identifying the various texts. Clearly not all the titles refer to discrete works and it sometimes appears that manuscripts with the same or similar text differ as far as title, beginning and ascription are concerned. Only a detailed examination of the separate manuscripts will determine the relationship between them and therefore the true extent of the Jaʿfarī corpus.

The following is a list of the works along with any relevant information.

## 1. *Miṣbāḥ al-Sharīʿa wa-Miftāḥ al-Ḥaqīqa* (The Lamp of Law and the Key of Truth)

This is a compilation of religio-ethical sayings, the British Museum catalogue stating that it is "a collection of thoughts and precepts relating to the rules and duties of religious life, ascribed to Jaʿfar al-Ṣādiq". It is divided into numerous *bābs*, each beginning "al-Ṣādiq said..."[20] The treatise has been published under the same title.[21]

## 2. *Tafsīr al-Imam Jaʿfar al-Ṣādiq* (Interpretation of the Qurʾān)

The manuscript held by the Oriental Library in Bankipore is apparently the work of a certain Muḥammad b. Ibrāhīm b. Jaʿfar al-Nuʿmān (10th century CE) who reportedly based it on

*Tafsīr al-Alḥām lil-Imām al-Ṣādiq* (Beirut, 1421/2000).

15 *Fihrist Makhṭūṭāt Dār al-Kutub al-Ẓāhiriyya* (Damascus, 1984) vol. 1, p. 34.

16 Ibid., vol. 1, pp. 23–4.

17 H.F.E. Karatay, *Topkapi Sarayi Müzesi Kütübphanesi Arapça Yazmalar Katalozu* (Istanbul, 1962) vol. 1, p. 82.

18 *Fihrist Makhṭūṭāt Dār al-Kutub al-Ẓāhiriyya* (Damascus, 1984) vol. 1, p. 24.

19 Fuat Sezgin, *Geschichte des Arabischen Schrifttums* (Leiden, 1967) vol. 1, pp. 529–31. See this for the locations of all manuscripts.

20 C. Rieu, *Supplement to the Catalogue of Arabic Manuscripts in the British Museum* (London, 1894) p. 147.

21 *Miṣbāḥ al-Sharīʿa wa Miftāḥ al-Ḥaqīqa* (Beirut, 1983) published by *Miṣbāḥ al-Sharīʿa wa Miftāḥ al-Ḥaqīqa*. It has also been translated into English under the title *Lantern of the Path* by Shaykh Fadhlallah Haeri (Qum, n.d.) available online at http://www.al-islam.org/lantern-of-the-path. The English translation has also been published in London by Element Books Ltd.

the sayings of al-Ṣādiq. It is arranged according to the *sūras* of the Qurʾān, although the whole of the Qurʾān is not included, rather only those words which require explanation.[22]

A book with the same title was compiled by Khaḍir Muḥammad Nabhā and published in 2007 in Beirut by Dār al-Hādī. It is not know what relation, if any, this has with the above manuscript.

## 3. *Kitāb al-Jafr* (The Book of Jafr)

Regarding this celebrated work, Ibn Khaldūn (d. 808/1406) remarks:

> As a basis for forecasts specifically concerning dynasties, one uses the *Kitāb al-Jafr*. People claim that it contains information about all these things in the form of traditions or astrological predictions. They do not think beyond this, and they do not know its origin or its basis. You should know that the *Kitāb al-Jafr* had its origin in the fact that Hārūn b. Saʿīd al-ʿIjlī, the leader of the Zaydiyya, had a book which he related from Jaʿfar al-Ṣādiq. The book contained information as to what would happen to the family of Muḥammad in general and to certain members of it in particular. This information was given to al-Ṣādiq and to other members of the family as an act of divine grace and through the removal of the veil (*kashf*) which is bestowed on saints like them. The book was in the possession of al-Ṣādiq and was written on the skin of a small ox. Hārūn al-ʿIjlī transmitted it on his authority, wrote it down and called it *al-Jafr* after the skin upon which it had been recorded, because *jafr* means a small [lamb or camel]. This name came to be title they used for the book. It contained an interpretation of the Qurʾān and remarkable statements concerning its inner meaning transmitted on the authority of Jaʿfar al-Ṣādiq. The book has not come down through continuous transmission and is not known as a book as such. All that is known of it is some stray remarks unaccompanied by any proofs. If the ascription to Jaʿfar al-Ṣādiq is correct, the work would have the exceptional authority of al-Ṣādiq himself or of members of his family who received acts of divine grace. It is indeed true that Jaʿfar warned some of his relatives about events that would occur to them and these things happened as he had predicted.[23]

## 4. *Ikhtilāj al-Aʿḍāʾ* (The Twitching of Limbs)

This deals with the involuntary movements of certain parts of the body and conjectures from these the future of the individuals concerned. The prophesies are from al-Ṣādiq, the prophet Daniel, Alexander the Great and the Persian and Byzantine sages. The various parts of the body from the crown of the head to the toes are detailed along with the respective interpretations of the above people. One manuscript begins:

> This is the explanation behind the twitching of limbs from five points of view. Jaʿfar al-Ṣādiq said that the twitching of the crown of the head indicates distinction and good memory. The prophet Daniel said that it indicates acquiring wealth from travel. Alexander said that it indicates a high rank among people. The Persian sages said that it indicates travel and gains. The Byzantine sages said that it indicates distant travel and protection from harm.

---

[22] Muiniddin Nadwi, *Catalogue of the Arabic and Persian Manuscripts in the Oriental Public Library at Bankipore* (Calcutta, 1932) 18, 143–4.

[23] ʿAbd al-Raḥmān Ibn Khaldūn, *Tārīkh Ibn Khaldūn: Kitāb al-ʿIbar wa Dīwān al-Mubtadāʾ wa-l-Khabar* (Beirut, 1956) vol. 1, p. 394.

It concludes:

> Jaʿfar al-Ṣādiq said that the twitching of the middle toe of the left foot indicates receiving a noble deed in travel. Daniel said that something hateful will be uttered. Alexander said that the man will acquire wealth easily. The Persian sages said that it indicates benefit and happiness... But God knows best.[24]

Other manuscripts are also extant which deal with the same subject but in which al-Ṣādiq plays no part.[25]

Numerous Arabic web pages also relate al-Ṣādiq's interpretations of the involuntary movement of certain parts of the body.[26] The affected part is listed alongside its significance. For example, a twitching in the right side of the temple indicates that the owner will be very happy or that someone close to him will die; a twitching in the lower part of the right eyelid indicates that people will speak well of the owner; a twitching in the left thigh indicates that the owner will come to possess a riding animal; and a twitching in the right heel indicates that the owner will be relieved of a worry.

## 5. *Hayākil al-Nūr [al-Sabʿa]* (The Seven Temples of Light)

This is a treatise on mysticism described as "[a] collection of religious and devotional formulae, talismans andc., entitled *al-Hayākil al-Sabʿa*, ascribed to the Imam Jaʿfar al-Ṣādiq, beginning:-

> A treatise in which are the seven Temples and an explanation of their benefits, related on he authority of the Imam Jaʿfar al-Ṣādiq on his father on his grandfather the Amīr al-Muʾminīn ʿAlī b. Abī Ṭālib. ʿAlī said: 'The Prophet of God gave me these seven Temples. He used to seek God's assistance with them in all his affairs and undertakings and never stopped using them either at night or during the day.'"[27]

## 6. *Khawāṣṣ al-Qurʾān al-ʿAẓīm* (Special Properties of the Holy Qurʾān)

This is a work on talismans relating the benefits of all the *sūras* of the Qurʾān. The beginning of one copy of the manuscript is as follows:

> The Imam Abū ʿAbd Allāh Jaʿfar al-Ṣādiq b. Muḥammad b. ʿAlī b. Zayn al-ʿĀbidīn b. al-Ḥusayn the martyr b. ʿAlī b. Abī Ṭālib said, "Whoever writes down *sūrat al-Baqara* and attaches it to himself will be freed of all pains. If it is attached to an infant, the child will be freed of pains, will be easily weaned and will not fear reptiles, with God's permission. If it is attached to an epileptic, the epilepsy will leave him, with God's permission. This *sūra* has countless benefits.

[24] *Die Handschriften-Verzeichnisse der Königlichen Bibliothek zu Berlin* (Berlin, 1891) vol. 3, p. 527.

[25] See ibid., vol. 3, pp. 572–3.

[26] See, for example, Muntadā Ḥawzat al-Sayyida Khadīja, viewed 3 April 2011, <http://khdegah.3arabiyate.net/t299–topic>.

[27] E.G. Browne, *A Hand-list of the Muhammadan Manuscripts, including all those in the Arabic Character, preserved in the Library of the University of Cambridge* (Cambridge, 1900) pp. 246–7. Another partial copy of the manuscript dating from the 16th century CE is held in the Bibliothèque Nationale in Paris. See the *Catalogue des Manuscrits Arabes* (Paris, 1883–95) vol. 2, p. 725.

The end of the manuscript reads:

> Whoever recites *sūrat al-Fātiḥa* every hour will be forgiven all his sins, and whatever disease it is recited over will be cured, with God's permission.[28]

Another manuscript with an identical title in the same collection begins:

> [Take a] paper bag of musk and some rose water. Put these in a reed tube (*qaṣab rīḥī*) which has been cut before sunrise and hardened with wax. When this is attached to a child he will be safe from the devil and all accidents. *Sūrat al-Nisāʾ*: On the authority of Jaʿfar al-Ṣādiq, that whoever writes it down and leaves it in his house for forty nights...

The manuscript ends:

> *Sūrat al-Qāriʿa*: If it is written down and attached to someone who is not well provided for, God will provide for him.[29]

There is another copy of the manuscript in the Königlichen Library in Berlin. This one begins:

> *Sūrat al-Fātiḥa*: Jaʿfar al-Ṣādiq said that whoever writes it down on a gazelle skin with musk and saffron and attaches it to himself will have protection.[30]

Evidently dealing with the same general area as the *Khawāṣṣ al-Qurʾān* is a further manuscript attributed to al-Ṣādiq and also located in the Königlichen Library in Berlin. It is called *Mukhtaṣar Mashārif al-Anwār wa-Maṭāliʿ al-Asrār* (The Abridged Hills of Lights and the Ladders of Secrets). It begins:

> On the authority of Jaʿfar al-Ṣādiq. He said that whoever recites the *Fātiḥa* forty times over a cup of water and sprinkles the water over a feverish face...

The text also refers to several magic seals and the use of magic words and letters.[31]

### 7. *Manāfiʿ Suwar al-Qurʾān* (Benefits of the Verses of the Qurʾān)

A note in the catalogue of manuscript holdings of the Vatican City states that the *Manāfiʿ Suwar al-Qurʾān* is spuriously ascribed to al-Ṣādiq.[32]

Although Sezgin lists this as a separate title, it appears to be identical to the *Khawāṣṣ al-Qurʾān*, above. Indeed, a manuscript of the *Khawāṣṣ al-Qurʾān* held in the Dār al-Kutub al-Ẓāhiriyya in Damascus ends "this concludes the *manāfiʿ suwar al-Qurʾān al-ʿAẓīm*".[33]

---

28 *Fihrist Makhṭūṭāt Dār al-Kutub al-Ẓāhiriyya* (Damascus, 1984) vol. 2, p. 118.

29 Ibid., vol. 2, p. 119. A composite version of the above two manuscripts held in the Dār al-Kutub al-Ẓāhiriyya along with an introduction is available online at Shabkat al-Sirāj fī al-Ṭarīq ilā Allah, viewed 3 April 2011,<http://www.alseraj.net/maktaba/kotob/quran/kawas/arabic/products/magazine/olum-a/07/003.htm>.

30 *Königlichen Bibliothek*, vol. 3, p. 525.

31 Ibid., vol. 3, pp. 525–6.

32 G. Levi della Vida, *Elenco dei Manoscritti Arabi Islamici della Biblioteca Vaticana* (Vatican City, n.d.) p. 116.

33 *Fihrist Makhṭūṭāt Dār al-Kutub al-Ẓāhiriyya* (Damascus, 1984) vol. 2, p. 118.

## 8. *Asrār al-Waḥy* (Secrets of Revelation)

There is no information on the nature and contents of this text.

## 9. *al-Adilla ʿalā al-Khāliq waʾl-Tadbīr* (Proofs of the Creator and His Providence)

"Proofs of the existence of the Creator and the governance of the world by Divine reason, deduced from the facts observed in the nature of man, of animals, in the inorganic world, in the universe, etc. The treatise, as stated in the heading and in the preface, is directed against the doctrines of the materialists (*dahriyyūn*); but it is not a controversial work, either in form or in spirit. The contents are said to have been derived from the teachings of Jaʿfar al-Ṣādiq, the sixth Shīʿī Imam, to whom such theosophic and occultist productions are usually ascribed; he revealed all his wisdom to his disciple, al-Mufaḍḍal b. ʿUmar, the well-known early Shīʿī saint. The real author of the compilation and the date of the composition are not given."[34]

The manuscript begins:

> What al-Mufaḍḍal b. ʿUmar related on our master Jaʿfar b. Muḥammad al-Ṣādiq in replying to the materialists... Muḥammad b. Sinān said that al-Mufaḍḍal b. ʿUmar told him: "One day in the early evening I was sitting in the garden between the tomb and the pulpit..."[35]

Muḥsin al-Amīn refers to this under the title *Tawḥīd al-Mufaḍḍal*.[36] It is indeed identical to the following *Kitāb al-Tawḥīd wa-l-Ihlīlaja* and the *Kitāb fī Ithbāt al-Ṣāniʿ*.

## 10. *Kitāb al-Tawḥīd wa-l-Ihlīlaja* (Book of the Unity of God and Myrobalan)

This is the same as *al-Adilla ʿalā al-Khāliq wa-l-Tadbīr* above. The modern scholar Muḥammad al-Ḥusayn al-Muẓaffar states that *al-Tawḥīd* is also called *al-Ihlīlaja* because in it al-Ṣādiq has a discussion about myrobalan (*ihlīlaja*) with an Indian doctor. al-Ṣādiq's debate with the Indian arises in the context of al-Mufaḍḍal asking the Imam whether any people deny the existence of God and requesting that he refute their position.[37] Elsewhere, Muḥsin al-Amīn states that the *Kitāb al-Ihlīlaja* deals with a discussion between al-Ṣādiq and an Indian in which the Indian is converted to monotheism.[38]

## 11. *Kitāb fī Ithbāt al-Ṣāniʿ* (Book on the Proof of the Creator)

This is probably more or less identical to *al-Adilla ʿalā al-Khāliq waʾl-Tadbīr* and *Kitāb al-Tawḥīd wa-l-Ihlīlaja* above.

---

[34] Wladimir Ivanow, *Catalogue of the Arabic Manuscripts in the Collection of the Royal Asiatic Society of Bengal* (Calcutta, 1939) p. 422.

[35] Ibid.

[36] *Tawḥīd al-Mufaḍḍal* was published in Beirut by the Dār Iḥyāʾ al-Turāth al-ʿArabī in 2002. It is also available online at Shabakat al-Sirāj fī al-Ṭarīq ilā Allāh, viewed 3 April 2011, <http://www.alseraj.net/maktaba/kotob...edalmafzal.exe>.

[37] Muḥammad al-Ḥusayn al-Muẓaffar, *al-Imam Jaʿfar al-Ṣādiq*, available online at Shabakat al-Qalam al-Islāmiyya, viewed 3 April 2011, <http://al-qalam.net/vb/showthread.php?t=941>, p. 164.

[38] al-Amīn, *Aʿyān al-Shīʿa*, 4:53.

### 12. *As'ilat al-Nabī, sa'ala Rabbahu bihā Laylat al-Miʿrāj* (What the Prophet asked God on the Night of the Miʿrāj)

Many traditions on the Prophet's *isrā'* (night journey) and *miʿrāj* (ascension to the heavens) are related on the authority of al-Ṣādiq. For example, the *Tafsīr* of ʿAlī b. Ibrāhīm al-Qummī (d. c. 307/919), one of the oldest works of Imamī Shīʿī Qur'ānic exegesis, contains a long and very detailed account of the *isrā'* and the *miʿrāj* attributed to him.[39] The present text is probably something similar.

### 13. *Munāẓarat al-Ṣādiq fī Tafḍīl bayna Abī Bakr wa-ʿAlī* (al-Ṣādiq's Discussion on the Comparison between Abū Bakr and ʿAlī)

In this, al-Ṣādiq prefers Abū Bakr to ʿAlī. It is stated to be of dubious authenticity.[40]

### 14. *al-Adʿiya al-Usbūʿiyya* (Weekly Supplications)

This is evidently a collection of supplications attributed to al-Ṣādiq.[41] A distinctive aspect of Imamī religious practice is the extremely important role accorded to supplications, that is, special prayers directed to God to request all manner of assistance and protection. The Imamīs have compiled numerous collections of supplications which are traced back to the Prophet Muḥammad, ʿAlī b. Abī Ṭālib and the other Imams, and occasionally Fāṭima and some of the earlier prophets including Abraham, Solomon and Moses. But none of these features nearly as prominently as does as al-Ṣādiq. Some of al-Ṣādiq's supplications may be seen, for example, in the long section in al-Majlisī's *Biḥār al-anwār* entitled *Muʿjizātuhu wa-istijābat daʿawātihi* ([al-Ṣādiq's] Miracles and the Answering of his Supplications)[42] and in the section of Ibn Shahrāshūb's *Manāqib Āl Abī Ṭālib* called *Fī istijābat daʿawātihi ʿalayhi al-salām* (On the Answering of [al-Ṣādiq's] Supplications).[43]

### 15. *Duʿā' al-Jawshan* (Supplication of the Armour)

*The Catalogue des Manuscrits Arabes* of the Bibliothèque Nationale in Paris lists this text, written in Mecca in 1004/1596, under "The Lives of the Patriarchs and the Prophets."[44] As the title suggests, however, it is actually a well known supplication for protection. It consists of one hundred sections each of which contains ten of the names of God. It begins:

---

[39] ʿAlī b. Ibrāhīm al-Qummī, *Tafsīr al-Qummī* (Najaf, 1387 AH) vol. 2, pp. 3–14.

[40] See *Fihrist Makhṭūṭāt Dār al-Kutub al-Ẓāhiriyya* (Damascus, 1947) p. 82. The text has been published in 24 pages under the title *Munāẓarat Jafar b. Muḥammad al-Ṣādiq maʿa al-Rāfiḍī fī Tafḍīl bayna Abī Bakr wa-ʿAlī* (Riyad, 2004).

[41] For an example of such a collection see Bāqir Sharīf al-Qurashī, *al-Ṣaḥīfa al-Ṣādiqiyya* (Beirut, 1989); 296 pages and also available online at Shabkat al-Sirāj fī al-Ṭarīq ilā Allah, viewed 3 April 2011, <http://www.alseraj.net/maktaba/kotob/new/book/al-sahifa/fehrs1.htm>.

[42] Muḥammad Bāqir al-Majlisī, *Biḥār al-Anwār* (Beirut, 1983), vol. 47, pp. 63–161.

[43] Muḥammad b. ʿAlī b. Shahrāshūb, *Manāqib Āl Abī Ṭālib* (Najaf, 1956) vol. 3, pp. 357–60.

[44] *Catalogue des Manuscrits Arabes* (Paris: Bibliothèque Nationale, Departement des Manuscrits, 1883–95) vol. 2, p. 343.

> Allah, I beseech You in Your name: Allah, Most Merciful, Most Compassionate, Most Generous, Self-Subsisting, Greatest, Eternal, All-Knowing, Forbearing, Wise. Praise be to You. There is no god but You, the Granter of all Succour. Protect us from the Fire, O Lord.[45]

### 16. *Duʿāʾ* (Supplication)

This is another supplication, perhaps identical to the above *Duʿāʾ al-Jawshan.*

### 17. *Kitāb al-Ṣirāṭ* (Book of the Path)

This is attributed to the ubiquitous al-Mufaḍḍal b. ʿUmar who is said to have received it orally from al-Ṣādiq. It explains the mystical meaning of the word *ṣirāṭ* ('path') and several other terms including *qamīṣāt* ('covers/cases') and *hayākil* ('temples'). The treatise is apparently esoteric and only intelligible to those versed in such matters. The copy in the Bibliothèque Nationale in Paris dates from approximately 1206/1791.[46]

The text has been published under the title *Kitāb al-Ṣirāṭ al-Mansūb ilā al-Mufaḍḍal b. ʿUmar al-Juʿfī* (The Book of the Path attributed to al-Mufaḍḍal b. ʿUmar al-Juʿfī).[47] The publisher's notes state that the book consists of a collection of traditions narrated to al-Mufaḍḍal by al-Ṣādiq concerning knowledge of 'the path' (that is, the narrow bridge over which Muslims believe all people must pass on the Day of Judgement to enter Paradise) and how believers can avoid the fate of those who disbelieve. The book also throws some light on the doctrines of the Shiʿite sect of the Nuṣayriyya. It is said to be based on a single surviving manuscript.

### 18. *Ḥirz* (Amulet)

A *ḥirz* is an amulet or 'charm case' worn on a necklace and containing religious sayings and prayers thought to protect the wearer. Such prayers are attributed to all the Imamī Imams. The one often attributed to al-Ṣādiq is as follows:

> In the name of God, the Compassionate the Merciful. O Creator of creation. O Giver of sustenance. O Opener of the seed. O Initiator of the breath of life. He who raises the dead to life and causes the living to die. The Everlasting. The Eternal. The One who brings forth the plants. Do with me as is your Will and not mine. You are all-protecting and all-forgiving.[48]

### 19. *al-Ḥikam al-Jaʿfariyya* (The Maxims of Jaʿfar)

This is a collection of religio-ethical maxims. It was published in Beirut in 1957 by al-Maṭbaʿa al-Kāthūlīkiyya. An example from the text is:

---

[45] For an English translation of the *Duʿāʾ al-Jawshan* see Ahlul Bayt Digital Islamic Library Project, viewed 3 April 2011, <http://www.al-islam.org/masoom/writings/duas/jawshankabir.html>.

[46] Ibid., 1:277.

[47] *Kitāb al-Ṣirāṭ al-Mansūb ilā al-Mufaḍḍal b. ʿUmar al-Juʿfī* (Beirut, 2004); 283 pages.

[48] For the Arabic, see, for example, Myali.Net Forum, viewed 3 April 2011, <http://www.myali.net/vb/showthread.php?p=235245>.

> With caution comes safety and with haste comes regret; and whoever begins something at the wrong time will complete it at the wrong time.[49]

### 20. *Risālat al-Waṣāyā wa-al-Fuṣūl* (Treatise on Prose Passages and Divisions)

This is the same as the alternatively titled *Risāla fī ʿIlm al-Ṣināʿa wa-l-Ḥajar al-Mukarram* (Treatise on Alchemy and the Revered Stone). It concerns the Philosopher's Stone, an imagined transmuting agent of great potency which could transform base metals into gold and silver, and the liquid from which was thought to prolong life and cure illnesses. The present treatise is stated to have been written by al-Ṣādiq as an instruction for one of his sons.[50] It has been translated and published in German by Julius Ruska who refutes the attribution to al-Ṣādiq.[51]

### 21. *Risāla fī l-Kīmīyāʾ* (Treatise on Alchemy)

This is perhaps an identical or similar text to the above *Risāla fī ʿIlm al-Ṣināʿa wa-l-Ḥajar al-Mukarram*. A treatise with the title *Risāla fī l-Kīmīyāʾ* is occasionally attributed to the somewhat mysterious founder of Islamic alchemy, Jābir b. Ḥayyān, who is said to have belonged to the circle of al-Ṣādiq.

### 22. *Taʿrīf Tadbīr al-Ḥajar* (Instruction for the Preparation of the Stone)

This work is perhaps also closely related to the *Risāla fī ʿIlm al-Ṣināʿa wa-al-Ḥajar al-Mukarram*. Once again, the stone referred is the Philosopher's Stone.

### 23. *Risāla fī Faḍl al-Ḥajar wa-l-Mūsā* (Treatise on the Benefit of the Stone and the Razor)

Sezgin includes this in his chapter on alchemy.[52] It is another treatise on alchemy dealing in part with the Philosopher's Stone.

### 24. *Risāla fīʾl-Iksīr* (Treatise on the Elixir)

Sezgin includes this in his chapter on alchemy.[53]

### 25. *Ikhtiyārāt al-Ayyām* (The Choosing of Days)

The copy of this held in the Dār al-Kutub al-Ẓāhiriyya in Damascus has the alternative title *Risāla yuʿlam minhā Ikhtiyārāt al-Ayyām al-Nasīḥa wa-l-Jayyida* (Treatise by which to learn the Choosing of Ill-omened and Good Days). It begins:

---

[49] See Shabakat al-Sirāj fī al-Ṭarīq ilā Allāh, viewed 3 April 2011, <http://www.alseraj.net/maktaba/kotob_new/book/al-sadiq/a129.htm>.

[50] Wilhelm Pertsch, *Die arabische Handschriften der herzöglichen Bibliothek zu Gotha* (Gotha, 1880), pp. 470–1.

[51] J. Ruska, *Arabischen Alchemisten vol. 2. Ga'far al-Ṣādiq der Sechste Imam* (Heidelberg, 1924).

[52] Sezgin, *Geschichte*, vol. 4, p. 131.

[53] Ibid.

> The writer of the treatise, may God be pleased with him, said, "The first day of the month in which God created Adam is good for audiences with the kings and sultans..."[54]

There is another copy in the Königlichen Library in Berlin under the title *Ikhtiyārat Ayyām al-Shahr al-ʿArabī ʿan Jaʿfar al-Ṣādiq* (The Choosing of the Days of the Arab Month on the Authority of Jaʿfar al-Ṣādiq). It consists of two pages each divided into two columns. In the right-hand column are the numbers 1–15 and 16–30, representing the days of the month. On the left it explains what those days are particularly suitable for and what they are not. Thus, by number 1 it says: "A good day for meeting the kings and princes"; by 4: "A good day for all affairs"; while by 5, it says: "A bad and objectionable day for everything."[55]

## 26. *Maḥmūdāt al-Ayyām wa-Madhmūmātuhā wa-Mutawassiṭātuhā fī Aḥwāl min kull Shahr* (The Commendable Days, the Objectionable Ones, and the Indifferent Ones, in the Affairs of Every Month)

This is clearly on the same theme as *Ikhtiyārat al-Ayyām* above, and may indeed be an alternative version of the same manuscript.

## 27. *Jadwal fī Madkhal al-Sinīn wa'l-Shuhūr wa'l-Ayyām* (Chart of the Beginning of Years, Months and Days)

A copy of the manuscript held by the library of Leiden consists of a chart for reckoning the years, months and days of the Muslim calendar, with the intention that this should serve accurately to place the various festivals, celebrations and fasts. Alongside this is a discussion between al-Ṣādiq and a certain ʿAbd allāh (i.e. an anonymous person or al-Ṣādiq's son ʿAbd allāh b. Jaʿfar) about the chart and in which al-Ṣādiq explains its workings.[56]

## 28. *Malḥama* (Divination)

The *Descriptive List of the Arabic Manuscripts* of the British Museum lists this under 'Works on Portents from Natural Phenomena.'[57] It is also described as a work of 'Wetterprophezeiungen' (prophesies from the weather).[58]

## 29. *al-Qurʿa* (The Casting of Lots/Rhapsodomancy)

This is described as a treatise on soothsaying or fortune telling.[59] It is also said to be a work of rhapsodomancy, that is, the arbitrary selection of a passage of writing and the use of this

---

54 *Fihrist Makhṭūṭāt Dār al-Kutub al-Ẓāhiriyya* (Damascus, 1969) p. 268.

55 *Königlichen Bibliothek*, vol. 3, p. 301. The text is available online at al-Wāḥāt al-Ṭullābiyya, viewed 3 April 2011, <http://www.alwahat.org/forums/index.php?showtopic=18531andmode=threadedandpid=154897>.

56 P. de Jong and M.J. de Goeje, *Catalogus Codicum Orientalium Bibliothecae Academiae Lugduno-Batavae* (Leiden, 1865–6) vol. 3, p. 82.

57 A.G. Ellis and E. Edwards, *A Descriptive List of the Arabic Manuscripts acquired by the Trustees of the British Museum since 1894* (London, 1912), p. 41.

58 *Die arabische Handschriften*, p. 142.

59 Sezgin, *Geschichte*, vol. 1, p. 531.

as a prediction of what will come to pass.[60] One copy of the manuscript begins with the words:

> The questions must first of all be reduced to a group of three letters.

This group of letters is used to indicate the paragraph containing the reply, which in turn is composed of *ḥadīth* and verses from the Qurʾān. The chapter dealing with how to reduce the questions to three letters is missing. It includes a prayer which must be recited before consulting the work.[61]

The manuscript collection of the Institute of Oriental Culture, University of Tokyo, has a copy of a manuscript entitled *Qurʿa fī ʿIlm al-Raml* (Lot Casting in Geomancy) also ascribed to al-Ṣādiq. The catalogue notes that there are several extant manuscripts with the same title (*qurʿa*) also ascribed to al-Ṣādiq. These have different beginnings and their relationship to the Tokyo text is unclear. As far as the Tokyo manuscript is concerned, it deals with a combination of lot casting (*qurʿa*) and geomancy (*ʿilm al-raml*). In some respects it is similar to the *Manāfiʿ Suwar al-Qurʾān* or *Khawāṣṣ· al-Qurʾān al-ʿAẓīm* mentioned above in that the divination is based on a Qurʾānic *sūra*. In the *Qurʿa*, the choice of the *sūra* is determined by the arrangement of little stones or kernels thrown on the ground. Folio 2r of the Tokyo text contains a table which is a graphical description of sixteen different kinds of arrangements resulting from the throwing of the stones or kernels. These sixteen different arrangements determine the division of the text into sixteen chapters.[62]

Dealing with a similar subject is a manuscript entitled *Risālat fī l-Raml* (Treatise on Geomancy) located in the Garrett Collection in Princeton and attributed to al-Ṣādiq. As the title suggests, it deals with geomancy or the making of predictions from the patterns formed when sand is thrown on the floor, or when dots are drawn it in and connected with lines.[63]

A book of 56 pages with the title *Qurʿat al-Imām Jaʿfar al-Ṣādiq* has been published in Arabic.[64]

## 30. *Risālat al-Faʾl* (Treatise on Omens)

This consists of a chart containing the letters of the Arabic alphabet. Appended to each letter are some verses, then a detailed explanation in prose. For example

> The letter *alif* demonstrates to the possessor of this *faʾl* that if in the middle of Friday he has pains in his head and aches in his joints and ribs, these will quickly be cured, God willing.[65]

[60] *Descriptive Catalogue of the Garrett Collection of Arabic Manuscripts in the Princeton University Library* (Princeton, n.d.), p. 445.

[61] *Catalogue des Manuscrits Arabes*, 2:476.

[62] See *Catalogue of the Arabic Manuscripts in the Daiber Collection*, Institute of Oriental Culture, University of Tokyo, available online (viewed 3 April 2011) at http://ricasdb.ioc.u-tokyo.ac.jp/daiber/fra_daiber.php?andms=135andtxtno=

[63] *Garrett Collection*, p. 297.

[64] *Qurʿat al-Imam Jaʿfar al-Ṣādiq* (Beirut, 1992).

[65] *Die arabischen Handschriften*, pp. 136–7.

Another manuscript of this in the same collection has the following introduction:

> This omen is the omen of the Qur'ān, belonging to Jaʿfar al-Ṣādiq. Whoever wants an omen from the Qur'ān must fulfil three conditions. The first is that he must be ritually clean. The second is that the Qur'ān must be complete. The third is that the man's belief and purpose should be pure.[66]

A further copy of the manuscript is composed of a number of circles which are used for predicting future events. With these are other circles enclosing letters of the alphabet in binary combination which are used for a related prophesy.[67]

### 31. *Sirāj al-Ẓulma fī Ṭibb al-A'imma*
### (The Lamp against Darkness on the Medical Science of the Imams)

This also appears with the alternative title *Risālat Ṭibb al-A'imma* (Treatise on the Medical Science of the Imams). The manuscript, written in 1074/1662, begins:

> Praise be to God. This book contains the medicine of the *Ahl al-Bayt*.[68]

The text is probably a collection of pieces of medical advice and remedies.

### 32. *al-Silk al-Nādir fī 'Ilm al-Awā'il wa-al-Awākhir*
### (The Precious Thread in Knowledge of Beginnings and Endings)

This is said to be a prophetic poem stated alternatively to have been composed by ʿAlī b. Abī Ṭālib, Jaʿfar al-Ṣādiq, the caliph Muʿtazz, or Yathrib.[69]

---

[66] Ibid., p. 37.

[67] E. Blochet, *Catalogue des Manuscrits Arabes* (Paris, 1925), p. 231.

[68] *Fihrist al-Makhṭūṭāt, Dār al-Kutub* (Cairo, 1961) vol. 1, p. 357.

[69] *A Handlist of Arabic Manuscripts, Chester Beatty Library* (Dublin, 1964) vol. 1, p. 92. Yathrib here may refer to the pre-Islamic figure of Yathrib b. Qātiyah.

# 3

# The Creeds of Aḥmad Ibn Ḥanbal

## 3.1 THE CREEDS OF AḤMAD IBN ḤANBAL

*Saud Al-Sarhan*

Creed (*ʿaqīdah*), here, refers to dogma or articles of faith:[1]

> A creed may take various forms: it may consist only of a few words or may be a whole treaties; it may be a doxology, a short phrase, or a work on dogmatics. This is as true of Islam as it is of Christianity; moreover, in both religions the short formula is anterior to the creed, which in its turn is anterior to the treatise on dogmatics.[2]

Wensinck notes that creeds represent the faith of the community as opposed to that of the sects. This means creeds reflect the struggle of the community,[3] and their elements are mostly conversional. There are always two parties: 'we', the community that holds the correct belief; and 'they', the sects (heresiarchs) that hold the false belief.

Riḍwān al-Sayyid indicates that the purpose of the traditionalists' creeds was to prove their identity through denying other beliefs.[4] This means that the attitude of 'us' was constructed on the basis of the attitudes of 'them':

> قال أبو داوود السجستاني: سمعت أحمد سئل: هل لهم رخصة أن يقول الرجل: كلام الله ثم يسكت؟
>
> قال: ولم يسكت؟
>
> لولا ما وقع الناس فيه كان يسعه السكوت، ولكن حيث تكلموا لأي شيء لا يتكلمون؟

> Abū Dāwūd al-Sijistānī reported that Aḥmad Ibn Ḥanbal was asked, "Is it acceptable for someone to say 'the Qur'ān is God's words' and remain silent [i.e., without adding 'and uncreated']?" Aḥmad answered, "Why do they stay silent? If there had not been [disagreement on the Qur'ān] among people, they could stay silent. But when they discuss [the Qur'ān], why do they not speak [and add 'uncreated']?"[5]

---

[1] W. Montgomery Watt, 'Akīda', *EI*², vol. 1, p. 332.

[2] A. J. Wensinck, *The Muslim creed: its genesis and historical development* (London, 1965), p. 1.

[3] Ibid., p. 102.

[4] Riḍwān al-Sayyid, 'Ahl al-Sunna wa al-Jamāʿah: Dirāsa fī al-takawwn al-ʿaqadī wa al-siyasī.' In *al-Jamāʿa wa al-mujtamaʿ wa al-dawla: sultat al-ʾaydiyulujiya fī al-majāl al-siyāsī al-ʿArabī al-Islāmī* (Beirut, 1997), p. 234.

[5] Sulaymān b. al-Ashʿath al-Sijistānī Abū Dāwūd, *Masāʾil al-imām Aḥmad* ([Cairo], 1999), p. 355.

The same idea can be found in a report narrated from Aḥmad by ʿUthmān al-Dārimī, who claims that

كنا نرى السكوت عن هذا قبل أن يخوض فيه هؤلاء، فلما أظهروه لم نجد بدّا من مخالفتهم والرد عليهم

> We used to choose to keep silent on this [matter] before they talked about it. However, when they expressed [their belief], we had no alternative but to differ from them and to refute them.[6]

Al-Sayyid considers the traditionalist creeds in the third A.H./ninth century to have appeared as a 'completed system' in order to answer the rationalists' questions and to preserve the beliefs of the common people (*al-ʿāmma*) by giving them a reliable and coherent text. Furthermore, the traditionalists did not attribute these creeds to themselves, but rather to the *salaf.* The aim of such attribution was to improve the creeds' legitimacy on the one hand, and to establish the 'real', continuing identity of the Muslims on the other.[7] All the traditionalist creeds start with a sentence claiming that the creed's contents represent the 'belief of *ahl al-Sunna wa-al-Jamāʿa*'; or, in other versions, 'these are the principles of the Sunna, on which the leaders of the pious early Muslims and the jurisprudents of all regions have reached a consensus', or 'the people of the Sunna reached consensus on …', or 'I found the people of knowledge (*ʿulamāʾ*) in the East and the West to believe in …'.

What is remarkable is that in some later traditionalists' creeds, the authority of the *salaf* was merged with or supplanted by an assertion of Aḥmad Ibn Ḥanbal's authority in matters of belief, and it was common to say 'this is what Aḥmad believes' instead of 'this is what the *salaf* believe'. Ibrāhīm al-Ḥarbī (d. 285/899), for example, states,

كل شيء أقول لكم: هذا قول أصحاب الحديث؛ فهو قول أحمد ابن حنبل، هو ألقى في قلوبنا منذ كنا غلمانا اتّباع
حديث رسول الله ... وأقاويل الصحابة، والاقتداء بالتابعين

> Whatever I tell you is the view of the traditionalists, and it is the view of Aḥmad Ibn Ḥanbal, who taught us, since we were young, to follow the traditions of God's Messenger … and the sayings of the Companions and to model ourselves after the Successors.[8]

Other scholars used the phrase 'I believe what Aḥmad believes' to confirm that their belief was correct. The famous example of this is the preeminent Sunnī theologian Abū al-Ḥasan al-Ashʿarī (d. 324/936), who states in his book *al-Ibāna* that he follows the doctrines of the Book, the Sunna, the Companions, the Successors and the traditionalists; then he insists on his adherence to Aḥmad Ibn Ḥanbal.[9] Moreover, some people submitted their creeds to Aḥmad in order to obtain his agreement and authority. Ibn Hāniʾ tells us this story:

---

[6] ʿUthmān b. Saʿīd al-Dārimī, *Naqḍ al-Imām Abī Saʿīd ʿUthmān b. Saʿīd ʿalā al Marīsī al Jahmī al-ʿanīd fīmā iftarā ʿalā Allāh ʿazza wa-jalla min al-tawḥīd*, v. 1, p. 538

[7] al-Sayyid, Riḍwān. *Ahl al-Sunna wa-al-Jamāʿa*. p. 258.

[8] Al-Ḥusayn b. Muḥammad Ibn Abī Yaʿlā Ibn al-Farrāʾ, *Ṭabaqāt al-Ḥanābila* (Riyadh, 1999), vol. 1, p. 234.

[9] ʿAlī b. Ismāʿīl al-Ashʿarī, *al-Ibāna ʿan uṣūl al-diyāna* (Cairo, 1977), pp. 20–21.

حضرت رجلاً عند أبي عبد الله وهو يسأله، فجعل الرجل يقول: يا أبا عبد الله، رأس الأمر وإجماع المسلمين على: أن الإيمان بالقدر خيره وشره حلوه ومره والتسليم لأمره والرضا بقضائه؟

فقال أبو عبد الله: نعم.

ثم قال له: والإيمان قول وعمل، يزيد وينقص؟

فقال: نعم.

ثم قال: والصلاة خلف كل بر وفاجر؟

قال: نعم.

قال: والجهاد مع السلطان والصبر تحت لوائه، ولا يخرج على السلطان بسيف ولا عصا. وألا يكفر أحداً إلا بذنب؟

قال أبو عبد الله: اسكت، من ترك الصلاة فقد كفر.

قال: والقرآن كلام الله غير مخلوق. ومن قال: إنه مخلوق فهو كافر؟

فقال: نعم.

قال: وأن الله، عز وجل، يرى في الآخرة؟

قال: نعم.

قال: وعذاب القبر ومنكر ونكير؟

قال أبو عبد الله: نؤمن بهذا كله، ومن أنكر واحدة من هذه فهو جهمي.

I came upon a man who was with Abū ʿAbd Allāh [Aḥmad Ibn Ḥanbal] and was asking him, "O Abū ʿAbd Allāh, the head of the matter [i.e., Islam] and the consensus of the Muslims is to believe in predestination, good or bad, sweet or bitter, and to surrender to His order and to be content with His decree?"
Abū ʿAbd Allāh said, "Yes."
Then [the man] said to him, "And faith comprises speech and action, and it increases and decreases?"
[Aḥmad] said, "Yes."
Then [the man] said, "And praying behind any [leader], pious or sinful?"
[Aḥmad] said, "Yes."
[The man] said, "And participating in *jihād* with the ruler and standing under his flag, and not rebelling against the ruler by sword or stick, and not calling anyone an infidel on account of a sin?"
Abū ʿAbd Allāh said, "Silence! Whoever does not pray is an unbeliever."
[The man] said, "And the Qurʾān is God's words, uncreated; and whoever says it is created is an unbeliever?"
[Aḥmad] said, "Yes."
[The man] said, "And God will be seen in the Hereafter?"
[Aḥmad] said, "Yes."
[The man] said, "And the chastisement of the grave, and Munkar and Nakīr?"
Abū ʿAbd Allāh said, "We believe in all of these, and whoever rejects one of them is a *Jahmī*."[10]

Another remarkable feature of the traditionalists' creeds is their similarity. In their main articles of belief, the creeds agree with each other not only in the contents of the articles,

[10] Isḥāq b. Ibrāhīm al- Naysābūrī Ibn Hāniʾ, *Masāʾil al-imām Aḥmad ibn Ḥanbal* (Al-Manṣūrah, 2008), pp. 409–10.

but even in their use of the same words to present these beliefs. These similarities were taken by some traditionalists as proof of the correctness of their beliefs. Abū al-Muẓaffar al-Samʿānī (d. 489/1096) claims that if the traditionalists' creeds are examined closely, all of them, across differences of place and time, exhibit the same belief, 'as if it had come from one heart and one tongue'. This similarity, according to al-Samʿānī, proves that the traditionalists hold the correct beliefs. They are not like the other sects, which have disagreements. Al-Samʿānī attributes this similarity to the fact that the traditionalists derive their beliefs from the Qurʾān and the Sunna and the traditional way of transmission (*ṭarīq al-naql*). In contrast, the 'innovators' derive their beliefs from rational methods (*al-maʿqūlāt waʾl-ārāʾ*), which leads them to dissension and disagreement.[11]

The earliest traditionalist creeds go back to the second half of the second A.H./eighth century, attributed to al-Awzāʿī (d. 157/774) and Sufyān al-Thawrī (d. 161/778). However, the reliability of these attributions is questionable, and the creeds were probably attributed to these scholars at a later date. The most reliably attributed creeds we have now date from the second quarter of the third A.H./ninth century. These include the creeds of al-Ḥumaydī (d. 219/834) and Muḥammad b. ʿUkkāsha al-Kirmānī (d. after 225/840).

Turning to the creeds of Aḥmad b. Ḥanbal, Laoust has identified and enumerated six creeds related to Aḥmad, all of which are found in Ibn Abī Yaʿlā's book *Ṭabaqāt al-Ḥanābila*.[12] Western scholars have accepted them as genuine and used them to study Aḥmad's theological views, even though some consider the creeds to be collations of Aḥmad's doctrines by members of his school rather than his own words.[13] In the following sections I examine each of these creeds and attempt to delineate their relationship to Aḥmad himself.

## *1. Creed I*

This is known as *Aqīdat al-Iṣṭakhrī*, referring to Aḥmad b. Jaʿfar al-Iṣṭakhrī al-Fārisī (d. not known)[14] who allegedly transmitted it from Aḥmad.[15] Abū Yaʿlā Ibn al-Farrāʾ quotes from this creed and calls it *Kitāb al-Risāla li-Aḥmad*.[16] A late manuscript entitled *Iʿtiqād ahl*

[11] Ismāʿīl b. Muhammad al-Iṣbahānī, *al-Ḥujja fī bayān al-maḥajja wa sharḥ ʿaqīdat ahl al-Sunna* (Riyad, 1999), vol. 1, pp. 224–7.

[12] ʿUbayd Allāh b. Muḥammad Ibn Baṭṭah, *al-Sharḥ wa-al-Ibāna ʿalā uṣūl al-sunna wa-al-diyāna = La Profession de foi d'ibn Baṭṭa* (Damas, 1958). p. xv–xvi.

[13] See: Laoust, in ibid.; and Christopher Melchert, *Ahmad ibn Hanbal* (Oxford, 2006), p. 83. In addition to Laoust and Melchert, these creeds are used widely by Western scholars. For instance, see: W. Montgomery Watt, *The formative period of Islamic thought* (Edinburgh, 1973), pp. 292–5; Wilferd Madelung, *Der Imam al-Qasim ibn Ibrahim und die Glaubenslehre der Zaiditen* (Berlin, 1965), pp. 225–8; Wilferd Madelung, *Religious trends in early Islamic Iran* (Albany, N.Y., 1988), pp. 22–5; M.A. Cook, *Commanding right and forbidding wrong in Islamic thought* (Cambridge, 2000), pp. 101–14; Wesley Williams, 'Aspects of the Creed of Imam Ahmad Ibn Hanbal: a Study of Anthropomorphism in Early Islamic Discourse'. *International Journal of Middle East Studies* vol. 34, no. 3 (2002), pp. 441–463.

[14] We do not have much information about him. See Ibn Abū Yaʿlā al-Farrāʾ, *Ṭabaqāt al-Ḥanābila* (Riyad, 1999) vol. 1, p. 54.

[15] Ibn Abū Yaʿlā, *Ṭabaqāt al-Ḥanābila*, vol. 1, pp. 54–74.

[16] Abū Yaʿlā Ibn al-Farrāʾ, *al-ʿUdda fī uṣūl al-fiqh* (n.p., 2002) vol. 2, p. 94.

*al-sunna wa'l-jamā'a* includes this creed, but in the chain of transmission it is called *Kitāb al-Sunna.*[17]

Presumably, the creed first appeared in Damascus at the end of the tenth century, based on the fact that all of its transmissions go back to ʿAbd Allāh b. Muḥammad al-Nahāwandī al-Malikī,[18] who transmitted it in Damascus. At the time when the creed appeared, Damascus was under Fāṭimid control.[19] Subsequently, the creed spread from Damascus and came to be known by Ḥanbalīs in Baghdad and Aṣfahān.[20]

The relevant points here are that this creed was attributed to Aḥmad by a Malikī follower, not a Ḥanbalī; under the authority of the Shīʿī Fāṭimids, not the Sunnī ʿAbbīsids; and in Damascus, not in Baghdad, where the school of the Ḥanbalīs was based.

The creed deals with number of theological issues:[21]

1. Faith (*īmān*) comprises speech, actions, intention and adherence to the Sunna. Faith increases and decreases, and it is permitted to insert conditionality in one's statement of faith (called *istithnā'*), provided this does not indicate doubt on the part of the believer. For example, one might say *anā mu'min in shā' Allāh*, 'I am a believer, God willing'. Such *istithnā'* is a path followed by the pious early Muslims *(al-salaf)*. According to the creed, acceptable responses to the question 'Are you a believer?' are 'I am a believer, God willing', or 'I hope that I am a believer', or 'I believe in God, His angels, His books and His Messengers'.
2. All of predestination (*qadar*), whether good or bad, sweet or bitter, comes from God, and all sins are due to predestination.
3. The community should not declare anyone of the 'people of the *qibla*' (i.e., those who pray towards the Kaʿba in Mecca) to be destined for Paradise, unless it is recorded in a tradition (*ḥadīth*) from the Prophet.
4. The caliphate belongs only to the Quraysh, which means that caliphs can come only from the Quraysh tribe; and people should obey their caliphs. The creed then presents the rights of the caliphs and the rights of the Muslim community, including the demand to avoid sedition (*fitna*) and the prohibition on calling any member of the people of the *qibla* an infidel on account of a sin, except if so designated in a Prophetic tradition.
5. The creed also includes the belief in the emergence of the *Dajjāl*, the afflictions of the grave, and all things that will happen after death and in the Hereafter, such as the pool (*ḥawḍ*), the broad way (*ṣirāṭ*), the trumpet (*ṣūr*) and intercession (*shafāʿa*). These things are known in later Islamic theology as *samʿiyyāt* (beliefs based only on transmitted texts).

---

[17] Aḥmad Ibn Ḥanbal (attrib.), *Iʿtiqād ahl al-Sunna wa'l-Jamāʿa*, MS. Berlin 1937 (fols. 63–70, 1089 A.H.), fols. 63A–64A.

[18] See ʿAlī b. al-Ḥasan Ibn ʿAsākir, *Tārīkh Madīnat Dimashq* (Beirut, n.d.), vol. 21, pp. 310–12; vol. 32, p. 175.

[19] See the entry of al-Nahāwandī in ibid. vol. 32, pp. 174–5.

[20] Several traditionists transmitted this creed from al-Nahāwandī, and took it out of Damascus, to Baghdad and Aṣfahān. See Abū Yaʿlā al-Farrā', *Ibṭāl al-Ta'wīlāt li-Akhbār al-Ṣifāt* (Kuwait, 1989) vol. 1, pp. 45–6, and Ibn Abū Yaʿlā, *Ṭabaqāt al-Ḥanābila.* Vol. 1, pp. 54–74.

[21] For a translation of this creed, see W. Montgomery Watt, *Muslim creeds*, pp. 29–40, and for a summary of it, see Watt, *The formative period of Islamic thought*, pp. 292–5.

6. The creed lists a large number of God's attributes. It even includes some extreme attributes which most Muslims might consider to constitute anthropomorphism, such as God's moving (*ḥaraka*) and laughing, His limit (*ḥadd*), and His having fingers and a mouth.
7. The creed contains the command to assert the good qualities of the Companions and to be silent concerning their faults. Furthermore, anyone who criticises them is an innovator and a *Rāfiḍī*, and should be asked to retract the criticism. If he does not, he should be jailed until death, or until he repents.
8. The creed is hostile towards rational jurisprudents (*aṣḥāb al-raʾy*) who rely on common sense and analogical reasoning (*qiyās*). The creed supports the traditionalists and *taqlīd* while declaring anyone who uses *raʾy* and *qiyās* to be an innovator and one who has strayed.
9. The creed contains a list of more than twelve "heretical sects" that are to be rejected, including the Murjiʾa, the Qadariyya, the Muʿtazila, the Rāfiḍa, the Zaydiyya, the Khawārij, the Manṣūriyya and the Ḥasaniyya.[22]
10. The creed makes mention of some additional points, such as stating a preference for Arabs over non-Arabs, and it confirms that profit and trade are licit.

The authenticity of this creed, that is, the correctness of its attribution to Aḥmad, is in doubt. It is most probably the creed of Ḥarb b. Ismāʿīl al-Kirmānī (d. 280/893), a student of Aḥmad Ibn Ḥanbal and one of the collectors of *masāʾil* from Aḥmad and others. This creed is included in Ḥarb's *Masāʾil*, in which he summarises his understanding of correct belief on the authority of his traditionalist masters:

هذا مذهب أئمة العلم وأصحاب الأثر وأهل السنة المعروفين بها، المتمسكين بعروقها المقتدى بهم فيها، وأدركت مَنْ أدركت من علماء أهل العراق والحجاز والشام وغيرهم عليها، فمن خالف شيئاً من هذه المذاهب أو طعن فيها أو عاب قائلها فهو مبتدع خارج من الجماعة زائل عن منهج السنة وسبيل الحق. وهو مذهب أحمد وإسحاق بن إبراهيم بن مخلد وعبد الله بن الزبير وسعيد بن منصور وغيرهم ممن جالسنا وأخذنا عنهم العلم.

> This is the *madhhab* of people of knowledge, the people of transmissions and the people of the Sunna, those who hold fast to its [i.e., the Sunna's] roots and are known by it, and through whom one can follow [the Sunna]; and I have known the scholars of Iraq, the Hijaz and the Levant and others to be in support of it. Hence, whosoever opposes any part of these doctrines, or refutes it or finds fault with anyone who endorses it, is an innovator and outside the community, a deviant from the way of the Sunna and the true path. Moreover, this is the *madhhab* of Aḥmad [Ibn Ḥanbal], Isḥāq b. Ibrahīm b. Makhlad [Ibn Rāhawayh], ʿAbd Allāh b. al-Zubayr [al-Ḥumaydī], Saʿīd b. Manṣūr and others with whom we sat and from whom we took knowledge.[23]

In his *Masāʾil* work, Ḥarb includes the creed under the title *bāb al-qawl fīʾl-madhhab*;[24] he follows it with approximately thirty-three chapters that present his evidence and the authority

---

[22] Melchert has studied these sects and the creed's attitude towards them in *Ahmad ibn Hanbal*, pp. 89–93; and idem, 'The Adversaries of Aḥmad Ibn Ḥanbal'. *Arabica* vol. 44, no. 2 (1997), pp. 234–253, particularly pp. 236–7.

[23] Ḥarb b. Ismāʿīl al-Kirmānī, *Masāʾil al-imām Aḥmad Ibn Ḥanbal wa-Isḥāq Ibn Rāhawayh* (Riyad, 2004), p. 355.

[24] Ibid,. pp. 355–66.

for the creed. From these chapters we can distinguish the various roots of the creed, which can be illustrated by the following examples.

On the subject of God's limit (*ḥadd*), Ḥarb declares in the creed,

> الله، تبارك وتعالى، على العرش، فوق السماء السابعة العليا، يعلم ذلك كله، وهو بائن من خلقه لايخلو من علمه مكان. ولله عرش، وللعرش حملة يحملونه، وله حد، الله أعلم بحده
>
> God, be He blessed and exalted, is on the throne, upon the seventh highest heaven, and knows all [things]. He is separate from His creation, and no place lies beyond His knowledge. God has a throne, and this throne has carriers to carry it; and He has a limit (*ḥadd*); God is the most aware of His own limit.[25]

In later chapters, Ḥarb makes clear the sources of his belief in the *ḥadd*. He states,

> I asked Isḥāq [Ibn Rāhawayh], "Is [God on] the throne with a *ḥadd*?" Isḥāq answered, "Yes, with a *ḥadd*." And he related to Ibn al-Mubārak: "He [God] on his own throne, separated from his creation, with a *ḥadd*."

Ḥarb then reports Ibn al-Mubārak's comment with his own chain of transmission (*isnād*).[26]

Another example is provided by Ḥarb discussion of the order of preference among the Companions:

> وخير الأمة بعد النبي، صلى الله عليه وسلم، أبو بكر وخيرهم بعد أبي بكر عمر ، وخيرهم بعد عمر عثمان.وقال قوم من أهل العلم والسنة: وخيرهم بعد عثمان علي. ووقف قوم على عثمان
>
> The best of the nation after the Prophet is Abū Bakr, and the best of them after Abū Bakr is ʿUmar, and the best of them after ʿUmar is ʿUthmān. Some Sunnī scholars (*ahl al-ʿilm wa-ahl al-Sunna*) say: the best of them after ʿUthmān is ʿAlī. Some others end at ʿUthmān.[27]

The details of this disagreement among the people of the Sunna are found in the later chapters of Ḥarb's *Masāʾil*, where Ḥarb claims that he asked Aḥmad Ibn Ḥanbal about the Companions, and the latter answered, "The best of the nation is Abū Bakr, followed by ʿUmar, then ʿUthmān; and ʿAlī is one of the caliphs." Similarly, some of the other traditionalists whom Ḥarb asked ended at ʿUthmān and did not count ʿAlī as the fourth-best Companion. These include Ibn al-Madīnī, Abū al-Rabīʿ al-Zahrānī and Muʿādh b. Muʿādh. Abū Thawr was quoted as saying, "Abū Bakr, then ʿUmar, then ʿUthmān, then the five, who are ʿAlī, Ṭalḥa, al-Zubayr, Saʿd and ʿAbd al-Raḥmān". On the other hand, Isḥāq Ibn Rāhawayh and Hudba b. Khālid state that ʿAlī is the fourth best of the Companions.[28] It was on the authority of these figures that Ḥarb wrote his creed, and because of the disagreement among them about counting ʿAlī as the fourth best of the Companions, he makes his creed explicit on this matter.

Finally, in his definition of certain sects (the Rāfiḍa, the Manṣūriyya and the Ḥasaniyya[29]),

---

[25] Ibid. p. 359.

[26] Ibid., p. 412.

[27] Ibid., p. 361.

[28] Ibid., p. 439.

[29] The name of this sect occurs in different forms: at one point it appears as Ḥasaniyya and at another as Khashabiyya. But as Ibn Asbāṭ and Ḥarb are talking about a Zaydī party, it is probably the Ḥasaniyya, referring to al-Ḥasan b. Ṣāliḥ Ibn Ḥayy (d.168/785), a Zaydī scholar.

Ḥarb was apparently relying on Yūsuf b. Asbāṭ's (d.195/811) definition, which he narrated in his *Masā'il*.[30]

However, Ḥarb does not always name his sources, especially for some extreme points of his creed. For instance, in his *Masā'il*, Ḥarb says, "God spoke to Moses and handed him the Torah from God's hand to his hand";[31] al-Iṣṭakhrī's version reads, "God spoke to Moses from his mouth."[32] Ḥarb does not give a source for the references to God's hand or mouth. Other examples include Ḥarb's statement, "Whoever rejects *taqlīd* and claims that he does not rely, in his belief, on another's authority, is impious, an innovator and an enemy of God and His Prophet."[33] Ḥarb also claims that God moves and laughs, and that He created Adam after His own image.[34] Yet he does not quote anyone in support of these points.

Apparently, the creed of Ḥarb b. Ismāʿīl was widely known by the title *al-Sunna wa'l-Jamāʿa* in the tenth-century Eastern Islamic world. Because this creed includes a list of 'innovator' parties and a statement of extreme anthropomorphism, it became an object of refutation and criticism by some Muʿtazilīs as well as by some Sunnīs. The Muʿtazilī scholar Abū al-Qāsīm al-Balkhī (d. 319/931) wrote a book to refute Ḥarb's creed and to criticise traditionists and traditionalists.[35] In response, al-Ḥusayn al-Rāmahurmuzī (d. 360/970-1) wrote a book, *al-Muḥaddith al-Faṣil bayn al-Rāwī wa-al-wāʿī*, to defend the traditionalists' methods and to refute al-Balkhī; yet he criticised Ḥarb for valuing transmission without understanding of meaning (*akthar min al-riywāya wa-aghfal al-istibṣār*).[36]

We can now address the extent to which this creed accurately represents Aḥmad's theology (*ʿaqīda*). As shown above, Ḥarb advocates not only the beliefs of Aḥmad, but the views of traditionalists in general in the third A.H./ninth century, a group to which Aḥmad belonged. Although this creed generally coincides with Aḥmad's beliefs, we cannot with complete certainty attribute it to Aḥmad. This is because it has other origins besides him, and apparently the words are not Aḥmad's but Ḥarb's.[37] In the fourteenth century, the Muslim historian al-Dhahabī strongly criticised this creed and argued that its attribution to Aḥmad was erroneous.[38] He also chastised the traditionists who transmitted the creed without subjecting it to criticism.[39] Similarly, Ibn al-Wazīr (d. 840/1436) offers a lengthy criticism designed to prove the falsity of this 'disapproved creed' (*al-ʿaqīda al-mukraha*).[40] These two scholars rejected the attribution of the creed to Aḥmad because it contains extreme views that they considered impossible for Aḥmad to believe in; in addition, the creed was transmitted through

[30] Ḥarb, *Masā'il al-imām Aḥmad*, pp. 437–38.

[31] Ibid., p. 360.

[32] Ibn Abū Yaʿlā al-Farrā', *Ṭabaqāt al-Ḥanābila*, vol. 1, p. 62.

[33] Ḥarb, *Masā'il al-imām Aḥmad*, p. 362.

[34] Ibid., p. 360.

[35] Yaqūt b. ʿAbd Allāh al-Ḥamawī, *Muʿjam al-Buldān* (Beirut, 1977) vol. 3, p. 296.

[36] al-Ḥusayn b. ʿAbd al-Raḥman al-Rāmahurmuzī, *al-Muḥaddith al-fasil bayna al-rāwī wa-al-wāʿī* (Beirut, 1971), pp. 309–11.

[37] Aḥmad b. ʿAbd al-Halīm Ibn Taymiyya, *al-Istiqama* (Riyadh, 1991), vol. 1, p. 73.

[38] Muḥammad b. Aḥmad al-Dhahabī, *Siyar aʿlām al-nubalā'* (Beirut, 1981), vol. 11, p. 286. al-Dhahabī, *Tārīkh al-Islām wa-wafayāt al-mashāhīr wa-al-aʿlam* (Beirut, 1987) vol. 18, p. 136.

[39] al-Dhahabī, *Siyar aʿlām al-nubalā'* vol. 11, pp. 302–3.

[40] Muḥammad b. Ibrāhīm Ibn al-Wazīr, *al-ʿAwāṣim wa al-qawāṣim fī al-dhabb ʿan sunnat Abī al-Qāsim* (Beirut, 1992) vol. 3, pp. 311–17.

untrustworthy individuals. Ibn Taymiyya also demonstrates suspicions of this creed.[41] On one hand, he knows Ḥarb's creed and quotes from it.[42] But on the other hand, he talks in some places about the two creeds (Ḥarb's and al-Iṣṭakhrī's) as one and criticises some of its articles by claiming that its transmitters are unknown individuals (*majāhīl*). Also, he argues that the creed does not appear in the books of those who are concerned with collecting Aḥmad's words, such as al-Khallāl, other Iraqis who knew Aḥmad's books or those who were well known for narrating Aḥmad's words.[43] Ibn Taymiyya's pupil Ibn al-Qayyim quotes most of the creed and relates it to Ḥarb, not to al-Iṣṭakhrī.[44]

In addition, another version of the creed was related to Muḥammad b. Wahb al-Qurashī (d. not known), who is claimed to have heard it from Aḥmad Ibn Ḥanbal.[45] This is obviously an edited and much later version of the creed, since the extreme anthropomorphic imagery of divine attributes (such as the mouth, edge and movement) has been removed.

## *2. Creed II*

This creed is related to Aḥmad by al-Ḥasan b. Ismāʿīl al-Rabaʿī (d. not known),[46] who claims that

قال لي أحمد بن حنبل، إمام أهل السنة والصابر تحت المحنة: أجمع تسعون رجلا من التابعين وأئمة المسلمين
وأئمة السلف وفقهاء الأمصار على أن السنة التي توفي عليها رسول الله.

> Aḥmad Ibn Ḥanbal, the leader of the people of the Sunna and the one who was patient during the Inquisition, said to me, "Ninety men of the Successors, the leaders of the Muslims, the leaders of the early Muslims and the jurisprudents of the regions have reached consensus on the Sunna [in whose practice] the Prophet died."[47]

This creed is the shortest among those attributed to Aḥmad Ibn Ḥanbal and it consists of brief comments on predestination, faith, and the belief that the Qurʾān is uncreated. Amongst the various theological issues discussed in the creed are obedience to the caliphs and the requirement to be patient under their rule, performing *jihād* with them and not fighting against them. The creed also deals with the order of preference among the Companions and lists them in the following order: Abū Bakr, ʿUmar, ʿUthmān, ʿAlī.

The creed was narrated in Baghdad in the late fifth A.H./eleventh century. Ibn Abū Yaʿlā (d. 526/1132) and Abū Ṭāhir al-Silafī (d. 576/1180) both narrated it from al-Mubārak b. ʿAbd al-Jabbār (d. 500/1107), who narrated it with his own *isnād* reaching back to al-Ḥasan al-Rabaʿī.[48] However, the creed had been known long before that and in many places as that

---

41 Ibn Taymiyya, *Iqtiḍāʾ al-ṣirāṭ al-mustaqīm li-mukhālafat aṣḥāb al-jaḥīm* (Riyad: 1998), vol. 1, p. 376.

42 Ibn Taymiyya, *Darʾ taʿāruḍ al-ʿaql waʾl-naql* (Riyad, 1979) vol. 2, p. 7, pp. 22–3

43 But as shown above, Abū Yaʿlā Ibn al-Farrāʾ quoted this creed.

44 Muḥammad b. Abī Bakr Ibn Qayyim al-Jawziyya, *Ḥādī al-arwāḥ ilā bilād al-afrāḥ* (Miṣr, 1962) vol. 2, pp. 826–42.

45 Aḥmad Ibn Ḥanbal (attrib.), *Iʿtiqād ahl al-Sunna wa-al-jamāʿa.*

46 Another unknown individual; see Ibn Abū Yaʿlā al-Farrāʾ, *Ṭabaqāt al-Ḥanābila*, vol. 1, p. 349.

47 Ibid., vol. 1, pp. 349–50.

48 Ibid., and Aḥmad b. Muḥammad al-Silafī, *Al-Mashyakha al-baghdādiyya*, MS. Escorial 1783, fol. 71B. Al-Silafī's version has seventy men instead of ninety, but this mistake is easy to make in Arabic writing.

declared in 225/840 by Muḥammad b. ʿUkkāsha al-Kirmānī, who sought to articulate the traditionalists' views on theology. Al-Kirmānī's creed can be found in the works of al-Malaṭī (d. ʿAsqalān 377/987), Naṣr al-Maqdisī (d. Damascus 490/1096), Ibn al-Bannāʾ (d. Baghdad 471/1087) and Ibn ʿAsākir (d. Damascus 571/1176).[49]

In his creed, al-Kirmānī claims that the "people of the Sunna" have reached a consensus on the articles of his creed, and he goes on to name more than thirty traditionalists who vouch for the validity of the creed. What is significant about al-Kirmānī's list is that while he counts Isḥāq Ibn Rāhwayh as one of the leaders of the people of the Sunna, Aḥmad is not mentioned. In addition, in order to prove the validity of his creed, al-Kirmānī asserts that in a dream he presented it three times before the Prophet Muḥammad, who agreed with the entire creed, with particular emphasis on two points: the preference for ʿUthmān over ʿAlī and abstention from debating the differences that arose among the Companions.

However, some traditionalists accused al-Kirmānī of being a fabricator, someone who lies in order to support the Sunna and to guide people to moral behaviour. Abū Zurʿa al-Rāzī, a famous traditionalist and a student of Aḥmad, met al-Kirmānī and described him as a "liar who does not know how to lie",[50] and Abū Zurʿa as well as others used the abovementioned dream to illustrate al-Kirmānī's lying tendencies. In sum, this creed is not Aḥmad's but was attributed to him at a later date. An interesting story shows that some traditionalists found it is necessary to have Aḥmad's agreement on this creed. Al-Malaṭī reports that the caliph al-Mutawakkil asked Aḥmad to present to him "the Sunna and the Jamāʿa" which Aḥmad had learned from the traditionalists, who had learned it from the Successors, who had learned it from the Companions, who had learned it from the Prophet. Aḥmad, according to the story, narrated to him this creed, together with an account of the dream.[51] This fabricated story illustrates the importance of Aḥmad's approval for the legitimacy to the traditionalists' creeds

### *3. Creed III*

The third creed is attributed to Aḥmad through ʿAbdūs b. Mālik al-ʿAṭṭār (d. not known). ʿAbdūs was a Baghdadi traditionalist who studied under Aḥmad, Ibn Maʿīn and other traditionalists in Baghdad.[52] According to al-Khallāl, Aḥmad respected him, and they remained on very friendly terms;[53] he was "someone whom Aḥmad trusted".[54]

---

[49] Muḥammad b. Aḥmad al-Malaṭī, *al-Tanbīh wa al-Radd ʿalā ahl al-ahwāʾ wa'l-bidaʿ* (Baghdad, 1968), pp. 14–17; al-Ḥasan b. Aḥmad Ibn al-Bannāʾ, *al-Mukhtār fī uṣūl al-sunna* (Medina, 2005), pp. 103–106; Naṣr b. Ibrāhīm al-Maqdisī, *Mukhtaṣar al-Ḥujja ʿalā tārik al-maḥajja* (Riyadh, 2005), vol. 2, pp. 381–88; Ibn ʿAsākir, *Tārīkh Madīnat Dimashq*, vol. 9, pp. 299–302. There are two significant studies of al-Kirmānī's creed, by Fahmī Jadʿān and Riḍwān al-Sayyid, respectively; however, both attribute it to Umayya b. ʿUthmān al-Ḍamrī. See Fahmī Jadʿān, *Riyāh al-ʿaṣr: qaḍāyā markaziyya wa-hiwārāt kāshifa* (Beirut, 2002), pp. 219–76; al-Sayyid, 'Ahl al-Sunna wa'l-Jamāʿa', pp. 252–68.

[50] ʿUbayd Allāh b. ʿAbd al-Karīm Abū Zurʿa al-Rāzī, 'Asʾilat al-Bardhaʿī' in *Abū Zurʿa al-Rāzī wa juhūduhu fī al-Sunna al-Nabawiyya: maʿa taḥqīq kitābihi al-Ḍuʿafāʾ wa ajwibatihi ʿalā asʾilat al-Bardhaʿī* (al-Manṣura, 1989) vol. 2, pp. 539.

[51] Al-Malaṭī, *al-Tanbīh*, p. 17.

[52] Aḥmad b. ʿAlī al-Khaṭīb al-Baghdadī, *Tarīkh Baghdād* (Beirut, 1966), vol. 12, p. 417.

[53] Ibn Abū Yaʿlā al-Farrāʾ, *Ṭabaqāt al-Ḥanābila*, vol. 2, p. 166.

[54] See al-Dhahabī, *Siyar aʿlām al-nubalāʾ*, vol. 11, p. 268.

This creed was transmitted by Muḥammad b. Sulaymān al-Jawharī (al-Minqarī) from ʿAbdūs, and by the first decade of the tenth century (the last decade of the third A.H. century) the creed was known in Iraq and Egypt on account of the efforts of al-Jawharī, who transmitted it in Egypt and presumably in Iraq, Syria and *al-Thughūr* (Antioch and Mopsuestis).[55] However, al-Jawharī was described as someone who confuses reports from authentic narrators, and he reports dubious narrations from weak authorities.[56]

This creed is mainly an attack on Muʿtazilī doctrines. It starts with the importance and the authority of the Sunna, stressing that people should adhere to it. It then refers to belief in predestination, *ruʾya* (the doctrine that the believers will see God in the Hereafter) and the uncreated nature of the Qurʾān. Next the creed addresses the doctrines of the *samʿiyyāt*, such as the pool, the scales (*mīzān*), and intercession. Concerning the order of preference among the Companions, this creed, like creed I, lists the Companions in the following order: Abū Bakr, ʿUmar and ʿUthmān, and after them the *aṣḥāb al-shūrā*, namely, ʿAlī, Ṭalḥa, al-Zubayr, ʿAbd al-Raḥman b. ʿAwf and Saʿd. The creed discusses the caliphs' rights and then goes on to declare that one ought to participate in the funerary prayer of and request divine forgiveness for any member of the people of the *qibla* who professes to believe in the one God. One must not, says the creed, refuse to pray at such a person's funeral on account of any sin the deceased has committed. Moreover, the creed warns against declaring that any particular member of the people of the *qibla* is headed for either Hell or Paradise because of his or her actions. The creed ends by explaining the meaning of *kufr*, *fusūq* and *nifāq*.

Interestingly, this creed was related through three different transmission chains to different authorities:

1. To Aḥmad Ibn Ḥanbal, as described above
2. To ʿAlī Ibn al-Madīnī, one of Aḥmad's teachers, who subsequently became Aḥmad's adversary because of his cooperation with Aḥmad Ibn Abī Duʾād[57]
3. To Aḥmad Ibn Ḥanbal, who transmitted it from ʿAlī Ibn al-Madīnī[58]

Between Aḥmad's and Ibn al-Madīnī's versions there are some differences, the most significant being the following:

1. In the version that was related to Aḥmad (AV) *uʾyat Allāh* is discussed in two places; these two places are not found in the version related to Ibn al-Madīnī (MV). At the time of the Inquisition, Ibn al-Madīnī was known for his relationship with Ibn Abī Duʾād and was accused by Aḥmad of helping Ibn Abī Duʾād by showing the latter the weakness of the transmissions of *aḥādīth al-ruʾya*.
2. MV contains a list of people about whom it says that a person's loving them is a sign

[55] Aḥmad b. Muḥammad al-Khallāl, *al-Sunna* (Riyad, 1989–99) vol. 1, p. 172, p. 174; Hibat Allāh b. al-Ḥasan al-Lālakāʾī, *Sharḥ uṣūl iʿtiqād Ahl al-Sunna waʾl-jamāʿa: min al-kitāb waʾl-Sunna wa-ijmāʿ al-ṣaḥāba waʾl-tābiʿīn min baʿdihim* (Riyāḍ, 1994) vol. 1, pp. 175–85; Al-Khaṭīb al-Baghdadī,. *al-Kifāya fī ʿilm al-riwāya* ([Cairo], 1972) p. 99; Ibn Abū Yaʿlā al-Farrāʾ, *Ṭabaqāt al-Ḥanābila* vol. 2, pp. 166–74. al-Maqdisī, *Mukhtaṣar al-Hujja ʿalā tārik al-maḥajja* vol. 1, p. 235.

[56] Muḥammad Ibn Ḥibbān ibn Aḥmad Ibn Ḥibbān, *Kitāb al-Majrūḥīn min al-muḥaddithīn* (al-Riyāḍ, 2000) vol. 2, p. 328.

[57] Al-Lālakāʾī, *Sharḥ uṣūl iʿtiqād Ahl al-Sunna waʾl-jamāʿa*. pp. 1: 185–192.

[58] Al-Maqdisī, *Mukhtaṣar al-Ḥujja*, vol. 1, p. 235.

of that person's being a Sunnī; the list includes Abū Hurayra and ʿUmar b. ʿAbd al-ʿAzīz, as well as others. By contrast, it is a bad sign if one loves Abū Ḥanīfa and his *raʾy*. This list is not found in AV.

This creed is similar, in many points, to *Sharḥ al-Sunnah*, the creed attributed to either Ghulām Khalīl or al-Barbahārī. The similarity between the two creeds is not limited to overlap in terms of the opinions they contain; it is even manifested in identical word choices.

It seems more likely that this creed is Ibn al-Madīnī's rather than Aḥmad's as transmitted by al-Jawharī, who was known for confusing transmissions. It is also more likely that the creed originated with Ibn al-Madīnī than that it originated with Aḥmad and was then related to Ibn al-Madīnī, because when the creed first appeared, it was normal for traditionalists to appeal to Aḥmad as a normative determinant of correct belief and to relate their beliefs to Aḥmad rather than to Ibn al-Madīnī. Moreover, had the creed been attributed to Ibn al-Madīnī, the parts on *ruʾya* would not have been removed. Since the belief in *ruʾya* was not added to MV, it is hard to believe that the creed was Aḥmad's and was then attributed to Ibn al-Madīnī. Another possibility is that one of Ibn al-Madīnī's and Aḥmad's students wrote the creed based on the authority of his traditionalist masters (as was the case with the creed of Ḥarb b. Ismāʿīl). Subsequently, it was attributed at one point to Aḥmad and at another to Ibn al-Madīnī.

### *4. Creed IV*

The fourth creed was related to Aḥmad through Muḥammad b. Ḥumayd al-Andrābī (d. not known).[59] It is transmitted from Aḥmad through three different paths:

1. By al-Andrābī, narrated in Ibn Abī Yaʿlā's *Ṭabaqāt al-Ḥanābila* without intervening transmitters[60]
2. By Muḥammad b. Yūnus al-Sarkhasī (d. not known), narrated by Ibn Abī Yaʿlā[61]
3. Al-Sarkhasī > al-Andrābī > Aḥmad, recorded by Ibn al-Jawzī[62]

However, of these transmitters, al-Andrābī and al-Sarskhasī are unknown.

This creed is one of the shortest, and it deals mainly with predestination, faith, the order of preference among the Companions and the belief that the Qurʾān is uncreated. Additionally, the creed mentions the rights of caliphs and amirs, the *samʿiyāt* and some practices not involving belief (*praxy* not *doxy*), such as trade, which is allowed, and the *takbīr* (declaring God's greatness), which ought to be preformed four times at funerals.

However, as one has come to expect with these creeds, in some early sources the creed is related not to Aḥmad Ibn Ḥanbal but to another traditionalist. In this case, the creed was

---

[59] Laoust reads the name as Muḥammad b. Ḥabīb al-Andarānī, and this form also appears in the old edition of *Ṭabaqāt* (al-Fiqī ed.), vol. 1, p. 294, but the editor of the new and more accurate edition (al-ʿUthaymīn) reads the name as Muḥammad b. Ḥumayd al-Andarābī, which is prevalent in other Ḥanbalī sources.

[60] Ibn Abū Yaʿlā al-Farrāʾ, *Ṭabaqāt al-Ḥanābila*, vol. 2, pp. 293–95.

[61] Ibid., vol. 2, pp. 392–94.

[62] Abūʾl-Faraj ʿAbd al-Raḥmān b. ʿAlī Ibn al-Jawzī, *Manāqib al-Imām Aḥmad Ibn Ḥanbal* (Egypt, 1979), pp. 222–24.

attributed to al-ʿAbbās b. Mūsā b. Miskawayh (d. not known), who, it is said, declared it to the caliph al-Wāthiq (r. 227–32/842–47) during the Inquisition. Al-ʿAbbās claimed that the caliph punished him, and after he declared the creed, the caliph punished him again and pulled out four of al-ʿAbbās's teeth and then released him. Al-ʿAbbās subsequently met with Aḥmad Ibn Ḥanbal, who thanked him for his patience under the Inquisition. Aḥmad, al-ʿAbbās claimed, said, "We should write it [i.e., the creed] on our mosques' doors and teach it to our children and family." Aḥmad ordered his son Ṣāliḥ to write the story of al-ʿAbbās on a white parchment (*raqq*) and keep it. This report, Aḥmad said, would be one of the best that Ṣāliḥ will ever write, and it will allow him to meet God on the path of the "people of the Sunna and the Jamāʿa".[63] This story is clearly a traditionalist myth about the Inquisition. Moreover, we have a third version of this creed, which is related to Bishr b. al-Ḥārith al-Ḥāfī (d. 227/841).[64] Altogether, the available evidence indicates that the authenticity of this creed can be seriously questioned.

### *5. Creed V*

The fifth creed is thought to be related to Aḥmad by Muḥammad b. ʿAwf al-Ḥimṣī (d. 272/885). Ibn Abī Yaʿlā claims that he found this creed written by Aḥmad al-Sinjī (d. after 400/1009), who narrated it via his own chain of transmission (*isnād*) from Aḥmad Ibn Ḥanbal (Ibn Abī Yaʿlā did not reproduce the *isnād*).[65]

This creed is likely to be a combination of two creeds The first is creed III, which is placed in the first part of this creed, and the second is a tract that displays extreme traditionalist theology. The extreme nature of the second creed can be illustrated by the following examples.

On the subject of the order of preference among the Companions, and in contrast to all

وخير الناس بعد رسول الله ... أبو بكر ثم عمر ثم عثمان ثم علي. فقلت له: يا أبا عبد الله، فإنهم يقولون: إنك وقفت على عثمان؟ فقال: كذبوا والله عليّ، إنما حدثتهم بحديث ابن عمر: 'كنا نفاضل بين أصحاب رسول الله ... ، كنا نقول: أبو بكر ثم عمر ثم عثمان، فيبلغ ذلك النبي ... فلا ينكره، ولم يقل النبي ... : لا تخايروا بعد هؤلاء بين أحد، ليس لأحدٍ في ذلك حجة، فمن وقف على عثمان ولم يربع بعلي فهو على غير السنة.

other *riwāyāt* from Aḥmad, Ibn ʿAwf asserts that Aḥmad said,

> The best person after the Messenger of God is Abū Bakr, then ʿUmar, then ʿUthmān and then ʿAlī". Then I [Ibn ʿAwf] said: 'O Abū ʿAbd Allāh, they claim that you end at ʿUthman." Aḥmad Aḥmad replied, "They have falsely attributed that to me. I have only related to them the *hadīth* of Ibn ʿUmar: 'We used to establish a preference among the Companions of the Messenger of God ..., saying Abū Bakr, then ʿUmar, then ʿUthman. The Prophet ... heard this and did not reject it.' [But Aḥmad added,] "The Prophet ... did not say one ought to refrain from assigning preference [to Companions] after these. Nobody has

[63] ʿUbayd Allāh b. Muḥammad Ibn Batta, *Kitāb al-Sharḥ wa'l-ibāna ʿalā uṣūl al-sunna wa'l-diyāna wa mujānabat al-mukhālifīn wa mubāyanat ahl al-ahwāʾ al-mariqīn.* (Mecca, 1984) vol. 6, pp. 284–6. The story, without the creed, is reported in al-Maqdisī, *Mukhtaṣar al-Ḥujja ʿalā tārik al-maḥajja* vol. 2, pp. 325–329.

[64] Al-Maqdisī, *Mukhtaṣar al-Ḥujja ʿalā tārik al-maḥajja*, vol. 2, pp. 394–96.

[65] Ibn Abī Yaʿlā, *Ṭabaqāt al-Ḥanābila*, vol. 2, p. 339.

> evidence of [the requirement to end at ʿUthman], and hence, whoever ends at ʿUthman and does not add ʿAlī as the fourth, is not in accordance with the Sunna.

This condemnation of those who end the list of the best Companions with ʿUthmān and do not include ʿAlī as the fourth-best Companion is not found in any other sources relating to Aḥmad. The majority (and the oldest) of the sources report that Aḥmad ended the list with ʿUthmān, while some other sources claim that Aḥmad accepted ʿAlī as the fourth in the list. However, to my knowledge no source except this creed ascribes to Aḥmad the view that anyone who does not acknowledge ʿAlī as the fourth-best Companion thereby contradicts the Sunna. Furthermore, al-Khallāl and then Abī Yaʿlā collected various *riwāyāt* from Aḥmad about this issue, and none of these contained Ibn ʿAwf's version.[66] It is more likely that this creed, which was not known to them (but became known later through Ibn Abī Yaʿlā), was written by Aḥmad al-Sinjī.

A second indication of the inauthenticity of the second part of this creed is the differences in the usage of *ḥadīths* in the first and second halves of the creed, respectively. While the first half, which resembles creed III, uses very well known and sound *ḥadīths*, the second half uses unknown and unsound *ḥadīths*. It is highly implausible that Aḥmad Ibn Ḥanbal, who was famous for his critique of *ḥadīths*, would have used such traditions. One of these questionable *ḥadīths* is that the Prophet forbade people to pray behind alongside the Qadariyya, the Murjiʾa, the Rāfiḍa and the Jahmiyya, and to pray at their funerals. Yet all of these parties were established only after the Prophet's death. In sum, this creed combines two creeds: the first part was probably influenced by creed III, and the second part seems to have been taken from an otherwise unknown extreme traditionalist creed.

### *6. Creed VI*

This creed is a letter from Aḥmad Ibn Ḥanbal to Musaddad b. Musarhad (d. 228/842–3), who had asked him about the Inquisition and the disagreements among people about *qadar*, *rafḍ*, *iʿtizāl*, the creation of Qurʾān and *irjāʾ*.[67]

The first part of this creed is dedicated to rejecting the doctrines of the Jahmiyya, the Muʿtazila and the Rāfiḍa. The second part deals with the *samʿiyyāt*, with certain practices which are not concerned with belief (more than those mentioned in creed IV) and with the order of preference among the Companions.

Regarding this creed, two points need to be made. First, in Ibn Abū Yaʿlā's and al-Maqdisī's versions of this creed, the order of preference among the Companions is given as follows: Abū Bakr, ʿUmar, ʿUthmān, ʿAlī. In Ibn al-Jawzī's version, by contrast, the list ends at ʿUthmān, without including ʿAlī as the fourth best of the Companions. In this version Aḥmad relies on Ibn ʿUmar's *ḥadīth* to establish the order of preference (see discussion of creed V above).

Second, in this creed Aḥmad mentions his disagreement with al-Shāfiʿī over the *takbīr* (declaring God's greatness) at funerals. Aḥmad says that the *takbīr* should be performed at

---

[66] See al-Khallāl, *al-Sunna*, vol. 2, pp. 404–11, and Muḥammad b. al-Ḥusayn Abū Yaʿlā al-Farrāʾ, *al-Masāʾil al-ʿaqadiyya min kitāb al-Riwāyatayn wa al-wajhayn: Masāʾil min uṣūl al-diyānāt* (Riyadh, 1999), pp. 41–51.

[67] Ibn Abū Yaʿlā al-Farrāʾ, *Ṭabaqāt al-Ḥanābila*, vol. 2, pp. 426–32; Ibn al-Jawzī, *Manāqib al-Imām Aḥmad*, pp. 224–29; and al-Maqdisī, *Mukhtaṣar al-Hujja*, vol. 2, pp. 366–79.

funerals four times, but if the *imām* adds a fifth repetition, one should add it with him. By contrast, al-Shāfiʿī held that if the *imām* repeats the *takbīr* five times, one should perform the prayer again.

The order of preference among the Companions is not the only difference which can be found in the various versions of this creed. For instance, in Abū Saʿīd al-Naqqāsh's (d. 414/1023) version,[68] which is presumably that used by Abū Yaʿlā,[69] Aḥmad says that "God comes down, every night, to the lowest heaven, and His throne is not unoccupied by Him". This sentence is not found in either of the versions we have now.

However, at some points of this creed, Aḥmad's doctrine can be identified as it is found in other *riwāyāt.* For example, in this creed the Jahmiyya are divided into three groups: the first who say the Qurʾān is created; the second who say the Qurʾān is God's word and do not specify whether it is created or uncreated (termed *wāqifa*); and the third who say the pronunciation of the Qurʾān (*lafẓ*) is created. This division is found in the creed and is attributed to Aḥmad's son Ṣāliḥ, but it is not found in the latter's *Masāʾil* work.[70] On the other hand, some points contrast with the mainstream of Aḥmad's *riwāyāt.* For example, in this creed Aḥmad defines the Rāfiḍa as those who prefer ʿAlī to Abū Bakr and say ʿAlī converted to Islam before Abū Bakr. In other *riwāyāt,* by contrast, Aḥmad defined the Rāfiḍa as those who not only prefer ʿAlī over Abū Bakr and ʿUmar but also curse them.[71]

ʿAbd al-Raḥmān b. Muḥammad b. Manda (d. 470/1078), the outstanding figure among the Ḥanbalīs in Iṣfahān in the fifth A.H./eleventh century, rejected the supposed authenticity of this letter on the basis that Aḥmad b. Muḥammad al-Bardhaʿī, who transmitted it from Aḥmad Ibn Ḥanbal, was unknown.[72] Ibn Taymiyya argued against Ibn Manda, claiming that the letter was well known among the Ḥanbalīs and the people of the Sunna, all of whom accept it. Moreover, Ibn Taymiyya added, Abī Yaʿlā Ibn al-Farrāʾ relied upon it and included it in his notes in his own handwriting.[73]

However, Aḥmad b. Muḥammad al-Bardhaʿī, as Ibn Mandah suggests, is an unknown transmitter, and his name is spelled differently in different sources. In some sources he is Aḥmad b. Muḥammad al-Barthaʿī al-Tamīmī,[74] in others he is al-Tamīmī al-Zarandī,[75] and in yet other sources he is al-Ḥāfiẓ Abūʾl-Ḥasan ʿAlī b. Muḥammad al-Barthaʿī.[76] Although Abū Yaʿlā Ibn al-Farrāʾ relied on this creed, it was not known to al-Khallāl or other Ḥanbalīs before Ibn al-Farrāʾ. The contradictions between the different versions of the creed thus reflect conflicts among the traditionalists on some aspects of theology, with each group modifying the creed to support its position.

---

[68] Aḥmad b. ʿAbd al-Halīm Ibn Taymiyya, *Majmūʿ fatáwá shaykh al-islám Aḥmad Ibn Taymiyya* (Riyadh, 1999), vol. 5, pp. 380–82.

[69] Abū Yaʿlā Ibn al-Farrāʾ, *Ibṭāl al-Taʾwīlāt*, vol. 1, p. 261.

[70] Ibn al-Jawzī, *Manāqib al-imām Aḥmad,* pp. 213–14.

[71] For these *riwāyāt,* see ʿAbd al-Ilāh b. Sulaymān al-Aḥmadī, *al-Masāʾil waʾl-rasāʾil al-marwiyya ʿan al-imām Aḥmad Ibn Ḥanbal fīʾ-ʿaqīda* (Riyadh, 1992), vol. 2, pp. 357–61.

[72] Ibn Taymiyya, *Majmūʿ fatāwā,* vol. 5, p. 396.

[73] Ibid.

[74] Ibn al-Jawzī, *Manāqib al-imām Aḥmad,* p. 224.

[75] Ibn Abī Yaʿlā, *Ṭabaqāt al-Ḥanābila,* vol. 2, p. 426.

[76] Al-Maqdisī, *Mukhtaṣar al-Ḥujja,* vol. 2, p. 366.

## *7. Conclusion*

My analysis indicates that these creeds, all attributed to Aḥmad, have in common a predominance of ninth-century theological concerns. One concludes, therefore, that these creeds are more likely to represent traditionalist theology in the third and fourth A.H./ninth and tenth centuries than Aḥmad's own beliefs. Even though Aḥmad's views, to the extent that they are known, correspond to the general views expressed in these creeds, it is difficult to attribute the wording or any single point within them to him unless we find it in other reliable sources. This applies particularly to the more extreme statements. It is noteworthy that these creeds epitomise how the authority of the *salaf* was fused with that of Aḥmad Ibn Ḥanbal, who became the unique authority for correct belief. This means that the *salaf* and Aḥmad Ibn Ḥanbal were used equally and reciprocally by later traditionalists as sources of doctrinal verification and authority.

One of the reliable sources is, however, a letter that Aḥmad wrote in reply to the caliph al-Mutawakkil's question about the Qur'ān.[77] According to al-Dhahabī,[78] this 'letter-creed' contains the most authoritative presentation of Aḥmad's belief and his method of arriving at it. In the 'letter-creed', Aḥmad was asked to present his theological views concerning the creation of the Qur'ān, after the caliph al-Mutawakkil had ended the Inquisition. Aḥmad starts with the assertion that the Qur'ān should not be a subject of *jidāl* (arguments); accordingly, he quotes reports from the Prophet and his Companions and their Successors in which *khuṣūmāt* (arguments) with innovators are disallowed. His main evidence for the Qur'ān's being uncreated is threefold:

1. The Qur'ān is part of God's knowledge (*ʿilm Allāh*), and God's knowledge is uncreated; hence, the Qur'ān is uncreated.
2. There is a difference between God's creation and His orders (*al-khalq wa'l-amr*), and the Qur'ān is part of God's orders; hence, the Qur'ān is uncreated.
3. The *salaf* held that the Qur'ān is uncreated.

Aḥmad ends his letter by declaring his method of belief:

لستُ بصاحب كلام، ولا أرى الكلام في شيء إلا ما كان في كتاب الله أو حديث عن النبي أو عن أصحابه أو عن التابعين. فأما غير ذلك فالكلام فيه غير محمود.

> I am not a theologian (*sāḥib al-kalām*), and I do not agree to discuss anything [in a theological way] unless it exists in the Book of God, or in a *ḥadīth* from the Prophet or from his Companions or from their Successors. Beyond these, any discussion [of an issue] is not praiseworthy.

[77] This letter was transmitted by Aḥmad's sons Ṣāliḥ and ʿAbd Allāh and by his disciple al-Marrūdhī, all of whom were with Aḥmad in Sāmarā' when he wrote the letter. See Ṣāliḥ b. Aḥmad Ibn Ḥanbal, *Sirat al-Imām Aḥmad Ibn Ḥanbal* (Alexandria, 1981), pp. 106–109; Ṣāliḥ b. Aḥmad Ibn Ḥanbal, *Masā'il al-Imām Aḥmad Ibn Ḥanbal* (Riyadh, 1999), pp. 238–53; ʿAbd Allāh b. Aḥmad Ibn Ḥanbal, *Kitāb al-Sunna* (Riyadh, 1994), vol. 1, pp. 134–40; al-Khallāl, *al-Sunna*, vol. 6, pp. 101–108; and Aḥmad b. ʿAbd Allāh al-Aṣfahānī, *Ḥilyat al-awliyā' wa-ṭabaqāt al-aṣfiyā'* (Beirut, 1988), vol. 9, pp. 116–19.

[78] Al-Dhahabī, *Siyar aʿlām al-nubalā'*, vol. 11, p. 286.

# 3.2. A RESPONSE TO SAUD AL-SARHAN'S *THE CREEDS OF AḤMAD IBN ḤANBAL*

*Christopher Melchert*

Henri Laoust first drew the attention of modern scholars to the six creeds attributed to Aḥmad ibn Ḥanbal in Ibn Abī Yaʿlá (d. 526/1133), *Ṭabaqāt al-ḥanābila*.[79] Already in the fourteenth century, al-Dhahabī (d. 748/1348?) questioned the attribution of Laoust's Creed I. Laoust himself stated that they must be regarded as to some degree a collective effort, inextricably comprising both Aḥmad's very words and the elaborations of others after him. Therefore, when Saud Al-Sarhan now questions the attribution to Aḥmad of every last one of them, this is to support the conventional view of modern scholarship, not to overturn it. But Al-Sarhan is the first to address their attribution in detail, and on this account his article must be considered a significant advance.

Al-Sarhan's principal methods are three. First, he looks for quotations of the creeds in later literature, mostly Ḥanbali, and seizes on attributions to other than Aḥmad. This looks to me like a version of the principle of *lectio difficilior* in textual criticism; that is, the presumption by which, faced with two readings equally acceptable on other grounds, we choose the more difficult text, supposing that a careless scribe will more likely substitute a familiar word for an unfamiliar than the other way around. With the attribution of Aḥmad's creeds, Al-Sarhan's reasoning is evidently that it must have been far more tempting to reassign texts from persons of middling or meagre fame to Aḥmad ibn Ḥanbal, eponym of the Ḥanbali school and great exemplar of Sunnism, than to reassign texts from Aḥmad to lesser names. So Al-Sarhan reassigns Creed I to Ḥarb al-Kirmānī (*fl.* mid-9th cent.), Creed III to ʿAlī ibn al-Madīnī (d. 234/849) or disciples of his, and Creed IV to al-ʿAbbās ibn Mūsá ibn Miskawayh (*fl.* early 9th cent.). It seems to me his argument here is strong, a notable improvement on Laoust's negative proof that the creeds are not mentioned in early lists of Aḥmad's works.

Secondly, Al-Sarhan investigates the purported transmitters of these creeds from Aḥmad. This is apparently a supplementary argument concerning Creeds I and III, the main one concerning Creeds II and VI. With this argument I am less comfortable. We lack the evidence on which basis these medieval critics made their judgements, and therefore must take their word for it. This is risky for two reasons. First, the medieval critics continually disagreed amongst themselves, confirming the extent to which their judgements were intuitive, not scientific. Secondly, their ratings of transmitters were generalizations, excluding neither

[79] Henri Laoust, 'Les premières professions de foi hanbalites', *Mélanges Louis Massignon*, 3 vols (Damascus, 1957), vol. 3, pp. 7–35, at pp. 12–15; idem, *La profession de foi d'Ibn Batta* (Damascus, 1958), pp. xv–xvi. The creeds are in Ibn Abī Yaʿlá, *Ṭabaqāt al-ḥanābila*, 2 vols (Cairo, 1371/1952), Creed I at vol. 1, pp. 24–36, II at vol. 1, pp. 130–1, III at vol. 1, pp. 241–6, IV at vol. 1, pp. 294–5 and pp. 329–30, V at vol.1, pp. 311–13, and VI at vol. 1, pp. 341-5.

occasional mistakes from transmitters pronounced trustworthy nor accurate transmission from others pronounced untrustworthy. *They* could go back to the evidence to assess individual cases, *we* less easily.

Thirdly, Al-Sarhan looks for contradictions either within creeds or between these creeds and others more reliably attributed to Aḥmad. This is his main argument concerning Creed V, a supplementary concerning VI. The first part of Creed V repeats III, he says, the second part appears to be too extreme for it to have come from Aḥmad. This is an argument of middling strength, I am inclined to think, for although it rests on the evidence before us, it is difficult to make conclusively. I am unconvinced that the first part of Creed V was taken from III. Here, for example, is how III rejects theological disputation:

> The *sunna* in our opinion is (known from) hadith (*āthār*) from the Messenger of God ... The *sunna* interprets the Qur'an, being evidence (for the meaning of) the Qur'an. There is no analogy (*qiyās*) in the *sunna*, examples are not to be made up for it, and it is not realized by minds or fancies, rather it is a matter of following and leaving off fancy.[80]

Here, then, is the corresponding passage of V, following a series of hadith reports that evidently contradict Sunni dogma about unbelief:

> We submit to them, even if we do not know their interpretation. We do not talk about them, engage in dispute over them, or interpret them. Rather, we relate them as they have come. We believe in them and know that they are true, as the Messenger of God . . . . said. We submit to them and do not reject them.[81]

This is not close enough to imply verbal dependence.

As for contradiction with other quotations, Al-Sarhan particularly objects to the quotation of Aḥmad at the end of Creed V by which it is contrary to the *sunna* to refrain from identifying ʿAlī as the fourth-best Companion.[82] I think Al-Sarhan goes too far when he says that 'no source, except this creed, ascribes to Aḥmad the view that anyone who does not say ʿAlī is the fourth best Companions is not "on the Sunna".' Al-Khallāl quotes Aḥmad ibn al-Ḥusayn ibn Ḥassān as reporting this response from Aḥmad to being told of a man who loved all the Companions but would not prefer any of them to any other: 'The *sunna* is that Abū Bakr, ʿUmar, ʿUthmān, and ʿAlī are preferred among the caliphs.'[83] However, there is inconsistency even among the *masāʾil* collections, which belong to the first generation of Ḥanbali literature and seem much more securely attributed than the six Creeds As I have developed elsewhere, Ṣāliḥ and ʿAbd Allāh report that Aḥmad specified Abū Bakr, ʿUmar, ʿUthmān, and ʿAlī as regards the caliphate (*al-khilāfa*), Abū Bakr, ʿUmar, and ʿUthmān as regards who was best (*l-tafḍīl*).[84] That is, he was certain that ʿAlī had been a genuine caliph in succession to ʿUthmān, contrary to the Umayyad view that Muʿāwiya had succeeded ʿUthmān with ʿAlī no more than an unsuccessful pretender. As for who was the best Companion after ʿUthmān,

[80] Ibn Abī Yaʿlá, *Ṭabaqāt*, vol. 1, p. 241.

[81] Ibn Abī Yaʿlá, *Ṭabaqāt*, vol. 1, p. 311.

[82] Ibn Abī Yaʿlá, *Ṭabaqāt*, vol.1, p. 313.

[83] Al-Khallāl, *al-Sunna*, 7 vols in 3 ed. (Riyadh, 1994/1415) vol. 2, p. 372.

[84] Ṣāliḥ ibn Aḥmad, *Masāʾil al-imam Aḥmad ibn Ḥanbal* (Riyadh, 1420/1999), no. 349; ʿAbd Allāh ibn Aḥmad, *Masāʾil al-imām Aḥmad ibn Ḥanbal* (Beirut, 1401/1981), p. 440. On the problems of *khilāfa* and *tafḍīl*, cf. Christopher Melchert, *Ahmad ibn Hanbal* (Oxford: Oneworld, 2006), pp. 93–8.

Aḥmad refused to say, probably from reluctance to take sides concerning the dispute between ʿAlī on the one hand, Ṭalḥa, al-Zubayr, and ʿĀʾisha on the other. By contrast, however, Abū Dāwūd and Ibn Hāniʾ report that Aḥmad specified Abū Bakr, ʿUmar, ʿUthmān, and ʿAlī in order as caliphs and the first of these three in order as the best, "but we do not rebuke whoever makes ʿAlī the fourth".[85] Al-Khallāl (d. 311/923) collected and synthesized almost all available accounts of Aḥmad's doctrine. He reports from several sources that Aḥmad said the best were, in order, Abū Bakr, ʿUmar, ʿUthmān, and ʿAlī; however, he then protests that by most accounts (*al-mashhūr*), he named only the first three.[86]

How to account for contradictions like this? Khallāl obviously preferred to believe that Aḥmad had one definite opinion, which must have been the one most widely reported. By this criterion, which has something to commend it when the reports are as early and securely attested as what Khallāl had to deal with, our Creed V certainly misrepresents Aḥmad, as Al-Sarhan believes, for it goes to an extreme weakly attested elsewhere (although not completely unattested). Alternatively, however, if somewhat less probably, it seems possible both that Aḥmad himself went back and forth on this point and that Aḥmad was too far ahead of majority opinion in Baghdadi Sunni circles in recognizing the claims of ʿAlī, so that the majority of reporters discreetly scaled back his commendation.

There are certainly indications in the early sources of uncertainty as to Aḥmad's position. ʿAbd Allāh quotes Aḥmad's longtime associate Muhannā ibn Yaḥyá (*fl.* earlier 9th cent.), 'I asked Aḥmad ibn Ḥanbal two years after he had been released from prison, "What do you say of the Qur'an?" He said, "It is the speech of God, increate. Whoever relates anything else of me, what he says is vain (*mubaṭṭal*)." I told him, "A certain person has said that you said, 'It is the speech of God', also that you told him 'It is neither create nor increate but rather the speech of God.'" Aḥmad said, "This is vanity, what you have said. I did not say this. Rather, it is the speech of God increate."'[87] In a story from al-Marrūdhī, we are told that Aḥmad's disciple Abū Ṭālib (presumably Aḥmad ibn Ḥumayd, d. 244/858–9) angered Aḥmad by writing to the people of Nisibis that he had declared, 'My pronunciation of the Qur'an is increate.' Trembling, Abū Ṭālib tried to excuse himself as having spoken only in his own name. Aḥmad told him, 'Do not relate this of yourself or of me. I have never heard a learnèd man say this.' He subsequently told various persons – four are named – that Aḥmad had forbidden it to be said that one's pronunciation of the Qur'an was increate. Fūrān (ʿAbd Allāh ibn Muḥammad ibn al-Muhājir, d. 256/870) was another disciple he upbraided for the same offence. Ibn Shaddād (*fl.* mid-9th cent.) crossed out the offending declaration in his notebook in Aḥmad's presence, substituting a less precise formula between the lines.[88] These incidents concerning the Qur'an certainly might have provided the literary model for Creed V's report of Aḥmad's exasperation at those who had misrepresented his position regarding ʿAlī.

[85] Abū Dāwūd, *Kitāb Masāʾil al-imām Aḥmad* (Cairo, 1353/1934, repr. Beirut, n.d.), p. 277; Ibn Hāniʾ, *Masāʾil al-imām Aḥmad ibn Ḥanbal*, 2 vols (Beirut, 1400) vol. 2, p. 169; also, despite ʿAbd Allāh's *Masāʾil*, ʿAbd Allāh ibn Aḥmad, *al-Sunna* (Mecca, 1349), p. 206 = (Beirut, 1414/1994), p. 235.

[86] Khallāl, *Sunna*, vol. 2, pp. 404–10.

[87] ʿAbd Allāh, *Sunna*, p. 61 (Mecca) = (Beirut) p. 70.

[88] Khallāl, *Sunna*, vol. 7, pp. 95–100 = 2 vols (Cairo, 1428/2007) vol. 2, pp. 335–8. The amended declaration is quoted without a framing story by Ibn Abī Yaʿlá, *Ṭabaqāt* vol. 1, p. 299, s.n. Muḥammad ibn Shaddād, although Khallāl calls him Ḥamdūn ibn al-Shaddād near the end of this passage.

They also show that attribution of theological views to Aḥmad by supposition was a recognized problem just as far back as our sources will take us. The problem of false attribution has received the most attention in the fields of law and hadith, where its extent has been subject to dispute.[89] To speak only of the ninth century, Norman Calder alleged massive pseudonymity in books of the Mālikī school (the *Mudawwana* of Saḥnūn) and the Shāfiī (the *Risāla* and *Umm* of the eponym himself and the *Mukhtaṣar* of al-Muzanī).[90] The more effective refutations have treated Mālik's *Muwaṭṭa'* of the previous century, and my own study confirms that ninth-century quotations of Shāfiʿī are not dependably accurate, although I have not made out reworking so drastic as Calder did.[91] Pseudonymous attribution of juridical positions to Aḥmad by subsequent Ḥanābila was a recognized problem in the school, where it was discussed under the technical name of *takhrīj*.[92] It was thought to be justified as extrapolation from positions securely known yet less authoritative than Aḥmad's express declaration in securely attested early texts.[93] As for its frequency, I myself have found that where Aḥmad's own position concerning some juridical problem is cited in a fifteenth-century collection of Ḥanbali opinions, there are multiple versions of it about a third of the time.[94] (Incidentally, Ibn Taymiyya is a late example of those who from time to time quote Aḥmad without citing any source to support a rule that no one in the school had hitherto so framed.[95] Ibn Taymiyya's acceptance of *takhrīj*, both express and implied, weakens the argument that his citing *al-Radd ʿalá al-jahmiyya* without denying its attribution to Aḥmad amounts to his endorsing it as verbatim quotation. I doubt the attribution, myself, mainly because its style of argumentation is so at odds with all other evidence of Aḥmad's regard for *kalām*, an application of Al-Sarhan's third method.)

My object here is to characterize the environment in which Aḥmad's putative creed was quoted; that is, an intellectual culture where 'Aḥmad said' might mean anything from 'he said, in these words, as I directly heard' to 'if he were here to answer our questions, this is,

[89] For reviews of the controversy over the authenticity of hadith, *v. Harald Motzki, The Origins of Islamic Jurisprudence* (trans. Marion H. Katz: Leiden, 2002), chap. 1, and Herbert Berg, *The Development of Exegesis in Early Islam* (Richmond, Surrey, 2000), chap. 2. For a review of controversies over the law, v. Christopher Melchert, 'The Early History of Islamic Law' in Herbert Berg (ed.), *Method and Theory in the Study of Islamic Origins* (Leiden, 2003), pp. 293–324.

[90] Norman Calder, *Studies in Early Muslim Jurisprudence* (Oxford, 1993), chaps. 1, 4, 5, 9.

[91] Christopher Melchert, 'The Meaning of *qāla 'l-Shāfiʿī* in Ninth-Century Sources' in James E. Montgomery (ed.) *'Abbasid Studies* (Leuven, 2004), pp. 277-301.

[92] For Ḥanbali discussions, v. for example ʿAbd al-Salām ibn Taymiyya (al-Majd, d. 652/1254?), et al., *al-Musawwada*, (Cairo, n.d., repr. Beirut, n.d.), pp. 527–9 = Silsilat al-Rasā'il al-Jāmiʿiyya 14, 2 vols (Riyad and Beirut, 1422/2001) vol. 2, pp. 941–3, and al-Mardāwī (d. 885/1480), *Qāʿida nāfiʿa jāmiʿa li-ṣifat al-riwāyāt al-manqūla ʿan al-imām Aḥmad*, appended to idem, *al-Inṣāf* 12 vols (Cairo, 1955–8, repr. Beirut, 1419/1998), vol. 12, pp. 177–218, esp. pp. 193–4, pp. 196–7. For an introductory survey, *v.* Wael B. Hallaq, '*Takhrīj* and the Construction of Juristic Authority' in Bernard G. Weiss (ed.), *Studies in Islamic Legal Theory* (Leiden, 2002), pp. 317–35. Hallaq finds that *takhrīj* was most intensively practised in the Shāfiʿī and Ḥanbali schools (p. 329).

[93] Ibn Taymiyya, *al-Qawāʿid al-nūrāniyya al-fihiyya* (Cairo, 1370/1951), p. 258.

[94] Christopher Melchert, 'Ibn Taymîyah and Ibn Qayyim al-Jawzîyah and the Ḥanbali School of Law', forthcoming in a collection of papers edited by Birgit Krawietz and Georges Tamer. The 15th-century collection is Mardāwī, *Inṣāf*.

[95] E.g. Mardāwī, *Inṣāf*, vol. 4, p. 155.

I believe, the gist of what he would say'. Pseudonymous attribution could be deprecated, strongly as in the case of Aḥmad on the pronunciation of the Qur'an, weakly as in the case of juridical *takhrīj* from the point of view of later-medieval Ḥanābila. I should guess that it tended to be more tolerant of pseudonymity than our intellectual culture in the present mainly because reliance on oral and manuscript transmission made it harder to avoid (textual fluidity and uncertainty of attribution were simply more familiar, everyday problems), secondarily because in that culture, compared with ours, authority resided much more in teachers, less in texts. Although I do not find Al-Sarhan's various arguments equally strong, I would say that, given the intellectual culture of the ninth century, the balance of probabilities is against our having in any of the six creeds an exact, unaltered transcription of his dictation.

The implication of Al-Sarhan's results for historians is mixed. On the one hand, the value of Aḥmad's creeds in documenting ninth-century Sunni theology is if anything increased, inasmuch as the products of a school can be expected to reflect more widely-held beliefs than the opinions of an individual. On the other hand, their value is somewhat lessened if we want to document Sunni opinion at precisely the middle of the ninth century, not, say, three-quarters of the way through it (sometimes, possibly, well into the tenth century).

As a test case, let me mention the creed attributed to the popular preacher Ghulām Khalīl (d. 275/888) in a twelfth-century manuscript and to the Ḥanbali leader al-Barbahārī (d. 329/941) in the biographical dictionary of Ibn Abī Yaʿlá (d. 526/1133).[96] I have argued for its attribution to Barbahārī. No anachronism patently rules out attribution to Ghulām Khalīl. The creed's specific warnings against those who speak of *shawq* (longing) and *maḥabba* (love) in relation to God seem to fit Ghulām Khalīl and his Sufi Inquisition.[97] However, they also might have led to misattribution to him, given his fame for persecuting Sufis (and little else). They moreover appear to be consistent with the teaching of Sahl al-Tustarī (d. 283/896?), whose disciple Barbahārī is said to have been. Its stress on commanding right and forbidding wrong (*al-amr bi-al-maʿrūf wa-al-nahy ʿan al-munkar*) is highly consistent with Barbahārī's continual involvement in rioting, less so with Ghulām Khalīl's Inquisition, which was something he persuaded the authorities to undertake. Its fierce opposition to speculative theology is also consistent with stories of Barbahārī's hostility to Abū al-Ḥasan al-Ashʿarī and Muʿtazili hostility to him, whereas Ghulām Khalīl is not known independently for hostility to *kalām*.[98] To the contrary, Laoust, followed by Jarrar and Günther (qq.v. for résumés of the creed), assumed practically without argument that the manuscript and Ibn Abī Yaʿlá are both correct, Barbahārī having simply appropriated the text as expressing his own views as well.[99] If

---

[96] Louis Massignon, *Recueil de texts inédits concernant l'histoire de la mystique en pays d'Islam* (Paris, 1929), pp. 212–14 (excerpt from Ẓāhiriyya *majāmiʿ* 13); Ibn Abī Yaʿlá, *Ṭabaqāt*, vol. 2, pp. 18–43.

[97] For this Inquisition, *v.* Louis Massignon, *The Passion of al-Hallāj*, 4 vols (Princeton, 1982), vol. 1, pp. 80–1; Carl Ernst, *Words of Ecstasy in Sufism* (Albany, 1985), p. 101; Richard Gramlich, *Alte Vorbilder des Sufitums* 1: *Scheiche des Westens* (Wiesbaden, 1996), pp. 383–5; and Christopher Melchert, 'The Transition From Asceticism to Mysticism at the Middle of the Ninth Century CE', *Studia Islamica* 83 (1996), pp. 51–70, at pp. 65–6.

[98] Sim., Christopher Melchert, 'The Ḥanābila and the Early Sufis', *Arabica* 48 (2001), pp. 352–67, at pp. 361–2.

[99] Laoust, *Profession*, xxix; Maher Jarrar and Sebastian Günther, 'Ġulām Ḫalīl und das *Kitāb Šarḥ*

Al-Sarhan is right about the six creeds attributed by Ibn Abī Yaʿlá to Aḥmad, then Ibn Abī Yaʿlá's attribution of this creed to Barbahārī must carry diminished weight. On the other hand, if Al-Sarhan's findings indicate that the six creeds attributed to Aḥmad are from later in the ninth century, it becomes harder to credit so much more elaborate a creed to Ghulām Khalīl: from Creed III in the later ninth century to Barbahārī's creed in the first third of the tenth to Ibn Baṭṭa's in the last quarter of the tenth is a more plausible progression than from Creed III to Ghulām Khalīl to Ibn Baṭṭa (here is Al-Sarhan's third method).

The attribution of the manuscript is not decisive evidence, either. Al-Sarhan brings up a faultily-attributed manuscript in connection with Creed V. Anyone who has worked with manuscripts knows they are liable, in descending order of frequency, (a) to bear a different title from that of other copies of the same work, (b) to lack the first and last folios, and (c) to be inscribed with an altogether erroneous attribution. For a Ḥanbali example, which has recently occupied my attention, let me mention the two known manuscripts of Aḥmad (actually ʿAbd Allāh ibn Aḥmad), *al-Zuhd*, which have exactly the same chain of transmission written out at the beginning even though they present texts slightly different from each other and scarcely a third as long as the text of *al-Zuhd* known to have circulated two centuries after the time of the last name on the given chain of transmission. That chain was obviously copied from another manuscript and does not represent the recent transmission history of either text.[100] Something of the sort could also account for the chain of transmission at the beginning of the manuscript of Ghulām Khalīl's creed, which traces it back to Ghulām Khalīl through Ṭabarī's disciple Aḥmad ibn Kāmil (d. 350/961 but said to have been 14 or 15 at the death of Ghulām Khalīl).

In sum, Al-Sarhan's re-attribution of Aḥmad's creeds does not revolutionize our understanding of the development of early Ḥanbali theology. However, if our knowledge of that development remains heavily speculative, it is much better to know it is so than to suppose it solidly grounded. For this clarification, Al-Sarhan is to be thanked.

---

*as-sunna*', *Zeitschrift der Deutschen Morgenländischen Gesellschaft* 153 (2003), pp. 11–36.

[100] Aḥmad, *al-Zuhd* (Mecca, 1357), on which all other editions are based except idem, *al-Zuhd*, 2 vols (Alexandria, 1980, then Beirut, 1981).

# 4

## Sayyid Niʿmatullāh al-Jazāʾirī and his (Literary) Anthologies

*Sajjad H. Rizvi*

Under Paul's direction, the Arabic and Islamic collection at the library here in Exeter has developed wonderfully and especially in areas of interest to me, namely philosophical texts and Shīʿī studies, we now probably have one of the best, if not the best, collections in the country. We and our students are quite lucky to have such a research collection at our disposal. Given our many conversations concerning sources and texts over the years since I have been in Exeter, the most appropriate piece to offer Paul in homage to his brilliant work as our specialist librarian is a short piece on a valuable Safavid source for our understanding of philosophy, mysticism, literature and Shīʿī thought in the early modern period.

Anthologies of literature understood broadly have been popular in Arabic for centuries and one needs not spend too much time proving or disproving it. Such belle-lettrist collections of anecdotes, stories, theological, mystical and philosophical arguments and general tales of delectation were often penned by prominent Islamic theologians. In the Safavid period which concerns us in this piece, we have the example of *al-Kashkūl* of Shaykh Bahāʾ al-Dīn al-ʿĀmilī (d. 1030/1621), the eminent Arab shaykh al-Islām of Isfahan, and at the end of the period, *al-Kashkūl* of Shaykh Yūsuf al-Baḥrānī (d. 1186/1772), the equally prominent Akhbārī thinker; the former covers stories and accounts varying from Sufism to mathematics to poetry, while the latter focuses on the literary and cultural heritage of Bahrain and Eastern Arabia, especially valuable given the denial of cultural expression and memory in these states in the contemporary.[1] Suffice it to say that these sources are of critical importance for the cultural, literary and intellectual history of the Safavid period.[2] These works were popular in their time and well attested in the manuscript traditions of the age and revealed the

[1] Bahāʾ al-Dīn al-ʿĀmilī, *al-Kashkūl*, 4 vols, (Beirut, 1983). There is an excellent study of this and other anthologies of al-ʿĀmilī: C.E. Bosworth, *Bahāʾ al-Dīn al-ʿĀmilī and His Literary Anthologies* (Manchester, 1989). Shaykh Yūsuf al-Baḥrānī, *al-Kashkūl*, 3 vols., (Karbala, 1961).

[2] For a brief discussion of their significance for the Safavid period, see Sajjad H. Rizvi, *Mullā Ṣadrā Shīrāzī: His Life and Works and the Sources for Safavid Philosophy* (Oxford, 2007), pp. 170–74.

networks, inner states and learned culture. They remain popular: even today on the streets in Najaf, Qum and Beirut one finds volumes of *al-Kashkūl* alongside legal manuals, works of sexology, the occult (*mujarrabāt* and *fawā'id* works) and popular spirituality. In the present article, I will examine one of these popular anthologies *al-Anwār al-Nuʿmāniyya* of the late Safavid scholar and student of the famous Mullā Muḥammad Bāqir Majlisī (d. 1110/1699), Sayyid Niʿmatullāh al-Jazā'irī and demonstrate its use as a source for the cultural and intellectual history of the period. Al-Jazā'irī was a prominent transnational Shīʿī intellectual, a leading light of the Akhbārī movement of his time, whose family continued to produce major Shīʿī scholars in Iran (related to the Marʿashī family including the late *marjiʿ* and bibliophile Sayyid Shihāb al-Dīn Marʿashī Najafī (d. 1992)), Iraq and India (especially Lucknow where his descendent Muftī Muḥammad ʿAbbās Shūshtarī was a major figure in the *uṣūlī* realignment in North India and his grandson Sayyid Ṭayyib al-Jazā'irī signalled a move back to Najaf). His work retained prominence and is widely available in Najaf, Qum and Lucknow; in all of these places he is considered to have been a local luminary.

Al-Jazā'iri is consistently praised in the Shīʿī biographical tradition as a polymath, a 'leading and unique master of Arabic, literature, law and *ḥadīth*'.[3] The nineteenth century biographer Khwānsārī chastises him for his Akhbārī leanings but praises his learning and his attack on decadent Sufism. The best source is his autobiography.[4] Sayyid Niʿmatullāh b. ʿAbdallāh al-Jazā'irī was born into a family of Ḥusaynī Mūsawī sayyids, who traced their ancestry to Sayyid ʿAbdallāh b. Mūsā al-Kāẓim and within a family who were sometimes known as Āl Shams al-Dīn, in the marshlands of Basra in Ṣabāghiyya between the Tigris and the Euphrates in 1050/1640 according to his own account.[5] He completed his early education in Ḥuwayza and then moved to study in Shiraz when he was eleven at the famed Madrasa-yi Manṣūriyya where his teachers included Shaykh Ibrāhīm (d. 1070/1661) son of the famed philosopher Mullā Ṣadrā, and two prominent Akhbārīs ʿAbd ʿAlī al-Ḥuwayzī (d. c. 1092/1681), author of *Light of the Two Weighty Things* (*Nūr al-thaqalayn*) a prominent Akhbārī exegesis of the Qur'ān, and Shaykh Jaʿfar b. Kamāl al-Dīn al-Baḥrānī (d. 1091/1680).[6] Having spent nine years in Shiraz and after the death of his father and a fire that destroyed the Madrasa-yi Manṣūriyya, he moved to Isfahan where he was a close student in *ḥadīth*, jurisprudence and theology of the renown tradent Muḥammad Bāqir Majlisī (d. 1110/1699), on whose monumental encyclopaedia of Shīʿī tradition, *Biḥār al-anwār*, he collaborated, the philosopher Āqā Jamāl al-Dīn b. Ḥusayn Khwānsārī (d. 1099/1689), the polymath Muḥsin Fayḍ Kāshānī (d. 1091/1680), the jurist Mullā Muḥammad Bāqir Sabzavārī (d. 1091/1681)

---

[3] Mīrzā Muḥammad Bāqir Khwānsārī, *Rawḍāt al-jannāt* (Beirut, 1991), vol. 8, pp. 138–39.

[4] Devin Stewart, 'The humor of the scholars: the autobiography of Niʿmat Allāh al-Jazā'irī (d. 1112/1701)', *Iranian Studies* vol. 22, no. 4 (1989), pp. 47–81.

[5] al-Jazā'irī, *al-Anwār al-Nuʿmāniyya* (Beirut, 2008), vol. 4, pp. 209–23. Other biographical sources include: al-Ḥurr al-ʿĀmilī (d. 1104/1693), *Amal al-āmil* (Najaf, 1966), vol. 2, p. 326; Mīrzā ʿAbdallāh al Afandī al-Iṣfahānī (d. 1129/c. 1717), *Riyāḍ al-ʿulamā' wa-ḥiyāḍ al-fuḍalā'* (Qum, 1981), vol. 5, p. 253; Shaykh Yūsuf al-Baḥrānī (d. 1186/1772), *Lu'lu'at al-Baḥrayn* (Najaf, 1966), p. 111; Sayyid ʿAbdallāh b. Nūr al-Dīn al-Jazā'irī al-Tustarī (d. 1173/1760, his grandson), *al-Ijāza al-kabīra* (Qum, 1989), pp. 70–77; Mīrzā Ḥusayn Nūrī (d. 1902), *Mustadrak al-wasā'il* (Qum, 1981), vol. 3, p. 404. Cf. Muḥammad al-Jazā'irī, *Nābigha-yi fiqh va ḥadīth: Sayyid Niʿmatallāh al-Jazā'irī* (Qum, 1997).

[6] al-Jazā'irī, *al-Anwār al-Nuʿmāniyya*, vol. 4, pp. 212–13.

and the Akhbārī Shaykh Ḥurr al-ʿĀmilī (d. 1104/1693).[7] In Isfahan, he studied in a *madrasa* in the bazaar and stayed in Majlisī's house for four years after which he was appointed as an instructor at a new *madrasa* founded in 1661 by Mīrzā Taqī Dawlatābādī. Having spent eight years in Isfahan in total, he went to pilgrimage to the shrine cities in Iraq. He moved back home briefly. Basra was nominally part of the Ottoman Empire but the governors were in dispute with their suzerain and following the Ottoman campaign of 1078/1668–69, he fled to Safavid realms.[8] Closely associated with the Safavid court, he was appointed Shaykh al-Islām of Tustar/Shūshtar (in modern Khūzistān province in Western Iran) and died there after an illness on 23 Shawwāl 1112/12 April 1701. In Isfahan and in Tustar, he trained a number of students including in particular members of his family. When he wrote his morose autobiography, he complained that at the early age of thirty-years he had suffered four calamities: first, the death of most of his friends, second, the death of his beloved son, third, the death of his children, and fourth, the envy of his peers, fifth, the hypocrisy and maltreatment at the hands of others, sixth, the lack of materials with which to write in a small town such as Shūshtar, and seventh, looking humbly at his life the absence of a juristic authority to whom he could direct people.[9] This latter suggests how his position on the debate between Akhbārīs and *uṣūlīs* was a moderate one.

He wrote a number of commentaries on major collections of *ḥadīth*: *Ghāyat al-marām fī sharḥ Tahdhīb al-aḥkām* of al-Ṭūsī (d. 460/1067), *Anīs al-waḥīd fī sharḥ al-Tawḥīd* of Ibn Bābawayh al-Shaykh al-Ṣadūq (d. 381/991) which was completed in Ḥuwayza in 1099/1698,[10] another *sharḥ* on *ʿUyūn akhbār al-Riḍā* of al-Ṣadūq, a *sharḥ* on the *Rawḍa* section of *al-Kāfī* of al-Kulaynī (d. 329/941), *Jawāhir al-ghawālī fī sharḥ ʿAwālī al-laʾālī* of Ibn Abī Jumhūr al-Aḥsāʾī (d. 906/1501) completed in Rajab 1105/February 1694 in which he commented upon the legal narrations and defended the probity of al-Aḥsāʾī, and *Kashf al-asrār fī sharḥ al-Istibṣār* of al-Ṭūsī.[11] He also wrote a *Nūr al-anwār fī sharḥ al-Ṣaḥīfa al-Sajjādiyya*,[12] a set of supplications attributed to Imam ʿAlī Zayn al-ʿĀbidīn that was growing in popularity in the Safavid period, a commentary on the Ninety-Nine Names of God (*Maqāmāt al-najāt fī sharḥ asmāʾ al-ḥusnā*), a hagiography of the Imams (*Riyāḍ al-abrār fī manāqib al-aʾimmat al-abrār*), and a popular history of the prophets *al-Nūr al-mubīn fī qiṣaṣ al-anbiyāʾ wa-al-mursalīn.*[13] His contemporary and co-student Mīrzā ʿAbdallāh Afandī notes that they were together in Isfahan and Mashhad as students and they later met in Basra and perfomed the pilgrimage to Mecca together, and that he had seen all of al-Jazāʾirī's works in Tustar where he had settled as the Safavid shaykh al-Islām.[14] Al-Jazāʾirī was also a prominent Akhbārī

7 al-Jazāʾirī, *al-Anwār al-Nuʿmāniyya*, vol. 4, p. 215.

8 al-Jazāʾirī, *al-Anwār al-Nuʿmāniyya*, vol. 4, p. 219.

9 al-Jazāʾirī, *al-Anwār al-Nuʿmāniyya*, vol. 4, pp. 221–22.

10 al-Jazāʾirī, *Nūr al-barāhīn fī bayān akhbār al-sāda al-ṭāhirīn aw Anīs al-waḥīd fī sharḥ al-tawḥīd*, 2 vols, (Qum, 1997).

11 al-Jazāʾirī, *Kashf al-asrār fī sharḥ al-Istibṣār*, 3 vols, (Qum, 1990–92). Cf. Ibn Abī Jumhūr al-Aḥsāʾī, *ʿAwālī al-laʾālī al-ʿaziziyya fī l-aḥādīth al-dīniyya*, 4 vols, (Qum, 1983–85) with a short treatise in defence by Sayyid Shihāb al-Dīn Marʿashī.

12 al-Jazāʾirī, *Nūr al-anwār fī sharḥ al-Ṣaḥīfa al-Sajjādiyya* (Beirut, 2000).

13 al-Jazāʾirī, *Qiṣaṣ al-anbiyāʾ* (Beirut, 1991).

14 Afandī, *Riyād al-ʿulamāʾ*, vol. 5, pp. 253–6.

whose commentaries on *ḥadīth* can be seen as vehicles for perpetuating that juristic method. In his *Source of Life* (*Manbaʿ al-ḥayāt*), he outlined a 'moderate' position, perhaps influenced by Majlisī critically engaging with the proposition on following the jurisprudence of a living *mujtahid* outlined by Zayn al-Dīn al-ʿĀmilī (al-Shahīd II, d. 966/1558), and arguing for the validity of continuing probative force (*ḥujjiyyah*) of the opinions of a dead *muḥaddith*/ *mujtahid*, a position condemned by uṣūlīs as *taqlīd al-mayyit* (following the opinions of a dead *mujtahid*).[15]

For our purposes, his most important work is *Lights upon Knowledge of the Human Realm* (*al-Anwār al-nuʿmāniyya fī maʿrifat al-nashʾa al-insāniyya*) which was completed in 1089/1678.[16] At the outset, al-Jazāʾirī explained his intention in writing the work:

> Having completed the two works *Ghāyat al-marām fī sharḥ tahdhīb al-aḥkām* and *Kashf al-asrār fī sharḥ al-istibṣār*, I devoted myself to writing a strange book in a wonderful style that had never been written by the ancients nor would the temperament of recent scholars have tolerated it, that would be a homily and intimate for the unschooled and a platform and discussion point for the scholar, from which everyone could benefit according to their ability, and by which everyone who wished to rise above his tenebrity could be enlightened. It contains detailed exposition of the states of man before his creation, and explains his condition until the day that he is buried and ends with his states when he enters the fire or the garden.[17]

Hence al-Jazāʾīrī produced an anthology that is a complete multi-faceted anthropology dealing with the triad of concerns that were central to philosophy, namely the whence, where and whither of man, as expounded in a famous saying of the first Shīʿī Imam ʿAlī b. Abī Ṭālib.[18] These three concerns map onto the three chapters or sections of the work: the first deals with God, Prophets and Imams and the origins of man; the second considers the nature of man, his practices, virtues and vices and includes extensive discussions of love, poverty and jokes; and the third shifts to eschatology and the end or culmination of man. The majority of the material is traditionalist based on sayings of the Prophet and the Imams but also there are other sources of a literary, Sufi and mystical nature even that are included – in fact in the introduction, he states that he cannot rely on the standard historical accounts produced by Sunnis because they are a corrupt pack of lies!

This indicates one of the central features of the social and cultural fabric of the Safavid period, namely the vehement promotion of Shīʿī doctrine alongside a rejection of both Sunni theology and the eponymous figures of their tradition in particular the early caliphs. The significance of the polemic within the Safavid-Ottoman conflict is clear as is the trend towards a more striking rise in such material towards the late Safavid period which contributed to the Sunni reaction that is often seen in the Afghan sack of Isfahan in 1722 and the

---

[15] al-Jazāʾirī, *Manbaʿ al-ḥayāt* in Muḥsin Fayḍ Kāshānī, *al-Shihāb al-thāqib fī wujūb ṣalāt al-jumʿa al-ʿaynī* (Qum, 1980), 33–36; cf. Robert Gleave, *Scripturalist Islam: The History and Doctrines of the Akhbārī Shīʿī School* (Leiden, 2007), pp. 194–204.

[16] There are numerous printings of this work.

[17] al-Jazāʾirī, *al-Anwār al-Nuʿmāniyya*, vol. 1, p. 11.

[18] See Sayyid ʿAlī al-Ḥaddād, *ʿĀrif fī-l-riḥāb al-qudsiyya: lamḥa ʿirfāniyya ʿan sīrat al-ʿārif al-kāmil al-Ḥājj al-Sayyid Hāshim al-Ḥaddād* (Beirut, 2007), p. 205.

dissolution of the empire.[19] Much of the first section (*al-bāb al-awwal*) of *Lights* is taken up with anti-Sunni polemics and rituals of loyalty and devotion to the family of the Prophet coupled with the dissociation and cursing of their enemies, which are part and parcel of the later Safavid period focusing the classic points of controversy. First, the Arab concern with purity of lineage and tribal affiliation meant that casting aspersion on their authenticity would bring into question any claims to authority within disputes. In a long section on the qualities of the first Shīʿī Imam and defending the daughter of the Prophet against her opponents, al-Jazāʾirī casts doubt upon the lineage, status and even sexuality of the early caliphs, drawing in particular on the work of the Sunni (although allegedly philo-Shīʿī) genealogist Abū Mundhir Hishām al-Kalbī (d. 203/819).[20] Abū Quḥāfa was a pauper so how could his son Abū Bakr have come into wealth so quickly? ʿUmar's grandparents were illegitimate and his father had his hand amputated for theft. He led the mob with brandishes to burn down the house of ʿAlī and Fāṭima after the Prophet's death. ʿUthmān's father was known to be effeminate (*takhannuth*) so he could not have been of legitimate birth.

Second, the popular promotion of Shīʿī Islam included not only the festivals and commemorations associated with their birth and martyrdom anniversaries but also the celebration of the demise of their enemies. From an early period, perhaps even in Būyid times when most of these celebrations began or in the medieval period, the ninth of Rabīʿ al-awwal became the celebration of the murder of ʿUmar. This was particularly disseminated in the Safavid period, sometimes by focusing on the shrine of his murderer Abū Luʾluʾ who is popularly known as Bābā Abū Shujāʿ and has a shrine in Kashan in Iran. Al-Jazāʾirī discusses the merits of such celebration.[21] Justifying the practice, he refers back to the period of the later Imams and to the tradents of Qum who he claims established the festival of what became known in Persian as *ʿumar-kushān.*

This is not to argue that al-Jazāʾirī's work is an infamous example of standard Safavid sectarian literature. It is, no doubt, a firm and at times sophisticated defence of Shīʿī doctrine, albeit not as nuanced and demonstrative as the massive efforts of his far relative Sayyid Nūrullāh al-Marʿashī al-Shūshtarī (d. 1019/1610) in his voluminous *Establishing the Truth and Obliterating Falsehood* (*Iḥqāq al-ḥaqq wa-izhāq al-bāṭil*) and his refutation of Mīrzā Makhdūm Sharīfī (d. 985/1578) entitled *The Calamities of the Enemies Refuting the Contradictions of the Rejectors* (*Maṣāʾib al-nawāṣib fī radd ʿalā Nawāqiḍ al-rawāfiḍ*).[22]

[19] See Adel Allouche, *The Origins and Development of the Ottoman-Safavid Conflict (906–962/1500–1555)* (Berlin, 1983); Michel Mazzaoui, *The Origins of the Ṣafawids: Šīʿism, Ṣūfism and the Ġulāt* (Wiesbaden, 1972); Jean Calmard, 'Les rituels Shiites et le pouvoir. L'imposition du shiisme safavide: eulogies et maledictions canoniques', in Jean Calmard (ed), *Etudes safavides* (Paris, 1993), pp. 109–50; idem, 'Shīʿī rituals and power II: The consolidation of Safavid Shiʿism', in Charles Melville (ed.), *Safavid Persia: The History and Politics of an Islamic Society* (London, 1996), pp. 139–90; Willem M. Floor, *The Afghan Occupation of Safavid Persia, 1721–1729* (Paris, 1998); Rasūl Jaʿfariyān, *Dīn va siyāsat dar dawra-yi ṣafavī* (Qum, 1370/1991); idem, *ʿIlal-i bar-uftādan-i Ṣafaviyyān* (Tehran, 1372/1993); idem, *Ṣafaviyya dar ʿarṣa-yi dīn, farhang va siyāsat* (Qum, 1379/2000); Michael Axworthy, *Sword of Persia: Nadir Shah from Tribal Warrior to Conquering Tyrant* (London, 2006), pp. 17–55.

[20] al-Jazāʾirī, *al-Anwār al-Nuʿmāniyya*, vol. 1, pp. 49–54.

[21] al-Jazāʾirī, *al-Anwār al-Nuʿmāniyya*, vol. 1, pp. 84–87.

[22] Sayyid Nūrullāh al-Shūshtarī, *Iḥqāq al-ḥaqq wa-izhāq al-bāṭil*, ed. Sayyid Shihāb al-Dīn Marʿashī Najafī and Sayyid Maḥmūd Marʿashī, 36 vols., (Qum, 1957–96); idem, *Maṣāʾib al-nawāṣib fī radd*

Throughout his work, al-Jazā'irī demonstrates a keen understanding of theology and philosophy, criticising major figures of Sunni thought such as the 'imam of the doubters' (*imām al-mushakkikīn*) Fakhr al-Dīn al-Rāzī (d. 606/1210). However, from the onset, al-Jazā'irī is sceptical about the claims of theology and philosophy. On the question of the existence of God that would often commence such a work, he states that there are many rational proofs notably those recounted in the works of (the Shīʿī philosophers in his eyes) Avicenna (d. 428/1037) and Naṣīr al-Dīn al-Ṭūsī (d. 672/1274) but that none of these 'proves' the existence of God. In this light, he cites an anecdote which seems rather contrived.[23] The famous philosopher Jalāl al-Dīn Davānī (d. 907/1502) was setting out to write a rational demonstration of the existence of God. His mother asked him what he was writing to which he replied that he was proving the existence of God. The mother expressed surprise at the simplicity of such an undertaking since there could not possibly be a doubt that there was a God. Of course, we now that Davānī wrote at least three separate treatises on the demonstration of the existence of God (*al-Risāla al-qadīma fī ithbāt al-wājib*, *al-Risāla al-ḥadītha fī ithbāt al-wājib* and *al-Zawrā'*) and given al-Jazā'irī's training he could not fail to know this.[24] But the anecdote is an important literary device for a rhetorical argument in favour of the common sense approach to faith. The only proofs for the existence of God are the existence and words of the Prophets and the Imams. And yet to cater for those with a somewhat theological frame of mind, he continues to cite a popular mode of the ontological argument based on the concept of perfection and God as the perfect being and the famous medieval doctrine of the impossibility of an actual infinite, corroborated by *ḥadīth*, not least the one most popular with philosophers and Sufis, namely God as the hidden treasure who desires to be known and hence creates so that he may be known.[25]

This flirtation with a more mystical inclined rationalism is evident in other discussions as well. His reconciliation of Prophetic and Imamic wisdom sayings with doctrines that are more properly Neoplatonic is reminiscent of other later Safavid figures who are more within the philosophical tradition such as Qāḍī Saʿīd Qummī (d. 1107/1696).[26] In his discussion of the realm of the divine throne and what exists beyond, he quotes sayings of the Imams and also refers approvingly to the cosmology of the famous Andalusian Sufi Ibn ʿArabī (d. 637/1240), condemned by other Shīʿī traditionalists as the 'destroyer of the faith' (*mumīt al-dīn*, a play on his name 'the reviver of the faith' *muḥyī l-dīn*), from his Meccan Revelations (*al-Futūḥāt al-Makkiyya*) as well as the *Philosophy of Illumination* (*Ḥikmat al-ishrāq*) of Shihāb al-Dīn Suhrawardī (d. 587/1191).[27] These works affirm the existence of an intermediate world, the imaginal realm (*ʿālam al-khayāl*) that is also properly disclosed to the mystic (in imitation of the Prophet and the Imams) and through which the mystic can understand this sensible realm (*ʿālam al-ḥiss*) 'as it truly is' and think beyond the throne to the intelligible

*ʿalā Nawāqiḍ al-rawāfiḍ*, ed. Q. al-ʿAṭṭār, 2 vols, (Qum, 2005).

[23] al-Jazā'irī, *al-Anwār al-Nuʿmāniyya*, vol. 1, 12.

[24] On these texts, see Jalāl al-Dīn Davānī, *Sabʿ rasā'il*, ed. Sayyid Aḥmad Tūysirkānī (Tehran, 2002).

[25] al-Jazā'irī, *al-Anwār al-Nuʿmāniyya*, vol. 1, pp. 15–16.

[26] For example, see Qummī, *Sharḥ al-arbaʿīn*, ed. Najaf-qulī Ḥabībī (Tehran, 1379/2000); idem, *al-Arbaʿīniyyāt li-kashf al-anwār al-qudsiyyāt*, ed. Najaf-qulī Ḥabībī (Tehran, 1381/2002).

[27] al-Jazā'irī, *al-Anwār al-Nuʿmāniyya*, vol. 1, pp. 125–27.

world (*ʿālam al-ʿaql*) of permanence and absolute truth. In another discussion on the nature of the spirit (*al-rūḥ*) and the soul (*al-nafs*), he conflates the *ḥadīth* on the pre-existence and volition of the former with the philosophical discussions of the latter, drawing upon the anthology of Bahāʾ al-Dīn al-ʿĀmilī.[28] The soul is an immaterial, separable and spiritual substance distinct from yet inextricably attached to the body; yet, it has a previous existential manifestation. In passing, he mentions and rejects the Illuminationist position on animals possessing rational souls and hence allowing for the possibility of metempsychosis. His position is thus not Platonic as such. Rather, he seems to approximate that of a philosopher of the previous generation, Mullā Ṣadrā (d. 1045/c. 1635), who is not explicitly mentioned anyway in the text: individual human souls come into existence with the birth of the body and they survive and are renewed with the subsequent bodies of purgatory, the judgement and the afterlife; however, the generic human soul, the 'Adamic soul' pre-exists bodies as it comes from the universal soul up in the intelligible realm. This is the previous atemporal realm of the 'dust' or 'particles' (*ʿālam al-dharr*) commonly described in the *ḥadīth*.[29]

Quoting philosophical and Sufi ideas approvingly does not entail approval of their traditions. Concomitant to the anti-Sufi tendency of the late Safavid period, led by his teacher Majlisī, al-Jazāʾirī includes a long tirade against Sufism.[30] Common to many Shīʿī polemics against Sufis (which can even be seen in more recent times), he associates Sufism with a denial of the rights of the family of the Prophet and collusion with their enemies (*nawāṣib*): 'the astonishing thing is how some of the Shiʿa can be inclined to this path while *knowing* that it is in opposition to the path of the people of the household (of the Prophet)'.[31] He quotes *ḥadīth* of the Imams condemning Sufis and Sufi practices. Sufis follow Sunni precedents and scholars such as al-Ghazālī (d. 505/1111) and Ibn ʿArabī (d. 637/1240) who were opposed to the way of the Imams. He gives colour to these accounts by narrating his own witness of Sufi practices at the two paramount shrines in Iran, associated as they were with the Dhahabī Sufi order, namely the shrine of Imam Riḍā in Mashhad and his brother Sayyid Aḥmad (known as Shāh-i Chirāgh) in Shiraz.[32] He attacks one famous Sufi (not named) who he claims gave a sermon at Mashhad stating that he had written the major compilations of Shīʿī *ḥadīth* and who encouraged deviant practices such as the loud chanting of God's names, singing, dancing, humming, dancing ecstatically next to the sarcophagus of the Imam, striking their heads on the tomb until blood flowed and so forth. In another account, he narrates the story of a celibate Sufi of Shiraz who frequented the shrine on Thursday nights with a handsome young boy (the implication is clear) singing loudly while wasting away the day in idleness. Sufis while away their time drinking and forsaking marriage while taking to boys. Socially, their ideas led to messianic fervour and revolt: sometimes they claim divinity, other times prophecy and sometimes the imamate. Sufi leaders are crooks

[28] al-Jazāʾirī, *al-Anwār al-Nuʿmāniyya*, vol. 1, pp. 196–205.

[29] al-Jazāʾirī, *al-Anwār al-Nuʿmāniyya*, vol. 1, pp. 117–124.

[30] al-Jazāʾirī, *al-Anwār al-Nuʿmāniyya*, vol. 1, pp. 193–216. Many of the themes that he discusses are commonplace in Safavid anti-Sufism. See Andrew Newman, 'Sufism and anti-Sufism in Safavid Iran: the authorship of the *Ḥadīqat al-Shīʿa* revisited', *Iran: Journal of the British Institute of Persian Studies* vol. 37 (1999), pp. 95–108.

[31] al-Jazāʾirī, *al-Anwār al-Nuʿmāniyya*, vol. 2, p. 194.

[32] al-Jazāʾirī, *al-Anwār al-Nuʿmāniyya*, vol. 2, pp. 195–96.

who claim to embrace poverty and enjoin it on their disciples who they rob. Sufis encourage people to act irrationally, common among the Sunnis but not the Shiʿa. He gives one example of a man who seeing Sufis playing with knives and fire, has a dream in which he claims the Imam ʿAlī b. al-Ḥusayn came to him and encouraged him to jump in a fire.[33] The carnival aspect of Sufi practices is thus a primary problem for al-Jazāʾirī at a time when there is an attempt to produce an alternative 'carnival' of Shīʿī practices. The contrary use of Sufi texts is striking. While earlier and elsewhere, al-Jazāʾirī quotes Ibn ʿArabī from the *Meccan Revelations* approvingly, here he condemns him for claiming in the same text to have ascended to heaven like the Prophet Muḥammad.[34] Similarly many passages on virtues and vices quote classical Sufis alongside the Imams such as stories on repentance associated with Abū Sulaymān al-Dārānī (d. 215/830) and Dhū-l-Nūn al-Miṣrī (d. 246/860).[35]

Despite his critique of the ecstatic practices of Sufis of his time, it is not the uncontrolled ecstasy that seems to worry al-Jazāʾirī. In a long discussion on love and its stages, he quotes stories of the excesses of lovers, practically the erotic lovers whose highest stage is that those effaced in the love of God, led by the master of them (*sayyid al-ʿāshiqīn*), Imam ʿAlī.[36] He cites one example from the shrine of Shāh-i Chirāgh in Shiraz from the 1070s/1660s that he witnessed. A naked man stood before the tomb and had a knife in each hand with which he was cutting away at his body. On investigation, it turned out that someone who loved passionately had left town and he knew not where so in his sorrow and enrapture he took to harming himself in this way. In another story, he relates from one of his teachers in Isfahan. A man was passionately in love with his friend who left Isfahan and moved to Bihbahān. One day, he set out to seek his friend and arrived on a Thursday night as people went out to the graveyards to visit the tombs of their loved ones. Once at the house of his friend, he saw himself in every aspect of his friend and realised that despite their physical separate they were in an act of union. Al-Jazāʾirī is quick to point out that union between lovers is a normal spiritual state of those realised selves and quite unlike the 'heresy' of Sufis.

The autobiography of al-Jazāʾirī and his harsh words about some of his opponents may give the impression of a sombre and morose individual. But the final section of the work has an extensive discussion on humour and jokes much of which sheds light upon the learned culture from which he emerged and elements of social life in his time.[37] He begins by commenting that the human spirit needs a balance between high intellectual pursuits that feed and sustain the rational soul and lighter material for everyday life from which the spirit takes pleasure. The butt of many of the jokes is ʿUmar as one would expect in the Safavid context; others are infamous figures known for their enmity to the family of the Prophet and the Shiʿa – many jokes revolve around encounters between Abū Ḥanīfa, eponymous founder of the Ḥanafī legal school that was dominant in the Ottoman Empire and Abū-l-Qāsim Muḥammad al-Aḥwal known as Muʾmin al-Ṭāq, the Shīʿī companion of Imam Jaʿfar al-Ṣādiq. In one joke, a Sunni asks an old man in Basra on whose authority they practice

[33] al-Jazāʾirī, *al-Anwār al-Nuʿmāniyya*, vol. 2, p. 206.

[34] al-Jazāʾirī, *al-Anwār al-Nuʿmāniyya*, vol. 2, p. 197.

[35] al-Jazāʾirī, *al-Anwār al-Nuʿmāniyya*, vol. 3, pp. 105–6.

[36] al-Jazāʾirī, *al-Anwār al-Nuʿmāniyya*, vol. 3, pp. 111–38, especially 115–16.

[37] *Nūr fī-al-mizāḥ wa-al-muṭāyabāt wa baʿḍ al-hazal wa baʿḍ al-muḍḥikāt* in Al-Jazāʾirī, *al-Anwār al-Nuʿmāniyya*, vol. 4, pp. 71–117.

temporary marriage (*mutʿa*).[38] The old man surprisingly answers that it was ʿUmar because despite his rejection of it, he famously went on the pulpit and attested to the licit and illicit being established by the Prophet but that he was forbidding the two mutʿas. The old man said that ʿUmar's confirmation of the Prophet's words was the authority for temporary marriage. Other jokes play on stereotypes such as the simple and weak Turk.[39] One Friday, the Turk is listening to the sermon in which the imam says that every time a believer has sex with his wife, a wall of a house in heaven is built for them. He goes home and tells his wife who decides to implement the advice. At night, she constantly wakes him up to complete the house in heaven after the third wall is erected, the tired Turk in response to his wife's fourth demand meekly says that everyone knows you have to wait for the mortar to dry or else building another wall will just make everything collapse.

*Al-Anwār* is a rich source for the learned culture and social, cultural and intellectual history of the Safavid period. Many more examples could be given about the superstitions concerning auspicious and inauspicious days, the raising and training of children, the nature of the curriculum, and funerary rituals to cite just a few further examples. To complement these discussions thus far, it is useful to consider his shorter anthology *Blooms of Spring* (*Zahr al-rabīʿ*), a work that has a more markedly literary bent. Unlike *Lights*, this is not a dense work but rather full of short jokes and anecdotes. The function of the text as before is to assist in fashioning an educated Safavid Shīʿī character and mindset. *Blooms* may well be the last work that he wrote, intending as little nourishment for the spirit after the rather depressing subjects of some of his other works:

> When I completed my last two works *Stages of Salvation* (*Maqāmāt al-najāt*) and *Reliever of the Distressed on the Rule to Flee from the Plague* (*Musakkin al-shajūn fī ḥukm al-firār min al-ṭāʿūn*), I took notice of the saying of al-Ṣādiq: "Spirits need to eat just as bodies need to eat so seek out elegant wisdom sayings for them".[40]

Some of his concerns remain consistent with Lights. For example, the text is full of pithy sayings of the Imams about their qualities and about their Shiʿa and replete with condemnations of Sunnis and of their heroes from the early period. Many of the anecdotes are light and jokey. Accounts begin with the description of *muṭāyiba* (a good, pleasant anecdote) or *athar* (a story). Similarly, a fair amount of material is deliberately and consciously culled from earlier such collections (which are his models for this type of literature) including *al-Kashkūl* of Bahāʾ al-Dīn al-ʿĀmilī (d. 1030/1621) and *Spring of the Righteous* (*Rabīʿ al-abrār*) of al-Zamakhsharī (d. 538/1144). Many fabulous tales from the ʿAbbasid period are cited as well. Another difference with *Lights* is the copious citation of verses.

A familiar theme is the quotation of anecdotes mocking companions held in esteem by Sunnis while at the same time quoting Sunni anthologies approvingly. Of the former, one example is the Shīʿī wise fool Bahlūl (said to be a companion of Imam al-Ṣādiq) mocking those who still argued for the authority of ʿĀʾisha, widow of the Prophet despite her action in rallying the battle of the Camel against ʿAlī.[41] Others who are juxtaposed and championed

38 al-Jazāʾirī, *al-Anwār al-Nuʿmāniyya*, vol. 4, p. 72.
39 al-Jazāʾirī, *al-Anwār al-Nuʿmāniyya*, vol. 4, pp. 73–74.
40 al-Jazāʾirī, *Zahr al-rabīʿ* (Beirut, 1994), p. 9.
41 al-Jazāʾirī, *Zahr al-rabīʿ*, p. 132. Bahlūl is often pitted against Abū Ḥanīfa.

include ʿAlī's companion Abū-l-Aswad al-Duʾalī against Muʿāwiya.[42] However, he has no qualms about quoting one of the anthologies of the famous Sunni theologian and anti-Shīʿī polemicist Ibn al-Jawzī (d. 597/1200), author of the *Devil's Deception* (*Talbīs Iblīs*) repeatedly.[43] One feature of the anti-Sunni polemic is relating physiognomy and the popular wisdom of reading faces with ugly famous Sunnis such as al-Jāḥiẓ.[44] Anti-Sufism is not a major theme of this work; he quotes a number of anecdotes from Sufi sources and about famous Sufis such as al-Ḥasan al-Baṣrī and Rābiʿa al-ʿAdawiyya.[45] In fact, in his later works, al-Jazāʾirī seems to have been more open to mystical speculation and cites Sufi sources extensively in *Stages of Salvation* and *Reliever of the Distressed* which were both completed around 1102/1691. Nonetheless, Al-Jazāʾirī's partiality against Sunnis is exemplified in a short anecdote:

> A Shīʿī man and a Sunni were arguing vehemently about who was most excellent after the Prophet and they agreed to the next person to come to them as an arbiter. So they both saw a man and approached him and the Shīʿī asked him: Judge between us – I say that the most excellent of creation after the Prophet is ʿAlī b. Abī Ṭālib. The man asked him: and what does this bastard (*walad zinā*) say? That shut the man (Sunni) up.[46]

Throughout the work, we see vices such as hypocrisy, false piety, ugliness, stupidity and the like associated with Sunnis as part of the Safavid sense of Shīʿī superiority. Hence it is the Shiʿa who are sincere, genuinely pious, beautiful and wise. These qualities and vices remain central to sectarian discourse even today.

Some anecdotes concern philosophers.[47] Someone asked a philosopher: who is the truthful one (*ṣiddīq*)? He replied that this is a name which has no meaning, an animal who does not exist. This anecdote has an implied critique of the Sunni usage of the title to describe Abū Bakr but also mocks the use of logic and definitions in philosophical discourse. Another anecdote probably culled from a Sufi source concerns a Greek philosopher, who is clearly Diogenes, who rejects the world and its possessions. One other example of philosopher cited in an anti-Sunni cause is the following definition:

> Philosophers prove their claim that stupidity is visible through the length of the beard on the face by the following. The beard grows from the brain. So one whose beard is excessively long, has few brains, and one who has few brains, has little intellect, and one whose intellect is limited is stupid.[48]

Of course, it would be misleading (even if tempting) to see al-Jazāʾirī merely as a peddler of Safavid Shīʿī propaganda. The popular jokes at the expense of Sunnis reveal a certain view of the world. But this is not for the scholars and the educated elite who need to engage at a more lofty intellectual level.

Texts are rarely the expressions of timeless individuals, disembodied minds engaged in

---

[42] al-Jazāʾirī, *Zahr al-rabīʿ*, p. 42.
[43] al-Jazāʾirī, *Zahr al-rabīʿ*, pp. 13–14, 131, *inter alii*.
[44] Al-Jazāʾirī, *Zahr al-rabīʿ*, pp. 16, 24.
[45] al-Jazāʾirī, *Zahr al-rabīʿ*, pp. 17, 115, 133.
[46] al-Jazāʾirī, *Zahr al-rabīʿ*, p. 92.
[47] al-Jazāʾirī, *Zahr al-rabīʿ*, p. 29–30.
[48] al-Jazāʾirī, *Zahr al-rabīʿ*, p. 135.

multilogical conversations. Even if they give an impression of engaging with figures, arguments and ideas across time, they are rooted in the intellectual, cultural and (dare I say) linguistic contexts and conventions of their time. Al-Jazāʾirī's anthologies are significant expression of Safavid ambience and of both the pain and joy of being Shīʿī in a confrontational world. As such they reflect the desires and anxieties of the author and his life and provide succour to his readers. Life jokes and anecdotes are dispersed among complicated theological and even philosophical arguments. But overall the attempt is to edify and to entertain the human spirit. As such, they reveal for else elements of their context and also do not fail to appeal to our own contemporary sensibilities.

# 5

# Majlis Readings in the Golden Age of Islam: Text and intertext

*Ian Richard Netton*

Plato's *Symposium* is the *locus classicus* for the *majlis*, the symposium and the later French salon. As *The Oxford Dictionary of the Classical World* notes: "Plato established the prose genre of the *Symposium*, an imagined dialogue of set speeches or discussions usually on themes appropriate to the occasion. Plato wrote on ideal love; Xenophon's *Symposium* is more realistic and less serious."[1] We shall have reason to examine both these works before proceeding to our Islamic text. For the Platonic Greek model establishes a paradigm for the general symposium, the Arab *majlis* and the French salon whose chief components are conviviality, conversation (both serious and pretentious) and drink of some kind or another. Intellectual, often deliberately 'clever', converse bonded the minds of those present; wine bonded their bodies and, often, their physical appetites! As Stanley Rosen puts it: "Wine drinking moves men beyond pleasure and confidence to the height of freedom in speech and action."[2] The mental and the physical co-mingled and were intended to do so: "Although symposia were places to indulge in the physical pleasures of food, drink and sex, they were also a place to cultivate the pleasures of the mind."[3]

Plato establishes, to use a Leavisite phrase, a great tradition; and if it is true that all philosophy is really just a series of footnotes to that Greek master, as A.N. Whitehead (1861–1947) long ago claimed,[4] then it is also true that all future symposia and salons must likewise acknowledge a huge debt to Plato. And the topic at the heart of all this is so often Love, *erōs*, a topic which, in Plato's *Symposium* gives rise to some of Socrates' longest speeches.[5]

---

1 John Roberts (ed.), *The Oxford Dictionary of the Classical World*, (Oxford, 2007), p. 736 *sv* "symposium literature".

2 Stanley Rosen, *Plato's Symposium*, (South Bend, Indiana,1999), p. 31.

3 Plato, *The Symposium* (ed. M.C. Howatson and Frisbee C.C. Sheffield; trans. M.C. Howatson: Cambridge, 2008), p. IX.

4 See A.R. Lacey, *Modern Philosophy: An Introduction*, (Boston, London and Henley, 1982), p. 10.

5 Michael C. Stokes, *Plato's Socratic Conversations: Drama and Dialectic in Three Dialogues*, (London, 1986), p. 114.

The *Symposium* of Plato (BC 429–347) has been variously characterised. Stanley Rosen understands the *Symposium* as "an evocation of the past, not in a historical but in a mythical sense."[6] It is also "a mediation of poetry and philosophy"[7] and, at the end of the *Symposium*, in the cold light of day Rosen concludes that "philosophy (together with its disciple [Socrates]) alone is left, neither to weep nor laugh, but soberly to rise up after a night of enthusiasm and continue in its customary ways."[8]

Howatson and Sheffield draw attention to the 'particularly dramatic' quality of the work: "It is set at the house of Agathon, a tragic poet celebrating his recent victory in 416 BC at one of the great dramatic festivals." They wryly conclude, however, that "there is no historical evidence for [this] celebration."[9] And even the Socrates of Plato's Symposium is suspect: Rowe insists that it is "unwise to insist on the historicity of the Socrates of the *Symposium*, except in broad terms."[10]

This essay proposes to examine Plato's *Symposium*, Xenophon's *Symposium*, and Molière's play *Les Précieuses Ridicules*. Set among these, and in pursuit of intertextual links, we will survey the text of al-Masʿūdī's *Arabic Symposium* as it appears in his seminal work *Murūj al-Dhahab* (Fields of Gold). In the process we will deploy a literary sieve of four distinct *topoi*: DRINK (that etymological essence of the classical *sumpósion*),[11] TEXTUAL STRUCTURE, THEME and SEMIOTICS. It will be demonstrated that the end product is an international web or intertext of Platonically-inspired Greek, Arab and French motifs, at the very heart of which lies the single *topos* of *erōs*, love.

The Greek word *erōs* embraces a spectrum of similar meanings with differing shades of intensity. It can mean simply 'love' but also 'love of a thing, desire for it', 'passionate joy', and it is also the name of one of the Greek Gods of love.[12] Indeed, Rosen notes that "according to Agathon's new teaching, Erōs is the happiest of gods because he is 'most beautiful and best'".[13]

Christopher Gill, in his 'Introduction' to his translation of Plato's *Symposium*, suggests, in addition to 'love', the stronger and more evocative translations 'desire' and 'passionate sexual desire'.[14]

Whichever translation is preferred, however, it should not be translated in the *Symposium* as mere 'platonic love' as we understand the term today,[15] lacking in all physical and sensual elements. Quite the contrary: most commentators have been moved to expound upon the

---

[6] Rosen, *Plato's Symposium*, p. 3.

[7] Ibid., p. 16.

[8] Ibid., p. 326.

[9] Plato, *Symposium*, ed. Howatson and Sheffield, p. vii, see also n. 3. See also Seth Benardete, *On Plato's Symposium/Über Platons Symposion*, Reihe 'Themen', Bd. 57, (Munich, 1994), pp. 12–14.

[10] Plato, *Symposium* [Dual Greek-English text], (trans. C.J. Rowe: Warminster, 1998), p. 1.

[11] See *An Intermediate Greek-English Lexicon*, founded upon the Seventh edn. of Liddell and Scott's *Greek-English Lexicon*, (Oxford, 1968), p. 763 *sv sumpósion* which is defined as 'a drinking party'.

[12] See ibid., p. 317 *sv erōs*.

[13] Rosen, *Plato's Symposium*, p. 174.

[14] Plato, *The Symposium*, (trans. Christopher Gill: London, 1999), pp. X–XI.

[15] Plato, *Symposium*, (trans. Robin Waterfield: Oxford, 2008), p. XI.

homoerotic elements in the text.[16] This is not to say that Socrates himself, philosopher-hero of *The Symposium* (died BC 399), despite his love of beautiful young men, was necessarily a practising homosexual or even bisexual. We know, at least from the textual evidence, that he was married to a rather difficult wife, Xanthippe,[17] that he didn't believe that a boy shared "the pleasures of sex with a man as a woman does" holding that the boy was "sober, facing a sexual drunk",[18] and that, in a sexual encounter with Alcibiades before the event of the symposium, Alcibiades had been unable to rouse Socrates sexually.[19]

But at *this* symposium it is clear that Socrates is surrounded by many who *are* physical lovers of young men and so the translation of *erōs* here must be much more sensual and specific than just 'love between friends'. The Arabic equivalents are *ḥubb* and *maḥabba* for ordinary 'love, affection, attachment' but *ʿishq* for 'ardour of love, passion' or *erōs*.[20] It is the latter which is at the heart of the discussions by *al-Masʿūdī* in his *Arabic Symposium*.

We have already noted that the Greek word *sumpósion* meant literally 'a drinking party'[21] and it was an institution of which Athenian high society was very fond.[22] The host and guests would usually be male and a typical party would consist of dinner, religious libations and post-prandial converse and drinking, often with music and dancers.[23] Robin Waterfield notes that "consumption of alcohol was indeed the main purpose of the party, but the evening meal would have been eaten first".[24] With 'important differences', Gill suggests some analogies between a Greek symposium and 'a modern private dinner-party'.[25] Drink is thus a key motif in the classical symposium, and what is intriguing about Plato's *Symposium* is the emphasis on moderation in wine drinking, at least to start with![26] Later, the arrival of a very drunk Alcibiades serves to lower the tone,[27] Socrates joins him in more drinking[28] and the whole symposium degenerates into a merry chaos with the entry of a group of revellers which precipitates the consumption of yet more 'large quantities of wine'.[29] The narrator and guest, Aristodemus, falls asleep (passes out?!) and when he awakes at daybreak, he

[16] See, for example, Waterfield in ibid., pp. XV–XVIII; Plato, *Symposium*, (trans. Gill), pp. XIII–XV.

[17] See Xenophon, *Symposium*, [Dual Greek-English text], (trans A.J. Bowen: Warminster, 1998), 2.10, pp. 32 (Greek text), 33 (English trans.).

[18] Ibid., 8.21, pp. 76 (Greek text), 77 (English trans.).

[19] Plato, *Symposium*, (trans. Gill), p. XXXVII; ibid., 219b–e, pp. 58–59; Plato, *Symposium*, (trans. Rowe), 219b–e, pp. 116 (Greek text), 117 (English trans.).

[20] Hans Wehr, *A Dictionary of Modern Written Arabic* (Wiesbaden/London, 1966), pp. 151, 152, 614 *sv ḥubb, maḥabba, ʿishq*.

[21] See above n. 11; see also Xenophon, *Conversations of Socrates*, (trans. Hugh Tredennick and Robin Waterfield: London, 1990), p. 219.

[22] See Xenophon, *Conversations*, p. 219; see also Simon Hornblower and Antony Spawforth (eds), *The Oxford Classical Dictionary* (Oxford, 1999), p. 1461 *sv* 'Symposium' (Oswyn Murray).

[23] Xenophon, *Conversations*, p. 219.

[24] Plato, *Symposium*, (trans. Waterfield), p. XIII.

[25] Plato, *Symposium*, (trans. Gill), p. XI.

[26] See Plato, *Symposium*, (trans. Rowe), pp. 5; 22 (Greek text), 23 (English trans.), 24 (Greek text), 25 (English trans.).

[27] Ibid., pp. 100 (Greek text), p. 101 (English trans.).

[28] Ibid., pp. 104 (Greek text), p. 105 (English trans.).

[29] Ibid., pp. 124 (Greek text), p. 125 (English trans.).

finds some of his fellows at the symposium, Agathon, Aristophanes and Socrates, still drinking![30]

The textual structure of Plato's *Symposium* is easily described, although it has been pointed out, quite rightly, that there is absolutely nothing normal about the dialogues of the *Symposium*.[31] Artificiality is of its essence. Fundamentally, it consists of the frame story[32] within which are six speeches on love[33] followed by the drunken speech of Alcibiades, a late-comer, who chooses to speak in praise of Socrates rather than love.[34] The first three speeches on *erōs* are delivered by Phaedrus, Pausanias and Eryximachus;[35] the next two by the great Greek dramatist Aristophanes (c. BC 448–380) and the symposium host, Agathon.[36] This is followed by Socrates' speech on *erōs* in which he introduces a sorcerer-type woman by the name of Diotima, who is possessed of considerable wisdom.[37] For Gill, this speech by Socrates "is the philosophical climax of the dialogue."[38] Finally, as we have already noted, Alcibiades, in the seventh major speech of the evening, chooses to change the subject somewhat![39]

Robin Waterfield has drawn attention to Plato's artistry in presenting the seven speeches: "There is the fact that each of the speeches is quite different from any other. Plato writes in seven different styles in the course of the dialogue…"[40] Bernardete considers Agathon's speech, structurally, as "the only conspicuously well-ordered speech in the *Symposium*. It is not only perfectly arranged, but it also states what it intends to do in a clear manner."[41]

However, of all the speeches, that with which most casual readers will be familiar is Aristophanes' famous explanation of the origins of the human race, the emergence of sexuality and the reasons why human beings fall in love.[42]

The guests at the symposium are all drawn from the cream of Athenian intellectual society. Indeed, the *Symposium* resembles nothing so much as a high-powered university seminar or conference with, perhaps, Socrates as the Keynote Speaker. There are present Phaedrus, a heroic poet, and Aristophanes, a dramatist and comic poet; there are the lawyer Pausanias

---

30 Ibid.

31 Benardete, *On Plato's Symposium/Über Platons Symposion*, p. 31.

32 Plato, *Symposium*, (trans. Rowe), p. 2.

33 See Benardete, *On Plato's Symposium*, p. 31.

34 Plato, *Symposium*, (trans. Rowe), p. 2.

35 See Plato, *Symposium*, (trans. Gill), pp. XX–XXIII; Plato, *Symposium*, (trans. Waterfield), pp. XXI–XXV.

36 See Plato, *Symposium*, (trans. Gill), pp. XXIV–XXVI; Plato, *Symposium*, (trans. Waterfield), pp. XXI–XXV.

37 Plato, *Symposium*, (trans. Rowe), p. 2; See Plato, *Symposium*, (trans. Gill), pp. XXVII–XXXV.

38 See Plato, *Symposium*, (trans. Gill), p. XXVII; Plato, *Symposium*, (trans. Waterfield), pp. XXV–XXXIV.

39 See Plato, *Symposium*, (trans. Gill), pp. XXXV–XXXIX; Plato, *Symposium*, (trans. Waterfield), pp. XXXVII–XL.

40 Plato, *Symposium*, (trans. Waterfield), p. XIX.

41 Benardete, *On Plato's Symposium*, p. 59.

42 See Plato, *Symposium*, (trans. Rowe), 189–194, pp. 48–58 (Greek text), 49–59 (English trans.).

and the medical doctor Eryximachus. The fêted dramatist Agathon is the host and, of course, there is the omni-present Platonic philosopher-hero, Socrates. The late-comer, Alcibiades, will later turn his manifold gifts to matters of war and, a year after the alleged symposium, persuade "the Athenians to embark on the doomed Sicilian expedition."[43] It is, indeed, a distinguished gathering and one the distinction of whose guests parallels the *Arabic Symposium* which al-Masʿūdī will later describe.

Rowe suggests that each of the first five speakers ( Phaedrus, Pausanias, Eryximachus, Aristophanes and Agathon) represents "a type as well as an individual".[44] Behind all, of course, we have the all-knowing, all-wise, philosopher-teacher, Socrates himself, in whom, in a very real sense, all "types" are merged in a universal figure of intellectual power.

The themes of Plato's *Symposium* are omnipresent and easy to identify: they include *erōs*, love, of course, in diverse senses embracing, notably, sexual desire,[45] philosophy,[46] the good,[47] beauty,[48] and the joys of wine.[49]

In terms of semiotics, the following statements are important:

- "Socrates will also have persuaded us that contemplation is the sort of good that can satisfy our desire for happiness, and thereby that philosophy – the love of wisdom – is the best expression of desire."[50] Here Socrates signals the best path to happiness.
- Socrates to Agathon: "Don't you think that what is good is also beautiful?"[51] Here Socrates signals an identification of the good and the beautiful.
- Diotima to Socrates: "Those who are happy are happy by virtue of possessing good things."[52] Here Diotima signals an identification of happiness and the good.

These are themes which are apparent throughout much of the Platonic corpus. They have an intertextual relationship with that broader corpus but the intertextual nature of the set speeches themselves in the *Symposium* has also been noted, even including the offbeat contribution of the drunken Alcibiades![53] Rowe quotes E. Stehle to the effect that "one could say that ideally the whole symposium should create one intertextual web",[54] and stresses that "not only does each successive speaker 'cap' the one before; they also repeatedly refer to each other ..."[55] This feature of intertextuality is an important motif for this essay, for it is one of the ways in which we shall link the works of Plato, Xenophon, al-Masʿūdī and Molière.

---

[43] Plato, *Symposium*, (ed.Howatson and Sheffield), pp. VII–VIII.

[44] Plato, *Symposium*, (trans Rowe), p. 9.

[45] Ibid., p. 5.

[46] Ibid., p. 4.

[47] Ibid., pp. 6–7.

[48] Ibid., p. 7.

[49] See Plato, *Symposium*, *passim*.

[50] Plato, *Symposium*, (ed. Howatson and Sheffield), p. XXV.

[51] Plato, *Symposium*, (trans. Rowe), 201c, pp. 74 (Greek text), 75 (English trans.).

[52] Ibid., 205, pp. 84 (Greek text), 85 (English trans.).

[53] Ibid., p. 8.

[54] E.Stehle, *Performance and Gender in Ancient Greece*, (Princeton, 1997), p. 222 cited in Plato, *Symposium*, (trans. Rowe), p. 8.

[55] Plato, *Symposium*, (trans. Rowe), p. 8.

*Erōs* may be the predominant theme and semiotic indicator in Plato's *Symposium* but, for Plato, it cannot be philosophically transcendent. The text, particularly in the Socratic conversations with Agathon and Diotima, shows us that *erōs* is ultimately neither to be regarded as beautiful nor good nor as a god.[56] There is an altogether higher plane above mere *erōs* which Socrates, and Plato through him, wishes to vaunt.

We continue our intertextual exploration with the *Symposium* of Xenophon (c. BC 430/428–c. 354). Now Xenophon was "an exact contemporary of Plato (429–347)."[57] A.J. Bowen notes that "Plato's *Symposium* was written not earlier than 384 [BC] and not later than 378"[58] and there is some scholarly debate as to whose *Symposium* actually came first.[59] However, since Xenophon's is considered the poor relation to Plato's,[60] we will accept the priority of Plato's *Symposium* in this essay while rejecting Bowen's rather odd comment that "neither *Symposium* contains much that is intellectual."[61] The profound themes and semiotics of Plato's work, adumbrated above, certainly give the lie to that statement, at least as far as *his* version is concerned. It may indeed be true that Socratic work is essentially apologetic[62] and that Xenophon's own version of the *Symposium* is episodic and leaves certain loose ends untied, but that detracts neither from the essential unity of Xenophon's work nor that author's achievement.[63]

What was Xenophon's purpose? A.J. Bowen answers as follows: "In [*The Symposium*] Xenophon was trying to catch the mood of a party whose topics of conversation could come and go in casual conversation, and where people could contribute for a while and be silent in between times, reacting to the moment according to their disposition."[64]

The topics of discussion at Xenophon's *Symposium* were diverse and eclectic. They ranged from scent and smell,[65] the nature of women,[66] and the thing one was most proud of,[67] to justice,[68] overindulgence[69] and – key intertextual link with Plato's *Symposium* – *erōs*.[70] Drink certainly has its role to play: "Sokrates said, 'Actually, gentlemen, drinking is something I very much approve of. Wine irrigates the spirit; it soothes irritability as mandragora soothes people, and it rouses thoughts of friendliness as oil does a fire.'"[71]

Structurally, the text of Xenophon's work may be "divided into nine unequal sections."[72]

---

[56] Benardete, *On Plato's Symposium*, p. 69.
[57] Xenophon, *Conversations*, p. 5.
[58] Xenophon, *Symposium*, (trans. Bowen), p. 9.
[59] See ibid., pp. 8–9, 19.
[60] See ibid., p. 8.
[61] Ibid.
[62] Ibid., p. 7.
[63] Ibid., p. 19.
[64] Ibid., p. 18.
[65] Ibid., 2.1–4 (Greek text)
[66] Ibid., 2.8–10 (Greek text)
[67] Ibid., 3.4–14; 4.9–63 (Greek text).
[68] Ibid., 4.1–4 (Greek text).
[69] Ibid., 6.1–10 (Greek text).
[70] Ibid., 8.1–43 (Greek text).
[71] Ibid., 2.24, pp. 36 (Greek text), p. 37 (English trans.).
[72] Ibid., pp. 5–7.

Socrates and others are guests in Kallias' house; also present is Autolykos who is admired by Kallias. All are struck dumb by Autolykos' beauty. "For the initiates of Erōs [Autolykos] was well worth contemplation."[73] They all eat and then there is music and discussion of the topics mentioned above. The leading themes of beauty and *erōs* are dominant at various times as in Plato's *Symposium*. The whole work ends with an entertainment, play or mime between a girl and boy enacting the passionate love between Ariadne and Dionysos: "They weren't just in fun, but were kissing truly mouth to mouth."[74] This so arouses all present that the symposium comes to an end and all go home, filled with erotic thoughts.[75]

Semiotically, the signals from Xenophon are often very similar to Plato's. For example, Socrates signals his preference for things of the *spirit* – "A spiritual passion is much better than a physically based passion"[76] – even though Tredennick and Waterfield suggest that "Xenophon presents Socrates as a modified, moral hedonist..."[77]

Goodness is both a theme and semiotic indicator;[78] but the 'chief unifying theme' which is signalled by the text is love.[79] Socrates speaks about love, Kallias loves Autolykos and, indeed, each of the guests present at this symposium seems to be 'in love'.[80] In this regard, however, what the text does signal is a massive 'contrast' between homosexual orientation and actual homosexual practice.[81] Socrates, despite the mutual attraction between his male disciples and himself, condemns the physical expression of homosexuality.[82] The text of Xenophon's *Symposium* suggests that the kind of homosexual spiritual attraction of which Socrates did approve was exploited by the sage 'for philosophical purposes'.[83] As with Plato's text, the principal theme and *signum* in Xenophon's work is love, *erōs*, and it is this motif which enables us to perceive and appreciate Socrates' innate goodness.[84]

Abū ʾl-Ḥasan al-Masʿūdī (283/896–345/956) is one of the most renowned and important proto-historians of the Abbasid age. Born in Baghdad, his fame rests on two surviving works: *Murūj al-Dhahab (Fields of Gold)* and *Kitāb al-Tanbīh (The Book of Indication)*.[85] It is the first of these volumes which concerns us here for it is in this that we find al-Masʿūdī's *Arabic Symposium*.[86]

---

[73] Ibid., 1.10, pp. 28 (Greek text), 29 (English trans.).

[74] Ibid., 9.5, pp. 84 (Greek text), 85 (English trans.).

[75] Ibid., 9.1–7, pp. 84 (Greek text), 85 (English trans.). See also ibid., pp. 5–7.

[76] Ibid., 8.12, pp. 74 (Greek text), 75 (English trans.).

[77] Xenophon, *Conversations*, p. 23.

[78] See ibid., p. 221.

[79] Ibid.

[80] Ibid.

[81] Ibid., p. 222.

[82] Ibid.

[83] Ibid., p. 223.

[84] Ibid., p. 224.

[85] Al-Masʿūdī, *The Meadows of Gold: The Abbasids*, (trans. and ed. Paul Lunde and Caroline Stone: London and New York, 1989), [Hereafter referred to as *Meadows*], p. 11 ('Introduction').

[86] See al-Masʿūdī, *Murūj al-Dhahab* (Beirut, 1966), [Hereafter referred to as *Murūj*], vol. 3, pp. 370–375. For a translation of this Arabic edn., with variant additions, see *Meadows*, pp. 109–114 and Julie Scott Meisami, "Masʿūdī on Love and the Fall of the Barmakids", *Journal of the Royal Asiatic Society*, no. 2, (1989), pp. 270–277. For a general introduction to the historiography of the period,

The Barmakid Yaḥyā b. Khālid (d. 189/805), already an enormously important figure in the empire having been both tutor and, later, wazīr to the caliph Hārūn al-Rashīd (*reg.* AD 786–809)[87] , holds a *majlis* which, to judge by the names of those who attend, must have been a highly prestigious event! Lunde and Stone translate the Arabic word *majlis* as 'symposiums'[88] while Meisami prefers the word "salon"[89] with all the later French connotations which that word possesses. I have chosen to translate *majlis* here as 'Arabic Symposium'.

Some doubt has been cast on whether this symposium actually took place and there are affinities here with the common doubts cast on the actual historicity of the Socratic symposium described in such loving detail by Plato.[90] Bell and Al-Shafie, for example, refer to al-Masʿūdī's 'account of a fictitious or semihistorical symposium' held by Yaḥyā.[91] However, in this essay we are concerned less with the actual historicity of the content of texts like Plato's *Symposium* and al-Masʿūdī's *Arabic Symposium* and more with these works as examples of *belles-lettres*, *adab*, and the intertext which operates between them.

At the beginning of al-Masʿūdī's *Arabic Symposium* Yaḥyā is lauded as an intellectual, thus transcending the political arena in which he normally operates, and one who is clearly fond of controversial debate, given the nature and diversity of those who participate in his symposium.[92] And the challenge that he throws down is that all should engage in a discussion of *ʿishq*, *erōs*, love.[93]

No specific reference is made to the *majlis* being a drinking party but it is at least possible that some wine would have been drunk by some of the participants. Al-Masʿūdī's text contains earlier references, before the detailed description of the *Arabic Symposium*, to the wine drinking habits of the caliph Hārūn with the Barmakids[94] and at least one of the participants in the actual *majlis* manifests a clear awareness of the effects of wine drinking in his comparisons with love: the fifth speaker, the Basran Muʿtazilī dialectician Ibrāhīm al-Naẓẓām (d. 231/845) declares:

> Oh Wazīr! Love is subtler than the mirage (*al-sarāb*) and more insidious than drink/wine (*al-sharāb*).[95]

---

see Tayeb El-Hibri, *Reinterpreting Islamic Historiography: Hārūn al-Rashīd and the Narrative of the ʿAbbāsid Caliphate*, (Cambridge, 1999); see also Ian Netton, 'The Passion of the Barmakids: Myth or Reality?' in Keith Cameron (ed.), *The Literary Portrayal of Passion Through the Ages*, (Lewiston/Queenston/Lampeter, 1996), pp. 29–38.

87 See Neguin Yavari, 'Mirrors for Princes or a Hall of Mirrors? Niẓām al-Mulk's *Siyar al-mulūk* Reconsidered', *Al-Masāq*, vol. 20, no. 1 (2008), p. 57; El-Hibri, *Reinterpreting*, p. 8. See also, Dimitri Gutas, 'Plato's symposium in the Arabic Tradition', *Oriens*, vol. 31 (1988), pp. 36–60.

88 *Meadows*, p. 109.

89 Meisami, 'Masʿūdī on Love', pp. 252, 271.

90 See Plato, *Symposium*, (trans. Rowe), p. 1.

91 Al-Daylamī, *A Treatise on Mystical Love*, (trans. Joseph Norment Bell and Hassan Mahmoud Abdul Latif Al-Shafie: Edinburgh, 2005), p. 49 n. 42.

92 *Murūj*, vol. 3, pp. 370–371; *Meadows*, p. 106.

93 *Murūj*, vol. 3, p. 371; *Meadows*, p. 109.

94 *Murūj*, vol. 3, p. 369; *Meadows*, p. 105.

95 *Murūj*, vol. 3, p. 372; *Meadows*, p. 110; Meisami, 'Masʿūdī on Love', p. 272.

However, if we are to believe the literature and not interpret it as mere polemic, not all the Barmakids were wine drinkers. The sobriety of Yaḥyā's father, al-Faḍl, is contrasted with Jaʿfar al-Barmakī's (c. 150/767–187/803) indulgence.[96] The conclusion is that we can only speculate as to the actual liquid refreshment available and drunk at the *majlis* held by Yaḥyā and portrayed by al-Masʿūdī.

The textual structure of this *majlis* is much easier to adumbrate. It comprises thirteen main speakers and divides stylistically into two principal sections.[97] It is intriguing that there is a dominance of Muʿtazilī and Twelver Shiʿite speakers and the latter, at least, may reflect al-Masʿūdī's own Shiʿite predilections[98] as much as any desire to portray the Barmakids in an ecumenical and tolerant light.[99]

Among the speakers we note some of the giant theologians of the Muʿtazila like Abū ʾl-Hudhayl al-ʿAllāf (d. 226/ 840) and Bishr ibn al-Muʿtamir (d. 210/ 825)[100] and in this display of a plethora of intellectual luminaries there are again close resemblances to the proto-*Symposium* of Plato. The whole structure of thirteen main speakers in al-Masʿūdī's *Arabic Symposium* is augmented by references to Hippocrates and Galen,[101] Plato's version of the creation of man clearly drawn from his *Symposium*,[102] Qurʾān and hadith,[103] the early Arab poet Jamīl al-ʿUdhrī (d. 82/701),[104] Sufism[105] and the Ismāʿīlīs.[106]

Al-Masʿūdī's overarching theme in his *Arabic Symposium* is *ʿishq*, passionate love. It is articulated in a mannered and competitive fashion, with direct (or indirect)[107] consciousness of Plato's model, though it is unclear whether the original direct or indirect consciousness is al-Masʿūdī's, as the author of this piece of *adab*, or Yaḥyā's, as the originator of this alleged *majlis*, or some unknown source of al -Masʿūdī's Platonic scenario.[108]

Commenting on this *leitmotiv* of 'passionate love', *ʿishq*, Meisami notes: "Despite their doctrinal differences, there is a remarkable uniformity in the definitions of love offered by the *mutakallimūn* [at the *Arabic Symposium*], which are in general brief and impressionistic. Almost without exception they stress spiritual and/or physical affinity as the cause of love."[109] Perhaps the most poignant articulation of the love motif, which vividly combines both the spiritual and the physical aspects of *ʿishq*, is that by Jamīl al-ʿUdhrī, quoted by al-Masʿūdī:

---

[96] See El-Hibri, *Reinterpreting*, pp. 35, 47.
[97] See Meisami, 'Masʿūdī on Love', pp. 253, 257.
[98] *Meadows*, p. 13 ('Introduction').
[99] Meisami, 'Masʿūdī on Love', p. 253.
[100] *Murūj*, vol. 3, p. 371; *Meadows*, pp. 109–110, 110–111; Meisami, 'Masʿūdī on Love', pp. 271, 272–273.
[101] *Murūj*, vol. 3, pp. 372, 374; *Meadows*, pp. 112, 113; Meisami, 'Masʿūdī on Love', pp. 274, 275.
[102] *Murūj*, vol. 3, p. 373; *Meadows*, pp.112, 113; Meisami, 'Masʿūdī on Love', p. 275.
[103] *Murūj*, vol. 3, p. 374; *Meadows*, p.113; Meisami, 'Masʿūdī on Love', p. 275.
[104] *Murūj*, vol. 3, p. 374, *Meadows*, p.113; Meisami, 'Masʿūdī on Love', p. 275.
[105] *Murūj*, vol. 3, p. 374; *Meadows*, p.114; Meisami, 'Masʿūdī on Love', p. 276–277.
[106] *Murūj*, vol. 3, p. 374; *Meadows*, p.114; Meisami, 'Masʿūdī on Love', p. 277.
[107] See Meisami, 'Masʿūdī on Love', p. 255 n. 8.
[108] See *Murūj*, Vol. 3, p. 373.
[109] Meisami, 'Masʿūdī on Love', p. 253.

My soul adhered to hers before our creation,
even before we were tiny sperm (*niṭāf*) or in the cradle.
Our love grew and prospered as we did
and, even if we died, our loving pledge will not die:
But it will survive through every trial
and be our visitor in the dark of the grave and the tomb.[110]

Meisami draws our attention to the fact that the *Arabic Symposium* deploys "a carefully ordered structure and the deliberate use of contrasting stylistic devices."[111] Such a statement immediately calls to mind Robin Waterfield's comment, cited earlier, "that each of the speeches [in Plato's *Symposium*] is quite different from any other. Plato writes in seven different styles in the course of the dialogue..."[112] Is al-Masʿūdī trying to do something similar? Again, with Meisami, we note the mainly 'unsystematic and fragmentary' nature of the statements by the Muslim protagonists at the *Arabic Symposium*, contrasting with the 'more continuous' and 'discursive' nature of the Zoroastrian's speech towards the end of the *majlis*.[113]

The semiotics of al-Masʿūdī's *Arabic Symposium* are diverse; we shall identify a few leading *signa*. We note that Meisami has already emphasised the prevailing stress on 'spiritual and/or physical affinity as the cause of love.'[114] The definitions may be diverse and, indeed, inventive, but there is this unity in diversity which Meisami pinpoints. Sexuality, whether homosexual or heterosexual, is not a leading motif or issue *per se* as it is in Plato's *Symposium*. And al-Masʿūdī acknowledges the digressionary nature of his *Arabic Symposium* within his broader history of the downfall of the Barmakid family,[115] whereas for both Plato and, indeed, Xenophon, their symposia are the principal foci of discourse.

What al-Masʿūdī does signal, *inter alia* through his own *dramatis personae*, is, paradoxically, both the fragile transience *and* the permanence of love: love is finer than a mirage but also lasts beyond the grave.[116]

Love can also be a severe illness, upsetting the balance of the four humours, and this is powerfully signalled in a remarkable passage detailing the humoral pathology resultant upon an over-inflamed love: the consequence may be suicide or death![117]

It is worth comparing this 'medical' section with the speech by the medical doctor Eryximachus in Plato's *Symposium*. While Aristophanes, whose turn it is to speak, has a fit of hiccups, Eryximachus takes his place. "Medical expertise," he claims, "to sum it up, is knowledge of the erotic affairs of the body in relation to filling up and emptying."[118] He refers to the opposites of hot and cold, bitter and sweet, dry and wet, associated with the

---

110 See *Murūj*, vol. 3, p. 374 (my trans.).

111 Meisami, 'Masʿūdī on Love', p. 252.

112 See above n. 40; Plato, *Symposium*, (trans. Waterfield), p. XIX.

113 Meisami, 'Masʿūdī on Love', p. 255; ibid., pp. 273–274; *Meadows*, pp. 111–112.

114 See Meisami, 'Masʿūdī on Love', p. 253.

115 *Murūj*, vol. 3, p. 375; see Meisami, 'Masʿūdī on Love', p. 252.

116 *Murūj*, vol. 3, pp. 372, 374.

117 *Murūj*, vol. 3, pp. 372–373. See also Peter E. Pormann and Emilie Savage-Smith, *Medieval Islamic Medicine*, (Edinburgh, 2007), esp. pp. 43–45.

118 Plato, *Symposium*, (trans. Rowe), 186c, pp. 42 (Greek text), 43, (English trans.).

humours[119] and, using a seasonal metaphor, insists that "when the lawless sort of Love comes more into power in relation to the seasons of the year, he does much damage and wrong. Plagues tend to arise from such things, and many other diseases of different kinds ..."[120] In both Plato and al-Masʿūdī, then, love may be a sign of alienation and illness, as well as a deep, unstoppable and mutual passion and bonding which lasts beyond the grave.

Finally, beyond this primary motif of love – good and bad – we note two further signs in al-Masʿūdī's text: firstly, the extremely tolerant, indeed 'interfaith', dimension of the *majlis*, the diversity of whose participants – Muslims of diverse sectarian groupings *and* a Zoroastrian – lead Meisami to comment on "the ecumenical nature of the vizier's salon."[121] Secondly, there is the display by Yaḥyā and his cronies of the sheer love of intellectual debate, however artificial and stylised that might be as presented by al-Masʿūdī as he deploys his craft as an *adīb*. The 'brilliance' of Yaḥyā's salon is there for all to see but al-Masʿūdī's digressive articulation of it as a piece of *adab*, within the framework of the Barmakid story, keeps us from boredom and serves to entertain.[122] It is a double aspect whose brilliance and artificiality resonate both in Plato's own *Symposium* as well as the later French salon.

The question remains: did al-Masʿūdī, or one of the participants in the *majlis* he describes, actually read, or even have access to, Plato's *Symposium*, either in the original Greek, in Arabic translation or in some adapted, transmogrified or bowdlerised version? What was in circulation?

The tenth century sufi Abū ʾl-Ḥasan ʿAlī b. Muḥammad al-Daylamī recounts a much shorter, but similar, set of definitions of *ʿishq* to those articulated at Yaḥyā's *majlis* in *Fields of Gold*.[123] Did he copy al-Masʿūdī, work from a common source or did both authors have direct or indirect[124] access to Plato's *Symposium* in one form or another?[125]

A fairly minimalist and cautious approach is suggested by Lois Anita Giffen: "Some of the early authors on love appear to have ... [drawn upon] Arabic translations of Greek works, if not from the Greek texts themselves, or from some work in Arabic containing extracts and summaries from Greek works."[126]

I would go slightly further than Giffen and suggest that there are sufficient clues in al-Masʿūdī's text to support the idea that he may well have had some kind of access to some kind of version of Plato's *Symposium*:

---

119 Ibid., 186d, pp. 44 (Greek text), 45 (English trans.).

120 Ibid., 188a–b, pp. 46 (Greek text), 47 (English trans.).

121 Meisami, 'Masʿūdī on Love', p. 253.

122 Ibid., p. 256.

123 See al-Daylamī, *Kitāb ʿAṭf al-Alif al-Maʾlūf ʿalā ʾl-Lām al-Maʿṭūf*, (ed. J.C. Vadet: Cairo, 1962), pp. 30–32; idem. *Treatise on Mystical Love*, pp. 49–51; Meisami, 'Masʿūdī on Love', in her footnotes (pp. 270–276) valuably indicates the principal similarities and differences between al-Masʿūdī's and al-Daylamī's texts on *ʿishq*.

124 See Joseph Norment Bell, *Love Theory in Later Hanbalite Islam*, (Albany NY, 1979), pp. 4, 5.

125 Ibid., p. 109.

126 Lois Anita Giffen, *Theory of Profane Love Among the Arabs: The Development of the Genre*, (London and New York, 1971–72), pp. 65, 143. See also R. Walzer, 'Aflāṭūn' *EI²*, v.1, pp. 234–236.

- Firstly, there is the creation of humanity story, originating in Aristophanes' account in Plato's *Symposium*.[127] However, this is by no means conclusive evidence on its own for this creation myth could have easily been mediated to al-Masʿūdī through a diversity of possible channels.[128]
- But Plato (*Aflāṭūn*) himself is mentioned by name towards the end of the dialogue.[129]
- We have already noted similarities between the views of the medical doctor Eryximachus expressed in Plato's *Symposium* and those adumbrated by al-Masʿūdī.[130]
- Alcibiades is (drunkenly!) extravagant in his praise of Socrates' moderation,[131] while al-Naẓẓām at al-Masʿūdī's *majlis* vaunts the merits of moderate love.[132] Indeed, the whole of al-Masʿūdī's text is suffused with a need for moderation.
- There is a strong competitive element in both texts: 'Each speaker attempts to outdo his predecessor'[133] in Plato's while the clashing grandiloquence among al-Masʿūdī's speakers indicates the same is true, even if the letter of Yaḥyā's initial challenging injunction to avoid actual dispute is observed.[134]
- There is an emphasis in both texts for the need of love to be rational and 'orderly'.[135]
- Intriguingly, but probably coincidentally, in Xenophon's *Symposium*, Philippos, the 'laughter-maker', fails to arouse any laughter among those assembled,[136] while in al-Masʿūdī's *Fields of Gold*, in a passage which occurs shortly before the description of the *Arabic Symposium*, Jaʿfar al-Barmakī's wit and humour similarly fail to stir a response in the notorious miser, philologist and grammarian al-Aṣmaʿī (died AD 828).[137]

It is, of course, impossible to speak absolutely and conclusively about al-Masʿūdī's actual access to Plato's – or indeed, for that matter, Xenophon's – *Symposium*. Scholars do, however, accept that he was familiar with the *Republic*, the *Timaeus* and the *Phaedrus*.[138]

---

127 See Plato, *Symposium*, (trans. Rowe), 189–193, pp. 48–56 (Greek text), 49–57 (English trans.); *Murūj*, vol. 3, p. 373.

128 See Meisami, 'Masʿūdī on Love', p. 255 n. 8.

129 *Murūj*, vol. 3, p. 375.

130 See above nn. 117–120.

131 See Benardete, *On Plato's Symposium*, pp. 89, 91; Plato, *Symposium*, (trans. Rowe), 215 ff, pp. 107 ff, esp. 216d, pp. 110 (Greek text), 111 (English trans.). See also ibid., 196c, pp. 64 (Greek text), 65 (English trans.).

132 *Murūj*, vol. 3, p. 372.

133 Plato, *Symposium*, (ed. Howatson and Sheffield), p. X.

134 *Murūj*, vol. 3, p. 371.

135 Plato, *Symposium*, trans. Rowe, 187d, pp. 46 (Greek text), 47 (English trans.); *Murūj*, vol. 3, p. 374.

136 See Xenophon, *Symposium*, trans. Bowen, 1.14, pp. 28 (Greek text), 29 (English translation); idem., *Conversations*, p. 229.

137 *Murūj*, vol. 3, p. 370.

138 See Ahmad M.H. Shboul, *Al-Masʿūdī and His World: A Muslim Humanist and His Interest in Non-Muslims*, (London, 1979), p. 43; Tarif Khalidi, *Islamic Historiography: The Histories of Masʿūdī*,

What we can say definitively is that Plato, Xenophon and al-Masʿūdī all espouse a literary tradition whose diverse intertextual, thematic and semiotic strands focus on the primary motifs of love and good conversation. And this "idea" of love and converse, precious though it might become, was at least a preliminary intellectual engine in the French salon as it developed in seventeenth century France. But in the process it involved the degeneration of the Platonic ideal and was cruelly but cleverly caricatured by that greatest of French comic dramatists, Molière (1622–1673), as we shall see.

The nature and actual impact of the French salon has been much debated by scholars and it is not proposed to enter that debate here.[139] There are numerous definitions of salons. Marc Ferro's is neat: "The salons constitute a kind of small private court initiated by aristocrats, usually created by women who gather the intellectual elite around them."[140] What is striking in this, which serves to set aside the salons in terms of pure definition from the symposia of Plato, Xenophon and al-Masʿūdī is the major leadership role of women within them. This constitutes, to use a term beloved by Foucault, a radical cultural 'epistemic break'.[141]

Sociability and good conversation were intrinsic to the operation of the salons[142] and both would have been much facilitated by the presence of good wine, or rather champagne.[143] It was, in Antoine Lilti's words, "à la fois comme la boisson privilégiée des soupers fins et comme une métaphore de la sociabilité et de la conversation."[144] And the conversation of the salons is characterised as having been of three kinds: "Le divertissement, la théâtralité, et la louange."[145]

Much has been written about the female denizens of the French salons;[146] and in many senses these aristocratic women embodied in themselves the very textuality of the salons not only in their conversation, whose types have been adumbrated above, but in their own writings. The salon was an arena both of 'literary critique and innovation.'[147] It was frequented by luminaries like the famous and prolific novelist Madame de Scudéry (1607–1701)[148] who

(Albany, NY, 1975), p. 52 n. 1. Al-Masʿūdī was also familiar with al-Fārābī's Platonic/Neoplatonic *al-Madīna al-Fāḍila* (see ibid., p. 96 n. 3). See also Richard Walzer, 'Platonism in Islamic Philosophy' in Ian Richard Netton (ed.), *Islamic Philosophy and Theology Volume 1: Legacies, Translations and Prototypes*, Critical Concepts in Islamic Thought, (London and New York, 2007), esp. p. 161; Franz Rosenthal, 'On the Knowledge of Plato's Philosophy in the Islamic World', *Islamic Culture*, vol. 14 (1940), pp. 378–422, esp. pp. 402, 419–420.

139 See Faith E. Beasley, *Salons, History and the Creation of Seventeenth-Century France*, Women and Gender in the Early Modern World, (Aldershot, 2006), esp. pp. 2–5; Antoine Lilti, *Le monde des salons: Sociabilité et mondanité à Paris au XVIII siècle*, (Paris, 2005); Carolyn C. Lougee, *Le Paradis des Femmes: Women, Salons and Social Stratification in Seventeenth-Century France*, (Princeton, NJ, 1976).

140 Beasley, *Salons*, p. 4 citing Marc Ferro, *Histoire de France*, (Paris, 2001), p. 622. See also Beasley, *Salons*, pp. 245, 317–318, 323; Lilti, *Monde des salons*, pp. 62–65.

141 See Lougee, *Paradis*, pp. 5, 6; Beasley, *Salons*, pp. 2, 175.

142 Beasley, *Salons*, p. 3.

143 See Lilti, *Monde des salons*, pp. 230–231.

144 Ibid., p. 230.

145 Ibid., pp. 275–287; see also Beasley, *Salons*, p. 3.

146 See Beasley, *Salons*, pp. 229, 247; Lougee, *Paradis*, pp. 116, 170.

147 Beasley, *Salons*, p. 235.

148 See, for example, her *Artamène ou le grand Cyrus* (10 vols) and her *Clélie* (10 vols) which were

tried to convey an image of "femme du monde et ... femme de lettres"[149] and the Marquise de Sévigné (1626–1696) who "frequently heard her own letters read aloud in salon gatherings."[150] Thus, in both the 'textuality' of the salon, and as two of its leading themes, literature and literary critique had prominent positions.

There are three dominant themes which we identify in salon life: the above mentioned discussion and dissection of literature with all the artifice and pretension which that might involve; politics and love. Lilti informs us that the "conversations politiques de salon sont particulièrement sensibles au temps court de l'evénement politique."[151] But perhaps the most interesting of our trinity of conversational *topoi* of literature, politics and love is love.[152]

Carolyn Lougee identifies Neoplatonism and its later Renaissance articulations as "the most important source of the cult of love"[153] and, wrongly, traces Neoplatonism back to Plato and his *Symposium*,[154] rather than emphasising the role of Plotinus. What she indicates, surely, is a revived Platonism. But it is her references to the *Symposium* and, in particular, the idea that "the highest type of human love was the perfect mutual love established in the revived Platonic myth of the Androgynes",[155] that is of interest to us here. For, in effect, and leaving aside the confusion of the terms 'Platonist' and 'Neoplatonist', Lougee locates the ultimate origin of the salon love motif, theory and praxis, in Plato's *Symposium*: "[The] built-in impermanence of love was antithetical to marriage in theory, and in practice this aspect of Neo-Platonism sanctioned the apparent infidelity which reigned in seventeenth-century salons."[156] She goes on to emphasise that what she is terming Neo-Platonism "was the theoretical progenitor of the salon in two other respects: in the special status with which it endowed women, and in its moralization of polite society."[157] This philosophy deriving from Plato could ultimately justify the salon's "pursuit of purely social ends: happiness, friendship, social polish, pleasure."[158] And the salons' associations with Plato which we have identified were consciously suggested in the Age of the Salon itself and are not simply the lucubrations of later scholars. The Marquise de Rambouillet (1588–1665), for example, famous for her *chambre bleu* salon, was identified by contemporaries with Plato himself![159]

Thus, too, we find the *préciosité* of the age, of which more anon, going hand-in-hand

the object of Molière's satire (Molière, *Don Juan and Other Plays*, (trans. George Graveley and Ian Maclean: Oxford, 2008), p. 391 n.7).

149 Lilti, *Monde des salons*, p. 116.

150 Beasley, *Salons*, p. 30, see also pp. 194, 203, 290; Lougee, *Paradis*, p. 163; Lilti, *Monde des salons*, p. 276. See Madame de Sévigné, *Selected Letters*, (trans. Leonard Tancock: London, 1982), esp. p. 14.

151 Lilti, *Monde des salons*, pp. 357–405, esp. p. 358.

152 See Lougee, *Paradis*, p. 79; Lilti, *Monde des salons*, pp. 239–249.

153 Lougee, *Paradis*, p. 34.

154 Ibid.

155 Ibid., p. 36.

156 Ibid., p. 37.

157 Ibid., p. 38.

158 Ibid., p. 38–39.

159 Beasley, *Salons*, p. 230.

with a conscious emulation of Plato as the *fons et origo* of the symposium.[160] Plato and *préciosité*? It was, in many respects, a sad degeneration of the Greek paradigm.

Beyond the themes, we may conclude this general analysis of the French salon with a brief listing of salon semiotics. The salons signalled the dominance, leadership and power of a certain class of aristocratic women especially in seventeenth century France. They signalled the precarious nature of love and the omnipresent desire to discuss love in all its ramifications. They signalled an infatuation with the idea of polite conversation which might rise to the heights of political and literary debate, or alternatively degenerate into the scurrilous and the precious. And it is this last aspect which deserves emphasis here in view of the direction which the salons took. For, as Beasley shows, "today seventeenth-century salons are synonymous with *précieuse* (precious), a term that is itself conflated not with culture but with ridicule due largely to Molière's satirical portraits of the women who frequented the salon milieu".[161]

We saw earlier that a major area in which the salons of France departed from the paradigm established by Plato, Xenophon and al-Masʿūdī was in the dominant voices of the women present. And although the speeches of those present at the Barmakid *majlis* in al-Masʿūdī's text may have deployed high-flown rhetorical definitions of '*ishq*, love, they were not subjected to later ridicule by their later literary or social Arabic peers. Yet a second major area of divergence from the Greek and Arabic paradigms in the French salons lies in the ridicule which their *préciosité* attracted.[162] *Salon* signalled *préciosité* which in turn signalled and inspired ridicule! It is true that scholars have disagreed over the exact roles of such luminaries as the Marquise de Rambouillet and Madame de Scudéry in inspiring the *préciosité* of the salons[163] and, in consequence, being the direct object of Molière's satire in *Les Précieuses Ridicules.*[164] But, in essence, the origins of, and models for, *préciosité* are unimportant. What we have, as a result of the satire, is a radical disjunction between the Greek models of Plato and Xenophon and the Arabic of al-Masʿūdī on the one hand, and the salons of seventeenth century France, as caricatured by Molière, on the other. And it is to one of his shorter, but nonetheless exquisite, satires that we will finally turn. For not only does Molière, greatest of all French comic writers, make *préciosité* a laughing stock;[165] he makes the very concept of salon a laughing stock as well.

*Les Précieuses Ridicules* received its first performance in 1659 and launched Molière on the highway to success as a comic playwright.[166] Farce and caricature it might have been but it was also exquisitely formed and "bore the stamp of his originality, keen observation and rich comic inventiveness."[167]

---

160 Molière, *Tartuffe and Other Plays*, (trans. with Introduction by Donald M.Frame: New York, Toronto and London, 1967), pp. 19–20.

161 Beasley, *Salons*, p. 2.

162 See Lougee, *Paradis*, pp. 7, 22–26, 79, 90–91, 99,169.

163 Beasley, *Salons*, p. 281, see also pp. 242, 290.

164 Ibid., pp. 281, 242.

165 Molière, *Tartuffe and Other Plays*, trans. Frame, pp. VII, 20; see David Shaw, *Molière: Les Précieuses ridicules* (London, 1986), p. 67.

166 Ibid., p. 19.

167 Ibid., p. X, p. 19. For the original French texts, which exist in multiple editions, see, for example,

In a nutshell, the story revolves round two p*récieuses*, Magdelon, daughter of Gorgibus and Cathos, niece of Gorgibus, both of whom are characterised by Molière as *précieuses ridicules.*[168] They are tricked into allowing into their house, and fêting, two common valets dressed up as the noble Marquis de Mascarille and the Vicomte de Jodelet. Structurally, this slight but perspicacious comedy is written in prose and comprises seventeen short scenes.[169] The very shortness of the work signals that it was designed for performance following a rather longer piece.[170] With little effort *Les Précieuses* observes the three classical "unities of time, place and action"[171] and David Shaw has commented upon its simple and beautiful construction[172] with its "three contrasting pairs of characters."[173]

While drink is not an obvious factor in the unexpected salon held for the two alleged noblemen by the two *précieuses*, it may well have been served on stage during the performance to oil the dramatic course of their pretentious and ridiculous conversation. Bronnie Treloar stresses that "much of the comic effect of *Les Précieuses Ridicules* springs from the ridiculous language."[174]

The overriding dramatic theme in *Les Précieuses* is the artifice of what the *précieuses* attempt. This is signalled by the extraordinary pretentious language which Molière puts into the mouths of his main characters. The whole play, indeed, is "a savage attack on the pretentiousness of the female denizens of bourgeois salons."[175] But there are other major themes implicit in the play as well: these include "marriage, social freedom and education for women" as well as "their role in society ... [and] their pretentions to literary creation."[176]

One of the most significant passages on marriage, love and courtship is put into the mouth of the key *précieuse*, Magdelon.

It begins:

> Mon père, voilà ma cousine qui vous dira, aussi bien que moi, que le marriage ne doit jamais arriver qu'après les autres aventures.[177]

With a key semiotic statement, the whole speech signals the fragility of love, the adventure of love and, indeed, the idea that love is a game. To take away the vicissitudes of the romance

---

Molière, *Les Précieuses ridicules*, (ed. Jacques Chupeau: Paris, 1998); Molière, *Les Précieuses ridicules*, (ed. Evelyne Amon: Paris, 2008).

168 *Les Précieuses*, (ed. Chupeau), p. 30; ibid., (ed. Amon), p. 26.

169 See *Les Précieuses*, passim; *Tartuffe and Other Plays*, (trans. Frame), p. 19.

170 Shaw, *Molière: Les Précieuses ridicules*, p. 19; Noel Peacock, *Molière: Les Femmes savantes*, (London, 1990), p. 71.

171 See Molière, *The Misanthrope and Other Plays*, (trans. John Wood and David Coward: London, 2000), p. XI.

172 Shaw, *Molière: Les Précieuses ridicules*, p. 33.

173 Ibid., p. 29.

174 Bronnie Treloar, *Molière: Les Précieuses ridicules*, (London, 1970), p. 29; see Shaw, *Molière: Les Précieuses ridicules*, pp. 30, 38.

175 Molière, *Don Juan and Other Plays*, p. XII.

176 Ibid., pp. XII–XIII.

177 *Les Précieuses*, (ed. Chupeau), pp. 36–37.

and the courtship and to focus solely on the marriage contract is too utterly bourgeois and not to be borne in the best salons![178]

The other signal sent by the protagonists in *Les Précieuses Ridicules* is an implicit, or even explicit, consciousness of a Platonic paradigm. In particular, Mascarille proclaims in Scene IX: "Je veux établir chez vous une Académie de beaux esprits."[179] But the noble ideal of the Platonic Academy, or symposium, is destroyed by the *préciosité* of the seventeenth century salon, and the latter is recognized for what it really is in Gorgibus' concluding speech at the end of the play in Scene XVII as he castigates his *precious* daughter and niece:

> Nous allons servir de fable et de risée à tout le monde ... Et vous, qui êtes cause de leur folie, sottes billevesées, pernicieux amusements des esprits oisifs, romans, vers, chansons, sonnets et sonnettes, puissiez-vous être à tous les diables![180]

Indeed, as Beasley neatly puts it, "the play offers a catalogue of all the general characteristics associated with many of the salons, such as women's desire to control marriage or reject it altogether, and to exert power over comportement and language according to models advanced primarily in Scudéry's popular novels, to which Molière explicitly refers."[181] It is entirely credible that it is Mlle de Scudéry who is the focus of Molière's attack in *Les Précieuses Ridicules*.[182]

It may be thought at first that we have come a long way from al-Masʿūdī's own Barmakid *majlis*. But nothing could be further from the truth. The seventeenth century French salon and al-Masʿūdī's medieval *majlis* swim in a common pool of artificial literary conceits and magniloquent boasting. Indeed, taking our four key *leitmotivs* of drink, structure and textuality, themes and semiotics, it is clear that several profound intertextual links may be established between Xenophon's *Symposium*, al-Masʿūdī's *Arabic Symposium* and the salon atmosphere, pretentious taste and artifice of Molière's *Les Précieuses Ridicules*, themes later to be revisited in Molière's 1672 play *Les Femmes Savantes*.[183] Over all hangs the brooding presence of Plato's own *Symposium*, master prototype and key paradigm.

---

[178] Ibid.; Molière, *The Misanthrope and Other Plays*, p. 9.

[179] Molière, *Les Précieuses*, (ed. Chupeau), p. 49.

[180] Ibid., pp. 75–76; Beasley, *Salons*, p. 45.

[181] Beasley, *Salons*, p. 45.

[182] Ibid., pp. 278–279; see Shaw, *Molière: Les Précieuses ridicules*, p. 42.

[183] Beasley, *Salons*, p. 46. For the French text, see Molière, *Le Bourgeois gentilhomme, Les Femmes savantes, Le Malade imaginaire*, (ed. George Couton: Paris, 1973), pp. 119–234. There is specific reference to Plato and his *Republic*: See the speech by Philaminte, *Les Femmes savantes*, Act iii, Scène 2, lines 847–848 in ibid., p. 184.

# 6

# Intellectual Gold? Oxford's *Book of Curiosities* and its importance for research on the Middle East and Islamic World

*Lesley Forbes**

## I

Paul Auchterlonie's distinguished career in Middle Eastern librarianship has focused primarily on printed and electronic resources relating to the Middle Eastern and Islamic World, rather than manuscripts. This contribution to his *Festschrift*, based on an early 13th-century copy of a work written between AD 1020 and 1050, might therefore seem an unusual choice to honour his achievements. Yet this is no ordinary manuscript. I hope to demonstrate that the *Book of Curiosities* is of major significance – an intellectual goldmine for research in many branches of Islamic Studies today. Its digital presence on the internet, along with the extensive research and professional programme that has been mounted since 2002 to interpret it, have made it accessible to the widest possible audience for further study.

The anonymous, recently discovered copy of the Arabic treatise at the centre of this article is entitled *Kitāb Gharāʾib al-funūn wa-mulaḥ al-ʿuyūn,* loosely translated as *The Book of Curiosities of the Sciences and Marvels for the Eyes*, or *Book of Curiosities* for short. It is a cosmography in 48 folios (96 pages), consisting of two books: Book I on the sky in ten chapters (fols 1a–22a) and Book II on the earth in 25 chapters (fols 22b–48b). The two books describe and illustrate the heavens and their influence upon events on earth, and the size and shape of the earth, its seas, islands, rivers, and the marvels and curiosities that inhabit it. The illustrative matter comprises over 30 astronomical diagrams, tables of stars and star-groups, lunar mansion maps and in-text illustrations in Book I, and in Book II two world maps, one rectangular and one circular; three maps of 'the great seas': the Indian

* Author's note: I am grateful to the Bodleian Libraries (formerly Oxford University Library Services) for making available to me for research for this article internal records created between 2000 and 2008 relating to the Medieval Islamic Views of the Cosmos project, and to Pamela Clemit for commenting on a draft of the article. I especially wish to thank Emilie Savage-Smith for her help and advice.

Ocean, the Mediterranean and the Caspian; four maps of Mediterranean islands and cities: Sicily, al-Mahdīyah, Tinnīs and Cyprus; five river maps: the Nile, the Euphrates, the Tigris, the Indus and the Oxus, plus five other illustrations and maps, including illustrations of a *wāqwāq* tree and an 'inhabited scroll', dating possibly from the 14th century.

The original 11th-century treatise is not known to us, although a number of other partial copies of the text, mostly unillustrated and produced relatively recently (in the 16th–18th centuries), have been identified.[1] In June 2002, its 400th-anniversary year, the Bodleian Library in Oxford acquired the only known plentifully illustrated copy, now shelf-marked MS. Arab. c. 90. This manuscript copy of Books I and II of the treatise is incomplete, however, for the copyist has omitted the eighth and ninth chapters of the second book, the manuscript has lost part of chapter 24 and all of chapter 25, and lacks a colophon. On the basis of internal textual evidence, the original treatise is thought to have been composed between 1020 and 1050, in Egypt, and, from the physical evidence, the Bodleian's manuscript copy to date from about 1200. Further details are available on the website devoted to the treatise, and to the Bodleian's manuscript copy of it, at http://www.bodley.ox.ac.uk/bookofcuriosities.

After a brief description of the manuscript itself, and the background to its acquisition, a summary of the work carried out under the five-year, Heritage Lottery funded, Medieval Islamic Views of the Cosmos project follows. I shall then describe some of the principal academic and other outputs that have been based on the *Book of Curiosities* in the short time that it has been available for study, and suggest some other potential areas of research for which it might be relevant.

## II

The story begins in October 2000, with the appearance at auction in London[2] of a very scruffy, grimy, battered, altogether unprepossessing manuscript, with a bird dropping on the front cover of its ill-fitting 18th- or 19th-century Ottoman binding. The manuscript was described in the sale catalogue as being produced probably in Iraq during the 14th century and was noted as being possibly related to a work with a longer title by Ibn al-ʿArabānī (d. c. 1450). Prior to this appearance in the saleroom, both the manuscript copy and the treatise it contained were unknown to scholars, having previously been in private ownership. In view of this, a few preliminary words may be appropriate about this exciting discovery and the early recognition in Oxford of its potential for extending and enhancing the world-view of medieval Islam.

Just before the sale, an Oxford colleague, Emilie Savage-Smith, had had the opportunity

[1] Manuscripts containing different parts of the text of *Kitāb Gharāʾib al-funūn wa-mulaḥ al-ʿuyūn* are held in Cairo, Damascus, Gotha, Milan, Oxford, and possibly Mosul. For an explanation of the relationship of these manuscripts to the *Book of Curiosities* see the section 'Afterlife of the treatise' via the *Book of Curiosities* link <http://www.bodley.ox.ac.uk/bookofcuriosities> (viewed 30th March 2011).

[2] Christie's London, *Islamic Art and Manuscripts*, lot 41, 10 October 2000.

to examine the manuscript. Her expert knowledge of Islamic science and cartography enabled her to see at once that it was a most remarkable manuscript – perhaps one of the most important Arabic scientific and historical manuscripts to have become available for a century. For it contains a fascinating series of early maps and astronomical diagrams, most of which, she knew, were unparalleled in any other Greek, Latin or Arabic material known today. As well as 13 double-page or full-page maps, all closely packed with labels, it includes many smaller maps, plans of Mediterranean cities, and diagrams illustrating orbits of the planets, winds and comets, and, as was later established, a substantial text based on 9th to 11th-century sources – Muslim astronomers, historians, scholars and travellers – over 20 of which are named, plus other material gathered by the unknown author. Jeremy Johns, an authority on Sicily and its history, quickly identified a double-page map depicting an *oval* island as the earliest and most detailed map known of Sicily (MS. Arab. c. 90, fols 32b–33a). Clearly this was a discovery of enormous significance for scholarship, touching on a wide range of disciplines, and for its potential to be explored and realised it needed to be in a public collection. By this time the manuscript had been sold to Sam Fogg, a London dealer in rare books and manuscripts, but shortly afterwards he offered to sell it to the Bodleian Library at a price well below its market value.

There followed an intense 18-month period of fundraising, consultations with experts on Islamic paper and palaeography, discussions with historians of medieval cartography and early astronomy, conservation and digitisation assessments, valuations for insurance, investigation of provenance issues, presentations, and grant-writing. During this period, we realised that simply acquiring this uniquely important manuscript was not enough; more was required if it were to be made accessible and for its riches to be exploited both for academia and the wider Muslim community. Little did we understand at this point that the real work had just begun. Generous donations towards the purchase price were received from a number of public and private bodies, as well as individuals.[3]

In June 2002 this activity culminated not only in the successful raising of the purchase price, enabling the Bodleian to acquire the manuscript to add to its already strong collection of Islamic scientific manuscripts, but also funding from the Heritage Lottery Fund to support the Medieval Islamic Views of the Cosmos (MIVC) project. This project, which I managed at the Bodleian Library, in close collaboration with Jeremy Johns and Emilie Savage-Smith of the Oriental Institute, University of Oxford, was designed to interpret the *Book of Curiosities*, to make it accessible and to ensure its dissemination to a wide audience. The grant covered conservation, digitisation, the construction of a website through which the manuscript could be published in digital form, with an edited transcription in Arabic, an English translation linked to notes, glossary of place and other names, an exhibition, the development of an outreach programme for schools, including a Teachers' Pack, and a study day for the general public. Thus, almost at a stroke, we were committed to what turned out to be a research and conservation project of some magnitude and considerable complexity

[3] The acquisition of the *Book of Curiosities* was made possible by generous donations from the Heritage Lottery Fund, the National Art Collections Fund, the Friends of the Bodleian Library, Saudi Aramco, several Oxford colleges (All Souls, Merton, New College, Nuffield, St Antony's, St Cross, St John's, Wadham, Wolfson), and a number of private individuals.

with ramifications glimpsed at the outset, but the extent of which could hardly have been foreseen.

An early task was to agree on a working English title for the treatise. At first it had been roughly rendered as *The Book of Strange Arts and Visual Delights,* then, more rhythmically, in tune with the Arabic title, *The Sciences' Strange Sights and the Eyes' Delights,* then again, more literally, *The Book of Curiosities of the Branches and Marvels from the Sources of Knowledge.* The final choice was *The Book of Curiosities of the Sciences and Marvels for the Eyes.* During the remainder of 2002 the project infrastructure was put into place. A research team was appointed (Emilie Savage-Smith and Yossef Rapoport) and started work in February 2003 on an ambitious programme for editing and translating the manuscript. Simultaneously, conservation and digitisation work was planned, timetabled and started, and ideas for the website discussed. Already from 2002, such was the interest in the manuscript, that talks were being given to academic groups, societies and at international meetings. In 2003 pressure increased as planning commenced on a major exhibition to be mounted at the Bodleian Library in 2004, a detailed specification for the website was drawn up, tenders invited and assessed and a choice made, graphic designs were commissioned and approved, and the first research article about the manuscript was published.[4]

Looking back, the year 2004 was a period of strenuous activity. Much of the first five months was devoted to detailed preparation and design of the exhibition 'Medieval Views of the Cosmos: Mapping Earth and Sky at the time of the *Book of Curiosities*', working alongside Dana Josephson and regular Bodleian Libraries Exhibitions staff. Conservation of the manuscript and its digitisation both before and after conservation also had to be completed by the time of the opening of the exhibition. The manuscript was disbound. In all, over 1350 hours of painstaking work, removing and sometimes replacing a hotchpotch of older repairs and strengthening the folios to enable them to be handled, was undertaken by Alison McKay and Sabina Pugh of the Bodleian Libraries Conservation workshop.[5] Pigments and inks were examined by Raman spectroscopy[6] and optical microscopy and found to be completely consistent with the suggested origin and age of the manuscript.

Drawing on the Bodleian's superb manuscript map collections, with the *Book of Curiosities* as the centrepiece, the exhibition set it in its historical context of European and Islamic map-making. Particular attention was devoted to helping visitors to understand the impact of medieval Islamic scholarship on Europe through explanatory wall and case panels, including specially created reproductions of key maps and diagrams with the Latin or Arabic place names or other labels overlaid with English translations. The exhibition, which featured some 67 items, 25 of them openings/folios from the *Book of Curiosities,* including ten items loaned by four other Oxford institutions, was mounted in the Exhibition Room of the Bodleian

[4] J. Johns and E. Savage-Smith, '*The Book of Curiosities*: a Newly Discovered Series of Islamic Maps', *Imago Mundi,* vol. 55 (2003), pp. 7–24 and plates 1–7; this article is now somewhat outdated.

[5] A. McKay and S. Pugh, 'Difficult decisions in the conservation of '*The Book of Curiosities*', a 13th-century Islamic manuscript', paper presented at the 14th Triennial meeting, 2005, ICOM Committee for Conservation preprints, pp. 215–222. <http://ora.ouls.ox.ac.uk/> (viewed 30th March 2011).

[6] T. Chaplin et al., 'Raman spectroscopic analysis of selected astronomical and cartographic folios from the early 13th-century Islamic 'Book of Curiosities of the Sciences and Marvels for the Eyes'', *Journal of Raman Spectroscopy,* vol. 37, no. 3 (August 2006), pp. 865–877.

Library between 7 June and 30 October 2004. It drew over 37,000 visitors, and many glowing tributes. By-products were an exhibition guide, an audio guide to the exhibition, weekly gallery talks by the two main researchers, as well as merchandise, a study day for the general public at the close of the exhibition, and a 122-page book with 59 colour illustrations[7] subsequently also translated into German[8] and Korean.[9]

The MIVC project, and particularly the exhibition, coincided with the Bodleian Library's desire to extend its product catalogue, and for the first time to bring academic concepts and images into a popular framework with a range of 'lifestyle' products. Thus in the summer of 2004, the 'Medieval harbour' themed gift collection (mugs, a silk scarf, trinket box, egg cups, notepaper, and of course postcards) was launched using the imams palaces and the al-Mahdīya harbour buildings (from fol. 34b of MS. Arab. c. 90) as a motif. It was fascinating to see how a carefully chosen image from an early medieval manuscript undergoing research for the first time, could be innovatively translated through design to create domestic products that would become part of everyday life in people's homes.

The project was originally envisaged as running for three years from 2002–2005, but in the end a further two years were required to complete the work. This was made possible by extra financial support from the Arts and Humanities Research Council, supplementing the Heritage Lottery Fund grant, along with much extra voluntary assistance. After the success of the exhibition, all efforts were devoted to pressing ahead with the research and interpretative programme, developing and populating the website, and writing, designing and printing the Teachers' Pack intended to link with Key Stage 3 (for 12–13 year olds) of the National Curriculum for History, Geography, English and Science.

These three areas of project work brought different challenges and pressures, demands for specialist expertise, for creative energy and imagination, and a need for much appreciated assistance from academic and Bodleian Libraries colleagues, and other professionals. Two further invited research papers that contributed significantly to awareness of the manuscript were published in late 2004[10] and early 2005.[11] These years were characterised by concentrated bursts of activity in order to complete all strands of the Heritage Lottery Fund programme by October 2007.

The website http://www.bodley.ox.ac.uk/bookofcuriosities is the main output of the project, and the basis for all ongoing research.[12] It enables access to the manuscript in fully digitised form, with an edited Arabic transcription, and an English translation. All maps and diagrams

---

[7] E. Edson and E. Savage-Smith, *Medieval Views of the Cosmos: Picturing the Universe in the Christian and Islamic Middle Ages* (Oxford, 2004).

[8] E. Edson, E. Savage-Smith and A.-D. von den Brincken, *Der mittelalterliche Kosmos: Karten der christlichen und islamischen Welt* (Darmstadt, 2005). This translation includes additional material.

[9] 중세, 하늘을 디자인하다 / E. 에드슨, E. 새비지 스미스 공저 ; 이정아 옮김 (n.p.2006).

[10] Y. Rapoport and E. Savage-Smith, 'Medieval Islamic View of the Cosmos: The Newly Discovered *Book of Curiosities*', *The Cartographic Journal,* vol. 41, no. 3 (December 2004), pp. 253–259.

[11] E. Savage-Smith, 'The Bodleian and the "Book of Curiosities"', *Oxford Magazine,* Noughth Week, (Hilary Term, 2005), pp. 4–7.

[12] E. Savage-Smith and Y. Rapoport (eds), *The Book of Curiosities: A critical edition.* World-Wide-Web publication, (March 2007). <http://www.bodley.ox.ac.uk/bookofcuriosities> (viewed 30th March 2011).

are displayed with mouse-overs allowing the user to see, in a new window, an Arabic transcription of each label (i.e. place-name or other text), a transliteration of it into Roman script, an English translation and identification of it. All these names (personal, place and star names) and the footnotes are fully searchable via the advanced search feature. There are summaries of the content of each chapter and downloadable explanatory diagrams of all maps and textual illustrations. There is a glossary of over 1600 place and personal names and references, with more being added as time permits. The website also includes background information about the manuscript and the project (summarising much of the information above), a downloadable User Guide to the website, downloadable PDFs of the Teachers' Pack, a full list of lectures, talks and publications based on the manuscript and acknowledgement of the help that many people have given to the project since 2000.

A primary aim of the MIVC project was to increase public awareness of the Islamic contribution to our common heritage, thereby contributing towards better understanding between society at large and Muslim communities. It was at times a labyrinthine path. By means of the website, the Teachers' Pack, the 2004 and other exhibitions, and continuing dissemination by lectures, and particularly through publications, it is to be hoped that this aim has been broadly achieved, though inevitably more remains to be done.

## III

Even before the formal acquisition of the manuscript by the Bodleian Library in June 2002, talks and papers on the manuscript were being given, and by early 2011 over 40 formal lectures/conference presentations had taken place, in the UK, Europe and North America. Alongside this, some 25 publications have appeared, or are in press. These lectures and publications are listed on the website, and some are referred to in the course of this article.

So far, published research has concentrated primarily on the larger maps and their cartographic and historical value. Only the circular world map usually associated with the Arab geographer al-Idrīsī (fl. 1154), who lived a century later than the date suggested for the composition of the *Book of Curiosities*, and the maps of the Nile and the Caspian Sea are known from other sources. All the other maps in Book II of the Bodleian manuscript are not attested anywhere else so far as is known. The *Book of Curiosities'* circular world map (MS. Arab. c. 90, fols 27b–28a) makes its own notable contribution, providing evidence (if it was an integral part of a treatise composed well before the Norman invasion of Sicily) that the circular world map, for so long linked with al-Idrīsī, had an independent existence at least a century earlier.

Each map demands specific examination and interpretation. Four[13] have had detailed exposure, inevitably largely raising more questions than answers. In form, the maps of the *Book of Curiosities* look very different from the maps we know today, and are richer in various ways than the uniform content presented in our contemporary maps. Itineraries of

---

[13] The Rectangular World Map and the maps of Sicily, the Indian Ocean and the Mediterranean Sea – see further below.

both overland and maritime routes are a feature of the *Book of Curiosities*. Each map has many 'labels' – 395 place names on one, 239 on another – there are a number of labels, the identification of which is still uncertain after eight years of research. Some labels, for example those on the maps of Cyprus, Tinnīs and the Indian Ocean, contain substantial portions of text, illuminating life and commerce in the 11th-century world.

The rectangular map of the inhabited world (MS. Arab. c. 90, fols 23b–24a) is unlike any other recorded ancient or medieval world map, having at the top a carefully executed graphic scale, and is discussed in some detail in two recent publications.[14;15] The map of the Indian Ocean uniquely depicts it as an enclosed narrow sea in two halves, which in our manuscript are wrongly joined up. It is a curious blend of Greek and Ptolemaic geographical ideas, local knowledge of sailors and merchants, and popular legend, and gives valuable detail of routes between China, Africa and western Asia.[16] The map of the Mediterranean Sea is the earliest extant map to present that Sea in such detail (118 islands depicted and 121 labels listing anchorages, bays, cities and fortresses), and has been used by scholars to exemplify the ancient conception of the Mediterranean.[17] The map of Sicily, which is represented as a flattened oval, is quite different from later triangular representations. Pre-Norman Palermo and its hinterland dominate the map, and the text relating to Sicily provides vital information for the dating of the treatise.[18] The 'map' of Cyprus is more a diagrammatic representation, and provides details of ports not previously attested, along with churches, harbours and their anchorage. It is the first detailed map of the island to be recorded. The 'map' of Tinnīs, in the Nile delta, is similarly diagrammatic, but with some pictorial elements and provides a wealth of information about the water supply for the textile industry for which the island was famous in the early medieval period. Tinnīs was evacuated in 1189–90 and destroyed in 1227, and this map is also the earliest and, indeed, the only known map of the city. The 'map' of al-Mahdīyah, built by the Fatimid caliphs as their capital in 916–921 is depicted in bird's eye view. It provides further evidence for the context and production of the manuscript, and is the only known representation of the city earlier than

---

14 A. Kaplony, 'Ist Europa eine Insel? Europa auf der rechteckigen Weltkarte des arabischen 'Book of Curiosities' (Kitāb Ġarā'ib al-funūn)', in I.Baumgärtner and H. Kugler (eds.), *Europa im Weltbild des Mittelalters (Orbis mediaevalis. Vorstellungswelten des Mittelalters, 10)* (Berlin, 2008), pp. 143–156.

15 Y. Rapoport and E. Savage-Smith, 'The *Book of Curiosities* and a Unique Map of the World' in R. Talbert and R. Unger (eds), *Cartography in Antiquity and the Middle Ages: Fresh Perspectives, New Methods* (Leiden, 2008), pp. 121–138 and plates IV–VI.

16 Y. Rapoport, 'The *Book of Curiosities*: A Medieval Islamic View of the East' in P. Forêt and A. Kaplony (eds), *Journey of Maps and Images on the Silk Road* (Leiden, 2008), pp. 155–171 and figs 8.1–8.5.

17 P. Horden and N. Purcell, 'AHR Forum: The Mediterranean and "the New Thalassology",' *The American Historical Review*, vol. 111, no. 3, (June 2006). pp. 722–740. <http://www.historycooperative.org/journals/ahr/111.3/horden.html> (viewed 30th March 2011).

18 J. Johns, 'Una nuova fonte per la geografia e la storia della Sicilia nell'XI secolo: il *Kitāb Ġarā'ib al-funūn wa-mulaḥ al-ʿuyūn*', in *La Sicile à l'époque islamique: questions de méthode et renouvellement récent des problématiques, Mélanges de l' école française de Rome (Moyen âge)*, vol. 116/1 (Rome, 2004), pp. 409–449.

the European engraving published in 1555.[19] Three recently published articles present a detailed assessment and interpretation of the mapping of the Mediterranean.[20]

Apart from the impact of all the studies mentioned above, it has become clear through research carried out during and since the MIVC project that the *Book of Curiosities* is of interest because it reveals new evidence for international commerce in the 11th century, particularly about the activities of Islamic merchants in the Eastern Mediterranean.[21] Travel and trade is everywhere evident in the maps of the *Book of Curiosities*. It is a significant new source for the history of pre-Crusader global trade networks, and presents some of the earliest Islamic mapping of Asia. The maps of the Mediterranean provide evidence that pre-Crusader Arab ships used to visit Byzantine ports regularly. To the East the maps of the Indian Ocean and the rivers give us an original picture of Muslim merchant networks around the Indian Ocean and the routes through which knowledge and commerce travelled back and forth between Africa, as far south as Mozambique and Zanzibar, China and western Asia. They also demonstrate that the overland routes across northern India towards southern China were much more important than was previously thought.

The mouse-overs used on the website for the map-labels offer an innovative technique for publishing historical maps. A printed edition of the *Book of Curiosities* is in preparation, with planned publication by Brill, Leiden, in their series *Islamic Philosophy, Theology and Science*, in 2014. This will include a colour facsimile of the whole manuscript, with edited Arabic text and English translation, all fully annotated, with glossaries, and will be accompanied by historical and interpretative essays. As well as serving the needs of scholars and university teachers by placing the work in its wider historical context, it is expected that this academic edition of the manuscript will attract an extensive readership among those interested in the extraordinary contribution of Muslim artists and scientists to our society.

Enough has been said, it is hoped, to indicate that the *Book of Curiosities* sheds light on an unusually wide and diverse range of subjects, and can provide a new stimulus to research in a whole variety of topics relating principally, but by no means entirely, to medieval Islamic civilisation.

Its spectacular series of unique astronomical illustrations and terrestrial maps make the

---

[19] C. Scepper (ed.), *Rerum à Carolo V. Cæsare Augusto in Africa bello gestarum commentarij* (Antwerp, 1555), map between fols 152v and 153r.

[20] Y. Rapoport, 'The View from the South: The Maps of the Book of Curiosities and the Commercial Revolution of the Eleventh Century', in R. Margariti, A. Sabra and P. Sijpesteijn (eds) *Histories of the Middle East: Studies in Middle Eastern Society, Economy and Law in Honor of A.L. Udovitch* (Leiden, 2011), pp. 183–212 and figs 1–3; E. Savage-Smith, 'The Book of Curiosities: An Eleventh-Century Egyptian View of the Lands of the Infidels', in K. Raaflaub and R. Talbert (eds) *Geography and Ethnography: Perceptions of the World in Pre-Modern Societies* (Oxford, 2010), pp. 291–310; E. Savage-Smith, 'Das Mittelmeer in der islamischen Kartographie des Mittelalters', in H. Baader and G. Wolf (eds) *Das Meer, der Tausch und die Grenzen der Repräsentation* (Zurich/Berlin, 2010), pp. 239–262.

[21] E. Savage-Smith, '1050: Assisting Arab-Byzantine trade' in P. Barber (ed.) *The Map Book* (London, 2005), pp. 48–9; E. Savage-Smith, 'Maps and trade' in M.M. Mango (ed.) *Byzantine trade (4th–12th centuries): the Archaeology of Local, Regional and International Exchange. Papers of the Thirty-eighth Spring Symposium of Byzantine Studies, Oxford, 2004. (Society for the Promotion of Byzantine Studies, 14)* (Ashgate, 2009), pp. 15–29.

Bodleian's *Book of Curiosities* a manuscript of permanent artistic and academic worth. The advantage of making such a primary source for research fully and freely available in digitised form is beginning to bear fruit, with evidence of wider use through the website. Studies discussing particular maps or matters mentioned in the treatise have begun to appear.[22] The website has been noticed by many blogs, some of which have mounted images of a number of the maps. More extensive websites, for example one relating to Islamic science, technology and civilization[23], have drawn more substantially on the *Book of Curiosities* website. It has been recognised by The Islamic Manuscripts Association (TIMA) as a serious user-focused digital manuscript resource for Islamic Studies. It has featured in courses taught at the universities in the UK, Europe, the Middle East and Australia.

Many topics have been raised during work on the MIVC project that require further exploration. While the primary geographical focus of the *Book of Curiosities* is on the Eastern Mediterranean, virtually every country in the Middle East and many countries in Africa, Asia and Europe are likely to be mentioned either on a map or in the text or both. There is, therefore, also much to interest regional Middle Eastern historians and historians of East Africa, South, Inner and East Asia. Both illustrations and text preserve materials gathered from Muslim astronomers, historians, scholars and travellers of the 9th–11th centuries, many of whose works are lost or preserved only in fragments.

The value of the *Book of Curiosities* in providing evidence for research in subjects such as archaeology, astronomy, economic history, maritime history, natural history, river and sea transport, travel, marvels, myths and curious information relating to the medieval world is clear. It contains abundant material relating to, for example, abandoned ports and harbours, star groups, constellations, the history of comets, medieval commerce, the medieval textile industry, foodstuffs, the bird population, fishes of the Mediterranean and medieval fishing, animals, plants, navigation, the churches of Cyprus, and boats of the Nile. Other subjects such as climate research, divination, population studies, social history, Fatimid history, reading material circulating in 11th-century Fatimid Egypt, the continued role of Coptic texts in the medieval Islamic world and undoubtedly many more could profitably be explored.

---

[22] J. Bloom, *Arts of the City Victorious: Islamic Art and Architecture in Fatimid North Africa and Egypt* (New Haven/London, 2007), pp. 46–47, and illus.; R. Galichian, *Countries South of the Caucasus in Medieval Maps: Armenia, Georgia and Azerbaijan* (Yerevan/London, 2007), pp. 108–113; F. Daftary and Z. Hirji *The Ismailis: An illustrated history* (London, 2008), pp. 76–77 and pp. 98–99, and illus.; L. Gari, 'About al-Shayzarī and Ibn Bassām: who preceded the other?' *Studies in Islam and the Middle East,* vol. 5, no. 1 (2008), pp. 1–4. <http://majalla.org/papers/2008/article3.pdf> (viewed 30th March 2011); T. Kahlaoui, 'Towards reconstructing the *Muqqadimah* following Ibn Khaldun's reading of the Idrisian text and maps', *Journal of North African Studies,* vol. 13, no.3 (2008), pp. 293–307; C. Koutelakēs, *Aigaio kai Chartes me anatreptikē matia:anamochleuontas tēn Historia tou Aigaiou apo tēn Proïstoria mechri sēmera: lathē, sphalmata metagraphes, skopimotētes, metallaxeis kai metakinēsis topōn* (The Aegean and its Maps from a radical viewpoint (Unearthing and Reconstructing its History) – mistakes, transcriptions, errors, considerations, transformations and displacements of locations) (Athens, 2008), pp. 67–96, and illus.; E. van Donzel and A. Schmidt, *Gog and Magog in Early Eastern Christian and Islamic Sources: Sallam's Quest for Alexander's Wall* (Leiden, 2010), pp. 177–181, and illus.

[23] <http://muslimheritage.com/topics> (via Manuscripts link) (viewed 30th March 2011).

Further study of the Bodleian Library's manuscript copy of the *Book of Curiosities* as an artefact would also be beneficial, not only to assist in building up a more detailed knowledge of the production of illustrated medieval Arabic manuscripts, but also for the study of the history of the book in general. As a result of some of the research carried out during the conservation of the manuscript, it could contribute evidence relating to, for example, paper, inks, pigments, the colour palette, and explanations of variations of colour, painting and overpainting techniques, quire makeup and the pattern of sewing techniques for binding.

Thanks to the intensive research programme and interpretative publications of the last eight years, specialists and non-specialists alike can now examine, appreciate and utilise this historically rich treatise with multi-disciplinary appeal. The easy availability of the whole manuscript, with supporting documentation and critical apparatus on the website, offers possibilities for any number of future teaching and research projects at many different levels.

As may be inferred, the three people originally involved were convinced from the outset of the potential academic and scientific importance of this previously unknown treatise. Not only for Islamic history, for medieval astronomy and cartography, and life, culture and trade between Christians and Muslims in the Mediterranean in the 11th century, but also as a resource for extending our understanding of the Islamic contribution to world knowledge.

The MIVC project was made possible by the indispensible support of the Heritage Lottery Fund (not forgetting those other generous donors who made possible the purchase of the manuscript, and the completion of the MIVC project). But without the skills, enthusiasm and commitment of the team of three scholars, Jeremy Johns, Yossef Rapoport and Emilie Savage-Smith, the *Kitāb Gharāʾib al-funūn wa-mulaḥ al-ʿuyūn* might well be lying in obscurity for another 100 years.

Now, in the light of eight years of research on the *Book of Curiosities*, a revision of the history of medieval cartography and astronomy is required. It is possible that Oxford's *Book of Curiosities of the Sciences and Marvels for the Eyes* may prove, in the words of the person who provided an early assessment of its worth, to be 'the type of codex that will be mined and interpreted almost without end'[24] – an intellectual gold mine indeed.

[24] Roger Martin-Mason, communication to the author, 30 October 2001.

# 7

# Translations of Naguib Mahfouz in English

*Rasheed El-Enany*

When Naguib Mahfouz became the first (and so far the only Arab Writer) to be accorded international recognition with the award to him of the Nobel Prize for literature in 1988, this did not come out of the blue. The age old Orientalist interest in classical literature was to be extended in the early decades of the twentieth century to modern Arabic literature, a natural result of the literary renaissance that was beginning to take root at that time at the hands of the modernisers or the 'enlightenment generation' as they came to be called in Arabic literary histories. The establishment in Arabic, thanks to that generation, of new literary genres such as the short story, the novel, drama and the literary essay was inevitably to attract the attention of western Arabists to the contemporary scene at the time, starting perhaps in the 1930s. Thus a translation by E.H. Paxton of the first part of Ṭāhā Ḥusayn's *Al-Ayyam* (1929) appeared in English under the title, *The Stream of Days*, only within three years of its first publication in Arabic, while Tawfīq Al-Ḥakīm's *Yawmiyyāt Nā'ib fī al-Aryāf* (1937) was rendered into English as *The Maze of Justice* by Abba Eban in 1947, ten years after the publication of the original. As for the first translation of a novel by Naguib Mahfouz, that had to wait until 1966 when Trevor Le Gassick published his translation of *Zuqāq al-Midaqq* as *Midaq Alley*, nearly 20 years after its appearance in Arabic in 1947. Mahfouz had by then already transcended his realistic phase to which *Midaq Alley* belonged and begun his 'modernist' phase, which was radically different both aesthetically and in subject matter. At that time Mahfouz had also become the unchallenged master of the Arabic novel following the publication of the *Trilogy* in 1956–7: the translation effort in English was clearly lagging badly behind.

For the purposes of translation, modern Arabic literature initially meant the novel and the short story; and more recently, mainly the novel only, after an apparent global dwindle of interest in the short story. On the other hand, modern poetry and the theatre have from the outset received scant attention from translators and publishers in the West. Regardless of the unequal fortune of different genres, the interest in modern Arabic literature born in the 1930s had to wait until the 1970s to see significant growth. This can be attributed in part at least to the increase of international preoccupation with the Middle East, following the two wars Arab-Israeli wars of 1967 and 1973 which led to a rise of interest in the Arab world, its language, culture and literature among specialists but also, to a lesser extent, the general public. Gradually the study and translation of modern Arabic literature and its exponents began to come to the fore, when until then Arabic was largely treated by Orientalists as a dead language like Latin and ancient Greek, with interest focused only on religious and classical literary heritage.

Thus when Mahfouz won the Nobel Prize in 1988, the number of his novels in English translation was no more than 13 as follows (Publication dates of original and translation are given between brackets in order):

1. *Zuqāq al-Midaqq* (1947) *Midaq Alley* (1966)
2. *Al-Marāyā* (1972) *Mirrors* (1977)
3. *Mirāmār* (1969) *Miramar* (1978)
4. *Al-Karnak* (1974) *Karnak Café* (1979)
5. *Awlād Ḥāratinā* (1959) *Children of Gebelawi* (1981, by Phillip Stewart); *Children of the Alley* (1996, new translation by Paul Theroux)
6. *Al-Liṣṣ wa-al-Kilāb* (1961) *The Thief and the Dogs* (1984)
7. *Afrāḥ al-Qubba* (1981) *Wedding Song* (1984)
8. *Al-Summān wa-al-Kharīf* (1962) *Autumn and the Quail* (1985)
9. *Bidāya wa-Nihāya* (1949) *The Beginning and the End* (1985)
10. *Ḥadrat al-Muḥtaram* (1975) *Respected Sir* (1986)
11. *Al-Shaḥḥādh* (1965) *The Beggar* (1986)
12. *Al-Ṭarīq* (1964) *The Search* (1987)
13. *Ḥikāyat Ḥāratinā* (1975) *The Fountain and the Tomb* (1988)

Now 26 years since the prize, all 33 novels by Mahfouz (counting *The Cairo Trilogy* as one not three novels) are in English translation, thanks to the effort of the American University Press in Cairo and its commissioned translators; who stepped up the production process in time for the centenary of Mahfouz's birth in December 2011, with no less than three titles published in 2010–11.

Mahfouz's major achievement as a contemporary Egyptian author from a point of view of circulation is his success in dismantling the barrier between the ordinary western reader and modern Arabic literature. Before the prize, he used to be published by small-circulation academic publishers, who targeted the students and staff of Middle Eastern Studies and special interest sections of the public with a curiosity about 'exotic' cultures and their literatures. After the prize, he was adopted by major, mainstream publishers, such as Doubleday, and his translated novels are now available from High Street bookshops and through book clubs, when in the past they had to be ordered through the publisher or sought after in specialist libraries and bookshops.

I cannot be certain whether translating the complete works of Mahfouz into English is a good thing or not. Not all that Mahfouz wrote merits translation. Indeed some of his oeuvre will not survive in the original Arabic. And he was the first to admit that with his customary modesty and realism, saying that on occasion he had no hesitation writing novels of no lasting value to deal with a current social or political concern. He has indeed written a few such novels, little read today in Arabic. However, all that has been rendered and published in English. But not all that is of the order of *The Cairo Trilogy, The Thief and the Dogs,* or *The Epic of the Harafish.* And as a Mahfouzian scholar and translator myself, I do have some trepidation concerning the long-term effect of this blanket translation of the author's work. There is, I fear, the danger that the best of his work will be submerged by the sheer quantity of availability, leaving the foreign reader at a loss, and likely to be put off the great because he had first fallen upon the mediocre. Although I do see this as a real danger, part of me is nonetheless delighted at the availability of Mahfouz's full oeuvre in English. For despite the fact that not all his works enjoy profundity or display high art, what is certain is that they all document with accuracy and vision the socio-political history of 20th century Egypt in a manner indispensable for any social scientist, let alone literary historian.

Let us however turn away from this debatable issue and focus attention on some of the existing translations of Mahfouz's best work in order to ponder the inevitable question whether the translation lives up to the style and content of the original. A good example to pick is the translation of *Bayna ʾl-Qaṣrayn* (1956), the first part of what came to be known later as, *The Trilogy*. Of his 33 novels, *The Trilogy* is widely regarded as his *magnum opus*. Written in the great tradition of realism, it is on a par with the great European masters of the nineteenth century, and represents the culmination of Mahfouz's realist stage, which began with *Khān al-Khalīlī* in 1945.

It is a great novel by any criterion. Not so unfortunately its English translation, *Palace Walk*, by William M. Hutchins and Olive E. Kenny, first published by Doubleday in 1990, which fails to capture the spirit of the Arabic text and does little justice to Mahfouz's style. What constitutes modern and spirited prose in Arabic has been rendered in a largely dated and stilted English register. This is particularly so in the translators' rendering of dialogue. Examples are literally on every page, but one will do. Here is what Khadīja says to her brothers trying to impress on them the importance of approaching their fearful father, Al-Sayyid Aḥmad ʿAbd al-Jawād with regard to the subject of allowing their banished mother to return to her home: "If we're all content to keep silent and wait, days and weeks may go by while she's separated from her house and consumed by grief. Yes, talking to Papa is an arduous task, but it's no more oppressive than keeping quiet ..."[1] This is not the idiom in which a girl who is hardly literate will speak; in fact it is hardly the idiom in which anybody would speak in a lifelike situation. It is however the idiom which the translators use uniformly for every character and every situation. Part of their problem of course lies in a peculiarity of Arabic, namely the gap between the spoken and written versions. Mahfouz uses *Fuṣḥā* (standard literary Arabic) for his dialogue, which when translated literally would perhaps, in fairness to the translators, sound something like what we have just heard. But then the Arab reader is used to this, and automatic mental compensation nullifies the gap on contact with the printed page. This is not to mention the fact that Mahfouz has progressively and through a conscious effort tried to bridge the gap between the two registers in his style by adopting structures and vocabulary common to both. The combined result of these facts is that there is no sense of artificiality experienced by the native speaker of Arabic reading Mahfouzian dialogue. Much less lucky is the reader of the English translation for whom what is often witty and racy prose in the original is rendered into lifeless and tardy English.

---

[1] Naguib Mahfouz, *Palace Walk* translated W.H. Hutchins and O.E. Kenny (London 1990), p. 121. Here is the Arabic text:

"إذا قنع كل منا بالسكوت والانتظار فربما تلاحقت الأيام والأسابيع وهي مبعدة عن بيتها حتى يضنيها الحزن.
أجل إن مخاطبة بابا في هذا الشأن مهمة شاقة ولكنها ليست أشق من السكوت الذي لا يليق بنا."

Another major problem which faced the translators and defeated them entirely is that of the high religious content of everyday spoken Arabic – something obviously without parallel in modern secularized English. Generations of Western translators of Arabic texts have failed to deal satisfactorily with this obstacle, the present ones being no exception. Their failure stems from their inability to realize that God's apparent omnipresence in the Arabic tongue is of a purely linguistic (and therefore idiomatic) nature. They tend to regard it as an expression of a universal and deep-rooted sense of religiosity and as such as part of the cultural flavour of the text translated that ought to be preserved. Or worse, they see it as an enhancement of the element of the exotic in the text and therefore an additional attraction for the western reader. Whatever their motive, it is in fact an illusion created partly by an exaggerated sense of the 'otherness' of the Arab culture and partly by the inadequate command of most western Arabists of colloquial Arabic.

Let us pick up one or two examples from the scores which clutter the English text and make it for the hapless reader at best cumbersome and at worst totally incomprehensible. What we have on one and the same page is an example of the use of the *basmala* (the Qur'anic phrase 'In the name of God, the Merciful, the Compassionate') twice, each time with a different idiomatic sense. And in each time, the translators miss the meaning, rendering it literally with disastrous results. Here is how. Al-Sayyid Aḥmad ʿAbd al-Jawād goes unannounced to visit a singer whose sexual favours he is after. She is taken aback to see him in her reception room: 'The moment the woman's eyes fell on him she stopped in astonishment and shouted, "In the name of God, the Compassionate, the Merciful! You!"[2] There is no intrinsic value in the letter of the expression used by the woman, which nonetheless is rendered literally by the translators. It is purely idiomatic and should have been translated into some English idiom expressing surprise, e.g. 'Oh my God! You!' It will help to look at the issue in question by reversing the situation. Take the English interjection of irritation, 'Jesus!' Surely 'Jesus' when used with the right intonation of annoyance will be seen as a purely linguistic quantity without any religious connotations and therefore if translated into Arabic will have to be rendered idiomatically with the correct equivalence. There is no choice in fact because Arabic does not happen to use the name of 'Jesus' to express irritation. Now God-based expressions in Arabic are exactly of the same nature and therefore should simply disappear in translation and make room for idiom in the target language. But the issue is evaded completely with catastrophic results in the present translation. Within two lines of the above example al-Sayyid Aḥmad runs his eyes lustfully over the woman's body and says: "In the name of God. God's will be done."[3] This again is the letter of the Arabic which in the context of the situation does not seem to mean anything in the translated text. The Arabic words are in fact a colloquial exclamatory phrase expressing admiration and ought to have been translated with an English exclamation to this effect.

Again, in the same scene, Al-Sayyid asks Zubayda, '*Naqraʾ al-Fātiḥa?*' (p. 109), which in idiomatic Arabic is an invitation to agree something between two parties and undertake to commit to it. However, the translators render it literally like this: 'Shall we recite the opening verse of the Qur'an?' (p. 96) This of course will make no sense to English language

[2] Naguib Mahfouz, *Palace Walk*, p. 92. The Arabic says: "باسم الله الرحمن الرحيم! أنت!

[3] The Arabic says: "باسم الله، ما شاء الله!"

readers in the context of the conversation, because they will be unaware of the idiomatic meaning, as sadly were the translators.

In another instance, Zubayda replies sarcastically to something Al-Sayyid has said thus: '*afādaka Allāh*!', a familiar colloquialism which Egyptians say by way of sarcasm when someone offers information that is already well known. This is translated as 'May God help you!' (p. 89), which is a serious utterance and has no meaning in the quick, witty repartee between Al-Sayyid and Zubayda. The truth is Mahfouz's wit and sense of humour are among the first casualties of his English translations, as exemplified in *The Cairo Trilogy*.

Apart from these frequent infelicities which stem from the philosophy of translation based on preserving the cultural content regardless, there are straightforward mistakes here and there which are probably attributable to the misreading of the meaning of the Arabic. One example is "When a generous man like you cheats, it isn't really cheating ...", (p. 90) which does not mean much. The Arabic in fact says "A generous man like you can be cheated but will not himself cheat.' (*al-karīm mithlaka, yusraq wa-lā yasraq*). On the same page when al-Sayyid Aḥmad refuses to accept from his mistress payment for goods purchased at his shop, he humorously asks his assistant to write in the accounts book 'Goods destroyed by an act of God.' Or so the translation would have us believe. The Arabic in fact says 'Goods destroyed by love,' (*baḍāʾiʿ atlafahā al-hawā!*), with a clear pun on '*hawāʾ*' (air), whose final *hamza* is softened in speech to a long 'a' sound, making it identical with '*hawā*' meaning 'love'. The witticism therefore consisting in entering in the accounts register 'goods destroyed by exposure to air/the elements', while also giving the real reason which is Al-Sayyid's failure to charge for the goods because of his 'passionate' designs on the woman. The pun, intrinsic to the particularity of Arabic vocabulary, probably had to be lost. The translators' compromise was probably the best that could be done in this particular circumstance, but the end product in the target language remains a good illustration of the diminishing of meaning in translation.

One is finally left with the feeling that the translation would have benefited a great deal and been spared many pitfalls if it had been thoroughly revised by a native speaker of Arabic with also excellent command of English. The above examples are based on spot checks, not a thorough page by page review. They are also all taken only from *Palace Walk*, the first volume of the *Trilogy*. But unfortunately leafing through the translations of the two other volumes, *Palace of Desire* (1991), and *Sugar Street* (1992) shows them, despite some change in the translators' names, to suffer from the same defects: stiff, artificial dialogue language that is no match for Mahfouz's lively, flowing dialogue; destruction of wit and humour wherever found; absurd adherence to the so-called 'cultural flavour' by literal as opposed to idiomatic translation of common religiously inspired phrases ; and ignorance of colloquial idiom generally resulting sometimes in nonsensical translation decisions. I shudder to think how much of this distortion in the translation of this great work a meticulous revision of its 1500 pages will produce.

The above however is not the worst thing that has happened to Mahfouz in translation. Worst of all is the translator who thinks he knows better than the author, and so takes the liberties of leaving out and adding to the source text in the translation. This is what the translator inflicts on Mahfouz's *Al-Ṭarīq* (1964; translated as *The Search* by Mohamed Islam; revised Magdi Wahba, 1987), one of the author's most important novels in the 1960s; a work so subtly constructed that even character names are chosen to contribute semantically to the total meaning. This delicate novel is approached by a translator using his pen as if it were the scalpel of a demented surgeon happily excising healthy parts of the body laid out in front of him. I remember the occasion when I first discovered the deficiency of this translation. I was discussing the novel with some of my British students relying on my knowledge of the Arabic text, not having read at the time the translation. On occasion, my references to certain passages perplexed the students who could not find the equivalent parts in the translation. This impelled me to undertake a thorough revision of the translation against the Arabic original. The liberties taken by the translator begin with the title, where 'al-Ṭarīq' is rendered as 'the search' rather than, the 'way', 'road', or 'path' as the Arabic says. But the liberties taken inside the text are far more serious, affecting the aesthetics of the work and its essential symbolism.

One example is the abridgement of the description of the blind beggar, situated outside the hotel where Ṣābir Al-Raḥīmī lodges, and the complete omission of the beggar's song in praise of the prophet, Muḥammad. This detracts from the symbolic function of the beggar. There is also the abridgement of the description of Ṣābir's move from Alexandria to Cairo, which stands symbolically for the Fall from Heaven to Earth. But the reduction of the description of the two cities through Ṣābir's consciousness destroys the symbolism.

The translation also loses a highly significant irony, the type Mahfouz is fond of, when the weapon of murder is changed by the translator from 'the leg of an ancient delivery chair' (*kursī wilāda atharī*) to a mere 'iron bar'. Thus the irony that is intended by the author, namely that what used to be a tool to facilitate birth or arrival into life has now turned into a murder weapon, a tool to force departure from life, is lost.

Finally, one universal loss in the translations of Mahfouz's novels is the loss suffered in translation of the allegorical connotations of proper names. Mahfouz was fond of choosing names for his characters that were at one and the same time the most normal of personal names but which also, because of their semantic value as Arabic words in their own right or clear derivatives, acted as keys to the characters that bore them, as indicators to their moral constitution or to their symbolic role in the story. For example, in *Al-Ṭarīq*, the protagonist's name, Ṣābir, is evocative of mankind's 'patient' quest throughout history for the absolute, for God, while his absent father's name, Sayyid Sayyid Al-Rahīmī clearly alludes to God by invoking two of his names in Islam 'al-Sayyid' (the Lord) and al-Raḥīm (the Merciful). There is hardly a novel by Mahfouz where character and place names are not consciously chosen to hint at something beyond just their simple function as names. But all this is lost in translation for the reader who naturally knows no Arabic. But this is nothing that translators can remedy, unless they provide annotation to explain the meaning of names. But this will be dangerous terrain which would lead translators into the realm of interpretation, a domain not really theirs.

In conclusion, many of the existing translations of Mahfouz's fiction leave much to be desired, including some of his most important works, notably the *Trilogy*. English is replete with re-translations of the great classics of literature, including some colossal works, such as Tolstoy's *War and Peace* and more recently Proust's *A la recherche du temps perdu*. It is natural that a publisher or translator is dissatisfied with the quality of a certain translation, and so undertakes a new one. I hope the day will come when this happens to Mahfouz's *Trilogy* and some other works, just as it happened with his *Awlād Ḥāratinā* and *Midaq Alley*, to date his only two novels with two translations each.

# PART 2

# TEXTS, CONTEXTS AND TRANSMISSIONS IN THE WEST

# 8

# The Lure of the Near East for European Travellers

*Derek Hopwood*[*]

These days most parts of the Mediterranean and Arab worlds are easily accessible to the European traveller. Travel there was once a rarity and the preserve of the upper moneyed classes, time consuming and difficult. Today a few hours are all that stand between the tourist holidaymaker and the edge of the desert or the heights of the Nile. Travel as a special activity lasting weeks, months or years barely exists nowadays except for the eccentric few who perform largely on television for the entertainment of the many. Travel was once an undertaking performed after great preparation and thought, not undertaken lightly, and certainly not frivolously. It had the serious purpose of education and enlightenment, a part of the formation of a lady or gentleman. It was intended to be rather like the Tibetan idea of pilgrimage – a journey from ignorance to enlightenment. It was a voyage made in order to experience other civilizations and to return with a modified sensibility and yet the traveller usually returned still convinced after all of the superiority of his own surroundings. It was a journey away from the familiar, the quotidian, to view the attractions of the foreign but so often, as George Moore wrote: "A man travels the world over in search of what he needs and returns home to find it" or as T.S. Eliot put it more succinctly in his poem East Croker: "In my end is my beginning". Thus, much travelling was undertaken secure in the expectation that a comfortable home was awaiting on return. Instilled in children from an early age is the longing for the familiar, the homely scene. However frightening and exotic the bedtime story may be, however far it may roam, the young listener is certain that he will eventually return home to the warmth and friendliness of his bedroom where the terrors of the imagined journey can be forgotten. Few fairy stories have unhappy endings and those that do are particularly disturbing.

Despite clinging to the idea of the security of home, there also seems to be implanted in the human psyche a feeling that somehow the grass is greener on the other side of the fence, that, as is said, happiness is another country. This may be because we are heirs to the

[*] This essay is a revised version of a lecture originally given at the Maison Française in Oxford in the series 'Rapports de voisinage'.

Romantic tradition of the nineteenth century which located happiness other than where we were. Unfortunately, however, travellers often returned home disillusioned with what they had found, discovering that the grass seemed greener precisely because it was on the other side of the fence. Perhaps this is why Robert Louis Stevenson (a long term exile!) claimed that it was better to travel hopefully than to arrive. You cannot be disillusioned with your destination if you never arrive. The French poet Charles Baudelaire described this curious paradox thus. "Life is a hospital where every patient is obsessed with changing beds. This one wants to suffer by the radiator; this one thinks he'll get better by the window. It seems to me that I'll always be well where I'm not". If the Romantic was melancholy, he took (as do we) his melancholy with him. A change of surroundings did not necessarily lead to a change of mood.

Travel was an opportunity to live vicariously, to participate in the lives of others in an exotic setting, often to live out a fantasy. Jean-Claude Vatin in his study of travellers to Egypt[1] lists four reasons for travel in the nineteenth century; exploration, experience, diversion, and '*éloignement*' (= 'getting away from it all'?). To these I would add travel stimulated by the urge to fantasize, to seek out the satisfaction of desires denied at home or to break the social norms of ones own society. (These desires in modern times have been channelled into excess drinking, drug taking and general anti-social behaviour abroad, no longer exactly taboo at home.) Such desires can be fired by discontent, alienation, disappointment in love, or some conflict to resolve – all have driven people at times to try to find solace or a solution abroad. Travel in these contexts is the search for somewhere beyond the usual range of experience.

We know about the experiences of nineteenth century travellers as many of them described their experiences in print. Their writings were often influenced by their personal emotions and points of view; i.e. the experience of travel was often transmuted through their own eyes. The countries they saw (or thought they saw) were transformed in their own image, becoming a contrived picture reflecting their personal obsessions or desires, fantasies or artistic needs.

To further define the common fantasies that travellers sought to live out, four types are discernable – that of escape (which is *éloignement* or *évasion),* of sexual experience (diversion), of acceptance (as a local), and of self (experience). Escape was a flight from the constraints of home life and /or inner problems. Alexander Kinglake, perhaps the best known of all 19th-century British travellers, wrote that "Travellers are driven to the Near East by a longing for the East very commonly felt by proud people when goaded by sorrow".[2] The Near East was also taken for granted as a place of sexual licence by some travellers who sought there willing women or boys, a search sometimes fulfilled. 'Acceptance' was something sought by longer term travellers; it was a desire to merge into the local population, to lose ones own personality for a time. The British disparagingly called this move 'going native', although often there was only the illusion of acceptance, when the locals were willing for a time to go along with the traveller's fantasy.

As for the 'self', travellers journeyed abroad in an attempt to come to terms with

---

[1] Jean-Claude Vatin, *La fuite en Egypte* (Cairo, 1989), p. 16.

[2] Sarah Searight, *The British in the Middle East* (London, 1979), p. 157.

themselves. Travel literature from the nineteenth century is full of the exploration of the inner self. The focus of travel is moved from the object visited or observed to the self. Buildings and monuments give pause for thought. Kinglake took this shift further: "A traveller is a creature not always looking at sights... he must, and he will, sing a sadly long strain about the Self."[3] We shall see other examples of this tendency later.

A final dimension of travel in the period is that of the desire to seek in order to appropriate. The strange and the distant moved travellers who had a great thirst for knowledge. Strange animals and plants were brought back, tales of 'primitive' men were spread and every corner of the globe fell into the sights of the intrepid traveller or explorer. Lives were put at risk as men (and occasionally women) set out for the remotest regions. To the Victorians nowhere was out of bounds and as the Empire expanded, to visit was to know, to experience at first hand an area, and perhaps to conquer and rule and add it to Her Majesty's possessions. The gaining of knowledge was the acquisition of power and many means were used to capture the remote and exotic in painting, in photographs, in exhibitions, and most immediately – militarily.

I have entitled this paper 'The lure of the Near East', not the Middle East which is a twentieth century concept. The Near East, largely a nineteenth century term, was not precisely defined, but it had particular connotations. The area was neighbour to Europe and included the Balkans, Greece and Turkey, and by extension Egypt and Palestine – the lands of the Roman and Ottoman Empires. All these were areas that attracted the European traveller. It was not co-terminous with the Orient. Although again this term was loosely used – the famous train, the Orient Express, terminated in Istanbul. Nor was it quite the Mediterranean, which has been both a unifying and dividing factor in European history. It has united through trade routes, empires and cultures at certain times, the Mare Nostrum of the Romans. At others, race and religion have divided it. As Albert Hourani vividly put it, the two shores have faced each "with a look of uneasy recognition". It was Italy's dream in the twentieth century to reunite it and at one time France, Britain, Italy and Spain occupied its entire southern coast. At one end Spain and Morocco meet and share history, at the other Constantinople bridges Europe and Asia. By the mid-nineteenth century the Suez Canal had tied in Egypt to European travel. Parts of the far shore of the sea seemed familiar to Europe; Egypt was an extension of classical Greece and Rome. Its monuments were known. The Holy Land was even more familiar through biblical acquaintance. But aspects of both areas were also rather mysterious and unknown as for long they had been occupied by Arabs and Muslims.

The whole area lured the European traveller and to cross the Alps going south to the Mediterranean was an emotional and imaginative journey. A visit to Egypt and Palestine was often an extension of the Grand Tour, going south from the sites of Italy (already a liberating experience for many travellers) or Greece. Dr Johnson had written as early as 1776: "A man who has not been in Italy is always conscious of an inferiority from not having seen what is expected he should see. The grand object of travelling is to see the shores of the Mediterranean".[4] Italy was already the beginning of the exotic for a man from the north. Romantics went there for the colour and light and to refurbish their imaginations.

---

[3] A. Kinglake, *Eothen* (Oxford, 1984), p. 4.

[4] Boswell's *Life of Johnson,* 11 April 1776.

Some travellers went to an area place largely invented in their own imagination. Louis Bernard, the French academic, criticized the Romantic traveller for inventing an Orient that had little in common with reality. In his view they had constructed an East that was mysterious, feminine, irrational and dominated, as opposed to the West that they believed was rational, masculine and dominating. This imagined region could be used as setting for literary works, written without the necessity of travelling there, as did Goethe and Victor Hugo and others.

Egypt had its own particular attraction for travellers; its monuments made a powerful appeal to the imagination. They were a living witness to a cradle of civilisation and gave them immediate contact with great themes, of life, of the afterlife, of religion, of gods and men. It contained the remnants of a great civilisation to be wondered at, a demonstration in contemporary Egypt of the continuity of life and society. The wondrous river Nile was a reminder of the constant renewal of life, of the rebirth of hope each year. It was a meeting with a history that was older than that of Greece and Rome. But it was viewed through the eyes of European condescension, for as eye-witnesses considered the ruins of ancient Egypt, they discerned in them a sad demonstration of the decay as contrasted with the dynamism of Europe. In their view Egypt had fallen into corruption and neglect.

Thus, visits to the Near East had a noticeable effect on European attitudes and thought. Travellers paused to ponder the rise and fall of empires, the spread of religions – in particular the triumph of Islam in the birthplace of Christianity – and the justification of Western empires. The contemporary Egyptian was viewed as a fallen version of his predecessor, a constant backdrop to the wonders of the Nile. Cairo was an alien background and Egyptian society remained closed to most outsiders. Egyptians were willing to share their monuments with foreign travellers but not their society. The apparent state of these societies forced outside observers to the conclusion that they were in need of reform and that Europe should intervene to carry it out in the name of altruism, in the name of Western Christian civilization and empire.

A dip into the writings of some of the better known British and French travellers to the Near East might help to elucidate some of the themes touched on above. One of the earliest was the well known French traveller and writer Constantine-Francois Volney. He visited the Near East in 1782 in the hope of seeing parts of the world where the ideas that governed the civilized world had grown up so that he could compare the greatness of the past with what was left. He spent seven months in Egypt and two years in Greater Syria. He published *Voyage en Syrie et en Egypte* in 1787,[5] a careful account of everything that he witnessed, and in 1791 a more reflective work, *Les Ruines, ou Méditations sur les révolutions des empires.*[6] He recorded the many the sites he visited, but did not place his own personality in the forefront of his writings; he was more concerned with the accuracy of his account. The literary critic, Sainte-Beuve, wrote that he regretted that there was so little of the author in *Voyage en Egypte et en Syrie*. He commented: "[H]is writing is dry and lacks colour, the book would have been more attractive had it been a simple narrative of a journey and so

[5] The latest edition of which is by Fayard (Paris, 1998).

[6] The latest edition of which is by Kessinger (Whitefish MT, 2009).

given the reader the feeling he was travelling with the author."[7] Volney, however, used the Near East to draw lessons from the history of Ottoman and Mamluk rule which he thought lawless tyrannies. He was also very hostile to Islam as a political system. He claimed that the ideal society should exist in accordance with natural principles of justice which was not the case in the Near East, except, he believed, in Lebanon where each man had the freedom to possess his land in security. Theses ideas influenced his own career in France and his book was studied by Napoleon before he set out to conquer and 'reform' Egypt. Volney considered the Near East an area ripe for French colonization and it was Napoleon who took the first concrete steps to achieve it. Although he failed totally, it was the French expedition and its publications that opened up the Near East to Europe. Egypt with the remains of its ancient civilization took root in the European mind.

The Near East was not the same after the little Corsican's visit. Anglo-French rivalry centred there and the new dynasty in Egypt turned more towards Europe than Istanbul. The *Description de l'Egypte*, compiled by the savants of the French expedition, listed, described and codified everything Egyptian and the French invasion was the first step in Egypt becoming a popular tourist destination. In the footsteps of Volney followed François Auguste Vicomte de Chateaubriand who visited the Near East in 1805–6. He was, however, very unlike his predecessor, a novelist whose novels emphasized introspection, generally of a pessimistic nature. Such elements in his work mark him out as a forerunner of the Romantic period. In the Near East he sought not scientific information, rather the exotic and attractive reality. He found there a locale sympathetic to his own private myths, obsessions and requirements. He asks the reader not to regard the account of his travels, *Itinéraire de Paris à Jérusalem* (1810–11), as travel literature per se but as 'mémoires d'une année de ma vie'. Despite long descriptions, his book is an exploration of himself in an exotic setting. He sighs: "Je parle éternellement de moi".[8] The Near East was for him an escape from French politics and a place to discover new imagery. But he cannot avoid commenting on the state of society as he sees it. He claims to be dismayed by the indiscipline of the locals. "Of liberty they know nothing; of propriety they have none; force is their god."[9] To him the Arab was civilized man fallen into a savage state. As a superior European traveller he took it upon himself to make judgements of this kind which later became common in writing throughout the 19th and 20th centuries.

Chateaubriand was a leader in this kind of soul searching journey during which he indulged in his private fantasies and self absorption. Somehow, the Near East encouraged him to reveal more of himself in his writings in the Romantic fashion. Some writers did not need to go abroad to do this but he set the trend for this type of journey of self discovery. He was followed by a number of other French traveller-authors who used the Near East for their own ends and to give their readers equally a glimpse of the exotic and of the writer's own inner strivings and torments. Alphonse de Lamartine was clearly in this mould. He said he had always longed for the Near East as an escape from the "gloomy days in the mists of

[7] A. Hourani, *Europe and the Middle East* (London, 1980), p. 84.

[8] F.R. Chateaubriand, *Itinéraire de Paris à Jérusalem* in *Œuvres complètes,* new edn. (Paris, 1939), p. 4.

[9] E. Said, *Orientalism* (London, 1995), p. 172.

the country of my birth" (not Northern France but the rather lovely countryside of southern Burgundy). The Near East was the patrie of his imagination and to travel there was "une grande acte de ma vie intérieure".[10] The area was for him a new source of inspiration and sensation. He made detailed notes of the various sites he visited, all coloured by his own personal inclinations. Lamartine like others did not hesitate to assert that the Near East was ripe for reform and regeneration with European help.

Gérard de Nerval was the essential Romantic poet, suffering from mental depression. His short life was touched by eccentricity, insanity and eventual suicide. He left a vivid account of his travels to the Near East in 1842/3. He was inspired to follow in the footsteps of other French Romantics to a region he believed he already knew and understood – his *patrie*. Once there, however, he felt strangely ill at ease as he did not find what he expected and found it difficult to interpret his findings. He wandered about looking for experiences in the Near East but was frustrated to discover that he was searching for the impossible. He was also attracted to the area by what he called the true feminine, an early seeker of the imagined exotic woman of the Near East. He was mesmerised by the veil and what he hoped lay behind it. He was again frustrated, never to lift the veil, and returned home convinced that Europeans should renounce the "voluptuous image created by our eighteenth century writers"[11] – words that largely fell on deaf ears.

An exact contemporary of de Nerval in the English speaking world was Alexander Kinglake who had published *Eothen* in 1844 – the classic book of English travel literature. It is a sensitive and witty account of things noted during his journey to the Near East and in English a new type of writing. He is the traveller who uses his journey to meditate upon himself and upon his own reactions. *Eothen* has remained one of the most popular books of Eastern travel evoking the life and texture of the area. Strangely, and it would seem irrationally, Edward Said is absolutely vitriolic about it. He calls it a "pathetic catalogue of pompous ethnocentricities and tiringly nondescript accounts of the Englishman's Near East".[12] "The Near East exists for the comparatively useless purpose of letting Kinglake take hold of himself." Said is a dissident voice in criticising a work that has fascinated generations of English readers. Perhaps he was irritated by the fact that the author saw the Near East a place ripe for British domination.

Gustave Flaubert did most in French literature to ignore de Nerval's plea. His goal was to foster the notion of the Near East as a place of sexual fantasy and experience. He claimed that he hated Northern France with its grey skies and mud. He was born for the Orient, eager to experience its supposed delights (particularly the sexual) in person. "Flaubert was finally going to know complete liberty, to find adventure and adventure naturally begins with *aventures*".[13] He set off for Egypt in 1849 and his subsequent book, *Notes de voyage*, is a mixture of lyrical passages, travel writing and descriptions of his sexual encounters. He also relays what happens when dreams collide with reality. His friend Maxime du Camp, who had encouraged him to undertake his journey, thought that Flaubert was quite depressed in

[10] A. de Lamartine, *Voyage en Orient* (Paris, 1887) vol. 1, p. 10.

[11] A. Behdad, *Belated travellers* (Durham, 1994), p. 31.

[12] Said, *Orientalism*, p. 193.

[13] G. Flaubert, *Voyage en Egypte* (Paris, 1991), p. 70.

Cairo and that the journey he had so cherished as a dream and whose realisation had seemed to him impossible had not satisfied him. Flaubert's reaction was not unlike that of others who visited the area with wildly exaggerated ideas of its blatant and available sexuality only to find the reality quite different. Such travellers had sought the Near East as an escape from restrictions at home. Flaubert did, however, draw on his Oriental experiences to write several novels on arrival back home.

It is stretching the concept of the Near East to include North Africa but it was an area of great interest to travellers from Europe, in particular the French. Close to Europe, exotic, brilliantly lit by the African sun, Algeria, later Tunisia, were under the control of the French and therefore experience could be had largely within protected limits. Maupassant, Gautier, Gide and Isabelle Eberhardt found a controlled exoticism there. Painters including Matisse, Delacroix and Gérôme were inspired by its light. The nearness of the Arab world in North Africa also attracted a whole series of British visitors, several of whom left slightly overheated accounts of a 'winter in Algeria'.

For the more daring, a trip into the not too distant desert added to the attractions of North Africa, but it was the British who made desert travel into a profession in areas adjacent to Egypt and Palestine. The endless sands exercised a strange and profound effect on the British, and their Bedouin inhabitants held a special place in British affection. Travel in the remoter deserts was a challenge. It was clearly unlike the more usual forms of tourism and sightseeing. A desert imposed its own harsh conditions and Europeans struggled to understand its nature. And they were fascinated by a society that could live in such conditions. Desert travel inspired great works of literature by authors such as Hogarth, Doughty and Bertram Thomas. The rigours of travel were overcome in order to experience something the travellers found clean, pure, and almost magical. There they could escape from the pressures of life as lived in Europe. Richard Burton went, he said, "to escape the prison-life of civilized Europe, to refresh body and mind".[14] The desert personified the lure of the Near East. But it was not for the faint-hearted traveller, for no casual visitor, as it posed challenges to be faced and conquered. In the daytime the expanses of the sands were immense. At night time in the dark the world was reduced to the confines of the mind. Desert travel demanded commitment and the ability to accept hardship. Richard Burton asked: "What can be more exciting, more sublime. Man's heart pounds in the breast at the thought of measuring his puny force with Nature's might and emerging triumphant from the trial".[15] Wilfrid Thesiger enjoyed the "vastness, the emptiness, the cleanness, the feeling of space".[16]

Some of these travellers tried to appropriate the desert to themselves, as a private retreat where they could escape from their problems. Thesiger was not the only one who needed to get away from the restraints of European life. The wild Isabelle Eberhardt found some solace in her Sahara. Gertrude Bell, Freya Stark, Gide, Wilfrid Blunt, and most famously, T.E. Lawrence all sought escape and relief amongst the endless dunes which became a "sounding box for their tortured psyches". [17] Maupassant described the lure of the desert thus:

[14] R.F. Burton, *The gold-mines of Midian and the ruined Midianite cities* (London, 1878), p. 1.
[15] P. Brent, *Far Arabia: explorers of the myth* (London, 1977), p. 21.
[16] M. Asher, *Thesiger: a biography* (London, 1994), p. 152.
[17] K. Tidrick, *Heart-beguiling Araby,* (Cambridge, 1981), p. 183.

"there ... one wishes for nothing, regrets nothing, aspires to nothing ... The calm landscape ... satisfies the eye, suffices the thought, satisfies the senses and the dream".[18]

Gertrude Bell, born into Victorian society, had to struggle all her life to follow her own path. By chance she found a way out through desert travel. Firstly, it was a challenge for a lone woman of independent mind, then, after a sadly failed love affair, it offered some relief. She admitted to a friend that the desert was an attempt to find a way out of an "irretrievable misfortune". There she was "taught at least some wisdom by solitude, taught submission, and how to bear pain without crying out".[19] She thought she was a different person in the Near East, but she still suffered. She, like Isabelle Eberhardt, never returned home though. T.E. Lawrence, no ordinary traveller himself, faced the desert both in his mind and physically. He wrote of it as a personal challenge in his rather enigmatic way: "It was pleasant to outface it directly, challenging its strength and conquering its extremity".[20]

St John Philby, who was elevated on his tombstone by his son to "greatest of Arabian explorers" – no mere traveller he, was obsessed with the desert from early on in his time in the Near East. He saw it even more personally than others. He did not just want to conquer; he wanted to possess it – "the bride of my constant desire".[21] He did so by exhaustive travels and minute recording of what he found. He, no temporary sojourner, spent most of his working life in the area and died there.

The background to travel is composed of scenery, both natural and man made, and of local inhabitants. We know that some visitors to Egypt believed the contemporary Arab to be a decadent descendant of his ancient forbears. Not so the inhabitant of the desert who was often admired, especially by a certain type of Briton. The British thought they had an especial affinity with the Bedouin who they believed to be civilized, hardy and loyal. Lawrence (somewhat ambivalently), John Glubb, Thesiger and others built a career on their relationships with the Bedouin. Thesiger exulted: "My travels in the Empty Quarter would have been pointless penance but for the comradeship of my Bedouin companions. I could not match them in physical endurance but with my family background, Eton and Oxford I did perhaps think I could match them in civilized behaviour".[22] There is the European traveller to the Near East lost in the world of his own imagination.

The lure of the Near East as exemplified in those travellers we have considered is now over. The tourist still likes to admire Egyptian antiquities, but from the pampered luxury of the Nile cruiser. Palestine is a highly developed Israel. Tunisia and Morocco offer deserts and Arabs, but are less exotic than further East (although it seems to matter little to modern tourists where they are as long as they have the minimum facilities of food and drink, shelter, sea and sand). Freya Stark was probably the last grand traveller of her age, Thesiger the last great desert explorer, and he lamented bitterly the passing of traditional society, the mechanization of the desert and the urbanization of the Bedouin. The places where European travellers might live out their own private fantasies have now largely passed away.

---

[18] G. de Maupassant, *Maupassant au Maghreb,* (Paris, 1982), p. 129.

[19] E. Burgoyne, *Gertrude Bell: from her personal papers,* (2 vv., London 1958, 61), i, p. 285.

[20] J. Wilson, *Lawrence of Arabia,* (London, 19890), p. 407.

[21] H. St J. Philby, *The empty quarter,* (London, 1933), p. xviii.

[22] W. Thesiger, *A life of my choice,* (London, 1987), p. 398.

# 9

# Charles Pellat and the *Encyclopaedia of Islam*: A personal reminiscence

*C. Edmund Bosworth*

My personal connection with Charles Pellat goes back to 1974, when Bernard Lewis, about to leave the School of Oriental and African Studies for Princeton, invited me to succeed him as Editor in Britain of the new edition of the *Encyclopaedia of Islam* and thus join the quadrumvirate of which Charles Pellat was by that time senior member. Pellat had been the Editorial Secretary for the French edition (since the *Encyclopaedia* was being published in parallel French and English editions) until 1956 and then, on the death of the French Editor, E. Lévi-Provençal, became his successor in that role.

Of course, I had long known Pellat by reputation as the leading French scholar in the field of Arabic literature and culture once the earlier generation of Massignon, Lévi-Provençal, Blachère and Massé had departed, and I possessed a copy of his magisterial *Le milieu baṣrien et la formation de Ǧāḥiẓ* which delineated in great detail the material and cultural background for his subsequent studies and translations of this most original and wide-ranging littérateur of ninth-century Baghdad.[1] It was, however, only when I could now participate in the deliberations of the Editorial Board that I was able actually to meet him.

At our half-yearly editorial meetings, held in rotation at Paris, Leiden, Manchester and Princeton, and then latterly in France only, something of the multi-facetted personality of Charles Pellat was revealed to me *en passant*, but it has only been through the posthumous publication of his autobiography, entrusted by him before his death in 1992 to his daughter, Mme Yvette Guilcher-Pellat,[2] that the fullness of his life and career can now be known to outsiders.

His family origins were modest. His grandfather had abandoned the constraints of rural life in the Dauphiné for work on the Algerian Railways system and the better prospects of life in Algeria. Hence it was in the Constantinois region of Algeria that Pellat was born in 1916. After 1924, his family moved to Morocco for work in the French Protectorate administration, and it was here that he first acquired a knowledge of Arabic – at first, of Moroccan dialect Arabic, in which he remained fluent all of his life, and then of the written classical and literary forms. Moreover, he acquired an equal knowledge of Berber (as the

[1] C. Pellat, *Le milieu baṣrien et la formation de Ǧāḥiẓ* (Paris, 1953).

[2] C. Pellat, *Une vie d'arabisant* (Paris 2007), pp. 167.

*EI²* article 'Berbers', much of which was written by him, attests),[3] and at one point in his career he could have become a Professor of Berber at the University of Algiers, had he not wisely realised that the profession of *arabisant* was going to offer far wider academic opportunities that of *berbérisant*.

He details in his autobiography the various steps in his education and the qualifications he acquired *seriatim*, all this not very intelligible to one not knowledgeable about what seems to have been, to outsiders at least, a labyrinthine French North African educational system. Military service, at first in North Africa and then after the outbreak of World War II, in the Near East, followed. He became chief of press and information at the Delegation of the High Commission in Damascus, got to know the Syrian literary milieu and its personalities and acquired a knowledge of Syrian colloquial Arabic. He mentioned to me that at one point he became *mustashār* or governor of Quneitra in the Golan Heights region of southern Syria (now, since 1967, under Israeli control). In 1941 he chose to be repatriated to France after the British and Free French invasion of Syria, together with the great majority of French government representatives and troops there. After the Germans had in November 1942 invaded the part of France under Vichy government control, his military career ended as a lieutenant and his academic career really began (although he records that, as an officer permanently on the reserve, he received official notification, some decades later and in the middle of his university career in Paris, when his military life had receded far into the background, of his theoretical promotion to lieutenant-colonel!). He was now able to present himself at the first post-war competition for *agrégation* in Arabic in 1946.

The unfolding of his academic career takes up the rest of his autobiography; first at the Lycée Louis-le-Grand in 1947, then in 1951 at the Ĝcole Nationale de Langues Orientales Vivantes, and finally at the Sorbonne/Paris IV, where in 1956 he became Professor of Arabic in what became the Department of Islamology. During his twenty-two years at the Sorbonne, he suffered many trials and tribulations. The events of May-June 1968 seemed to him likely to bring about the negation of all that a University stood for: scholarly integrity, the disinterested pursuit of knowledge for its own sake, courtesy towards and respect for one's colleagues. He had to make much of his own career, once his patron and encourager Lévi-Provençal was no more, in the face of unrelenting opposition and what seems to have been pure malevolence on the part of an influential figure in the French Arabist world, R. Blachère. When the chair of Arabic at the Collège de France fell vacant in 1975 with the retirement of Henri Laoust, Pellat seemed, from his experience and academic record, the obvious person, but in the event it was a younger man, André Miquel, who was appointed. Pellat states that Miquel's candidature was put forward by Jacques Berque ("qui ne me portait pas dans son coeur, probablement parce que j'avais une réputation de patriotisme qui ne convenait pas aux intellectuels"). French academic life at this time seems to outsiders to have been incredibly cut-throat, and political motives may indeed have played a part here. Pellat was disliked by the left, although he always enjoyed the respect of, and had cordial relations with, the greatest French Islamic historian of the time, Claude Cahen. Pellat describes him as a friend, even though Cahen remained a firm Communist to the end of his life; it was Cahen who presented Pellat's candidature for the Académie des Inscriptions et Belles-Lettres, mentioned just below.

---

[3] *EI2* (Leiden, 1960), vol. 1, pp. 1173–87

In compensation for this setback to his career, Pellat was able in 1986 to achieve a notable mark of recognition, election to the Académie des Inscriptions et Belles Lettres (he had been since 1973 a member of the Académie des Sciences d'Outremer, but was to find the AIBL a more congenial, higher-level, intellectual home than the ASO, whose membership was sprinkled with retired generals and admirals).

Pellat was much in demand as a speaker and participant in conferences and colloquia in European centres of learning and in virtually every Arabophone country from Mauritania to Iraq. Tunisia had a special place in his affections, and it was a Tunisian colleague, Ferhat Dachraoui, who organised in his honour a collection of *Mélanges*, published in 1989 in *Cahiers de la Tunisie*, XXXV, no. 139–40 (*Numéro spécial. Mélanges Charles Pellat*). Both during his Sorbonne years and afterwards in retirement, Pellat's scholarly output was, I came to realise, prodigious. Thus, he became aware that, whilst a rising scholar could get articles published in academic journals and, when he became established, get full-scale books likewise issued, there was an intermediate stage when it was difficult to get dissertations or monographs of modest length into print. Hence he inaugurated a series of Publications du Département d'Islamologie, economically produced as reproduced typescript and manuscript, of which he kindly gave me a set, and these ran to six volumes, published in 1976–78 before his decision to retire in 1978. Vols II–VI ranged in subject from a translation of and study on Ibn al-Muqaffaᶜ's *Risāla fī 'l-Ṣaḥāba* to one on d'Herbelot's pioneer *Encyclopaedia of Islam* from the later seventeenth century, his famous *Bibliothèque orientale*.[4] As well as this Ibn al-Muqaffaᶜ monograph, his own output included large-scale projects such as texts and translations of various works of Jāḥiẓ[5] and a freshly edited and revised text and translation of Maṣᶜūdī's extended History, the *Murūj al-dhahab* or 'Meadows of Gold'.[6]

All this was in addition to his unceasing and unrelenting work on the *Encyclopaedia*, with himself as Editor, aided by Mme Nurit as his indefatigable secretary.

After the end of World War II, it was some time before the European academic world, like everything else in those dreary post-war years, got back to any semblance of normality. The first edition of the *Encyclopaedia of Islam* had been published, in four volumes and a supplement, by E.J. Brill at Leiden over 1908–1938. The periodic International Conferences of Orientalists, which had begun in the later nineteenth century, were revived, and at the first postwar conference in Paris in 1948, it was decided to embark on a new edition of the *EI*, since much of the earlier volumes of the *EI*¹ at least had become outdated. The original *EI* had been published in three languages, German, French and English. In the immediate postwar climate, there was no question of a German edition; over the following years, German colleagues came to accept this with a good grace, and were to make solid and valued contributions to the new project. Moreover, in these same postwar years, it became clear

[4] Ch. Pellat, *Ibn al-Muqaffaᶜ, mort vers 140/767* 'Conseilleur' du calife (Paris, 1976); Henri Laurens, *Aux source de l'orientalisme. La Bibliotèque Orientale de Barthélemi d'Herbelot* (Paris, 1976).

[5] The most notable here being his French translation of the *Kitāb al-Bukhalāᵓ*, *Le Livre des avares de Ǧāḥiẓ* (Paris, 1951) and those in his *The Life and Works of Jāḥiẓ Translations of Selected Texts,* English tr. D.M. Hawke (London 1969). See also his 'Nouvel Essai d'inventaire de l'oevre ǧāḥizienne', *Arabica*, 31.2 (1984), pp. 117–64.

[6] Text: *Les Praires d'or/Murūj al-Dhahab wa-maᶜādin al-jawhar*, 7 vols. (Beirut, 1966–79); French Translation, *Les praires d'or*, 5 vols (Paris, 1962–98)

that, given the share of the United States in the achieving of victory and the general trend of circumstances across the world, the English language, whether of a British or American variety, was going to become more and more the international language of communication. Presumably sensing this trend, it soon became clear that French orientalists would stand out for a two-language new edition of the *EI*, and Lévi-Provençal expressly stated that, if there was not to be a French-language version, the contribution of French scholars could not be counted upon.

So the project went ahead in both English and French. In the event, about two-thirds of articles contributed were originally in English, or translated into English in the first place, and one-third in French, or translated into French in the first place. Of course, since every article had to be translated into the other language, an article contributed in say German or Spanish or Italian ended up in three versions (it was a matter of regret that, in these Cold War years, the Russian Communist régime would not allow any Russian scholars to participate in this bourgeois undertaking, when in the past the *EI*[1] had benefited from articles by such outstanding authorities as Barthold, Berthels and Kratchkovsky). These complexities of translation and editing go a long way in explaining the slowness of publication, with over fifty years needed to complete the project in its eleven volumes and supplement and an index volume.

As noted above, Pellat assumed membership of the Editorial Committee of the *EI* in 1956, and it was to take up a large share of his life right up to his death in 1992, his place as a co-Editor and as guiding spirit behind the French edition being then taken by his old colleague from the ENLOV, Gérard Lecomte, regrettably functioning for only two years till his own death, but thereafter, by Thierry Bianquis of the University of Lyons, who was to see the project through to the end and who is happily still with us.

As mentioned at the outset, I myself came into the *EI* project in the mid-1970s. Our twice-yearly editorial meetings moved around, and came to include Leiden, Paris, Manchester, Princeton and then Harvard, once Wolfhart Heinrichs of Harvard University and Peri Bearman of the Harvard Law School had joined our editorial board. Our meetings in France were at first held at Pellat's own Department d'Islamologie in the Sorbonne but then, after his retirement, in the elegant surroundings of the Château de Morigny, in the Île de France near Ğtampes, a country house which had been bequeathed by its noble owners to their alma mater, the Sorbonne, as a centre for meetings and conferences. Its smooth running was now the responsibility of Pellat's faithful secretary, Mme Nurit, who had been appointed Administrator of the Château (it was, alas, eventually to be sold off by the Sorbonne). In addition to the attendant gastronomic delights, our sessions there were always packed with activity: reviewing progress of the *Encyclopaedia*, sorting out problems and allocating articles to contributors. Nevertheless, there was time for the Editors to get to know each other in the relaxing surroundings of the house and its grounds. Hence I gradually came to learn something of Charles Pellat's mode of life as Editor: how he had worked assiduously each morning from 5.00 am onwards on the editing of typescripts received and on the translation into French of those arriving in English, Spanish, Italian, etc., until he had gone off to the Sorbonne to fulfil his teaching duties. During that time he had to write out everything by hand lest the clattering of his typewriter awake the rest of the household (this would not, of course, be a problem today when word-processing can be done on a virtually silent computer!). The resultant French manuscript versions of articles sometimes gave problems to the publisher Brill's typesetters in Leiden, and our Dutch colleague Emeri van Donzel would have to be called into Brill's offices to elucidate; but the difficulties here seem to have been surmounted over the course of time as his hand became more familiar to them.

In the course of our editorial sessions, I also came to realise and appreciate his strong French patriotism, and his love for the French language and desire to protect it, as far as possible, from the inexorable pressures of what was increasingly becoming a global, English language-dominated world. Our editorial proceedings, wherever we were, were always conducted in French, which was perfectly acceptable except that I myself sometimes got lost in the abstruse technical vocabulary of financial matters. I know that he always insisted, whenever possible, on speaking French when in anglophone milieux (though his reading knowledge of English was excellent; he was a great reader of the detective stories of Agatha Christie in their original tongue), which must have caused him problems at times. He told us that when, in 1972, he had visited Rajshahi University in what had just recently become Bangladesh, he had, as elsewhere in India (including the Osmania University in Hyderabad), given his lectures and spoken with University colleagues in Arabic. I assume that, whilst travelling around the subcontinent, he had aid from French consular and diplomatic personnel; the numbers of arabophone or francophone actual airport staff at an airport like Dacca must have been minimal, if not indeed non-existent. Nevertheless, he could express himself adequately in spoken English when pressed. He coped – at the outset, with some trepidation, as he expresses it in his autobiography – first with an invitation to a colloquium at Princeton University in 1966 and then shortly afterwards, with a further invitation to give a complete, four-week course of twenty-four lectures in total on the history of the Arabic language and on literature and *adab*, these to be given in English. Towards the end of the course, he records, the students asked him to speak in Arabic, so that he had to translate his written English text spontaneously into Arabic, certainly a feat for someone who avows in his autobiography again, clearly with vastly exaggerated modesty, to have no gift for languages!

His feeling for France, its history and cultural heritage, was obvious, but it was tinged with a certain nostalgia. He cannot have found much of later twentieth-century France, the France of Mitterand and socialism, with its accommodation, at least initially, with the Communists, congenial. I remember discussing with him on one occasion (perhaps in the bicentennial year of 1989) the pros and cons of the French Revolution and its subsequent effects. He expressed the view that, if left alone, late eighteenth-century France would in the course of time have evolved peacefully into something like a modern constitutional state, as eighteenth and nineteenth-century Britain had done after the *Sturm und Drang* of the seventeenth century: this without the upheavals, violence and slaughter of the Revolution, and its deleterious effects on Europe as a whole, and the consequent eight decades or so of continued military coups and personal animosities within France itself. Regarding his own beliefs, he once told us, rather despairingly, "en principe, je suis royaliste – mais quel roi?"

I always admired him, not only for his intellectual eminence, but also for his dedication, integrity and firmness of purpose in furthering the cause of the *Encyclopaedia of Islam*, and these are the qualities above all for which I remember him; it is only regrettable that he did not live to see the completion of the great work to which he devoted so much of his life.

# 10

# Arabic Printing in Scotland: An historical sketch

*Geoffrey Roper*

Among the many areas of interest and knowledge which Paul Auchterlonie developed during his long bibliographical career is the history of printing and publishing in the languages of the Middle East. This brief sketch is an attempt to throw some light on the use of Arabic in books printed and published in his own native land. It is also a belated contribution to the celebrations of the 500th anniversary of Scotland's first printed book (1508).

In an earlier article, in which I gave an account of Arabic printing and publishing in England up to the early 19th century, I observed that "Britain was a relative late-comer to Arabic typography, as indeed it was in the development of printing generally. Furthermore, its production of Arabic books remained at a lower level than that of its main European rivals, both in quantity and in quality, at least until the 19th century".[1] What was true of England, and of Britain in general, was even more so of Scotland. It has been remarked that by the time that printing was introduced there, after the age of incunabula, the markets for Renaissance classical and scholarly literature had been cornered by other European countries, and as a consequence "the earliest Edinburgh books were on the whole of a homelier interest".[2] Moreover, before 1700 Scottish printers were "entirely dependent on European and English types and ornaments".[3] These limitations certainly played a part in the late development and, as we shall see, quite restricted use of Arabic printing, a situation which lasted long after 1700.

The first two and a half centuries of printing in Scotland were dominated, typographically speaking, first by black letter (Gothic) and subsequently by various roman and italic styles introduced from England and elsewhere; Greek also made its appearance in the 16th century.[4]

[1] G. Roper, 'Arabic Printing and Publishing in England before 1820', *British Society for Middle Eastern Studies Bulletin*, Vol.12 (1985), pp. 12–32.

[2] W. Beattie, *The Scottish Tradition in Printed Books*, (Edinburgh, 1949), p. 1.

[3] ibid., p. 2. Cf. also J.C. Smail, *Printing in Scotland 1507–1947* (Dundee, 1963), p. 12.

[4] R. Dickson and J.P. Edmond, *Annals of Scottish Printing: from the Introduction of the Art in 1507 to the Beginning of the Seventeenth Century* (Cambridge, 1890), vol. 1.

The first non-European script was, as elsewhere, Hebrew, which was used in two works by the radical Aberdeen clergyman and scholar John Row (c. 1598–1672): a grammar, *הדקדוק קצור = Hebrææ Linguæ Institutiones compendiosissimæ et facillimæ*, and a vocabulary, *הדברים אלף = Χιλιας Hebraica, seu, vocabularium continens præcipuas radices linguæ Hebrææ.* These were printed and published together in Glasgow by the University printer George Anderson, in 1644.

But, as far as we can tell, no books printed in this period contained any Arabic script. Without scrutinising them all, we cannot be absolutely certain, but the published surveys[5] make no mention of Arabic, and the enumerative bibliographies[6] do not seem to contain any titles which indicate the likelihood of Arabic being used.

In the 18th century there was a massive improvement in Scottish typography, with printers producing high-quality books for the academics and intellectuals of the Scottish Enlightenment. Notable among them was the Foulis Press in Glasgow (1742–75), which produced fine editions of both classical and vernacular literature: it was renowned for its Greek typography, and also used Hebrew in at least one of its books[7]. But Arabic remained beyond its scope, and the editions of Arabic texts, which had become a notable feature of the output of a number of scholarly printers in other European countries, were notable in Scotland by their absence.

In 1758 appeared the first Scottish book, as far as we can ascertain, to contain Arabic: another Hebrew grammar, *Grammatica Linguæ Hebrææ, cum notis et variis quæstionibus philologicis.* It was printed not in Glasgow, but in Edinburgh, by the firm of Hamilton, Balfour and Neill, one of a series of shifting partnerships formed by Patrick Neill (founder of a long-lived dynasty of Edinburgh printers which lasted into the second half of the 20th century), who had been printer to the University since 1754.[8] The author was James Robertson (1714–95), one of the first Scottish Orientalists, who was a graduate of Leiden University and pupil of the celebrated Jan Jacob Schultens[9]. He was Professor of Oriental Languages in the University, and his book is stated to be 'In Usum Juventutis Academicae'. On pp. [ix–xi] (or 255–256, according to the list of contents), there is a table of Arabic equivalents of the letters of the Hebrew alphabet; there are also some Arabic words scattered in the text and footnotes, but it certainly cannot be considered to be an Arabic book as such. The types used appear to be those cut by the celebrated London type designer William Caslon in the early 1720s. Caslon's types were in general much favoured by Scottish printers in the 18th century,[10] so when Arabic was required it would have been natural for Neill and

[5] J.P. Edmond, *The Aberdeen printers: Edward Ruban to James Nicol, 1620–1736* (Aberdeen, 1886); Dickson and Edmond, *Annals*; J.P. Edmond, *Bibliographical Gleanings, 1890–93: being Additions and Corrections to the* Annals of Scottish Printing (Edinburgh, 1894); A.F. Johnson, 'Type-designs and type-founding in Scotland', *Edinburgh Bibliographical Society Transactions*, vol. 2 (1946), pp. 255–261; A. Kamm, *Scottish Printed Books, 1508–2008* (Dingwall and Edinburgh, 2008).

[6] H.G. Aldis, *A list of books printed in Scotland before 1700* (Edinburgh, 1904, rp. with additions 1970).

[7] P. Gaskell, *A Bibliography of the Foulis Press* (London, 1964, rp. Winchester, 1986), p. 506, #504.

[8] Neill and Company, *The Printing-House of Neill* (Edinburgh, 1917).

[9] C. Fell-Smith, 'Robertson, James (1714–1795)', rev. P. Carter, *Oxford Dictionary of National Biography* (Oxford, 2004), online database, viewed 14 March 2011 <http://www.oxforddnb.com/view/article/23797>.

[10] Johnson, 'Type-designs and type-founding', p. 258.

his colleagues to acquire a fount from the Caslon foundry. The inexperience of the printers in setting Arabic is probably the reason for the use of incorrect letter-forms in places.

In 1770 another work by Robertson appeared: *Clavis Pentateuchi; sive analysis omnium vocum Hebraicarum suo ordine in Pentateucho Moseos occurrentium: una cum versione Latina et Anglica: notis criticis et philologicis adjectis.* Although this is primarily an analysis of the Hebrew version of the Pentateuch, Robertson decided to demonstrate his erudition by including a 72-page 'Dissertatio de Origine, Antiquitate, Conservatione, Indole, et Utilitate, Linguæ Arabicæ' [Dissertation on the origin, antiquity, preservation, nature and utility of the Arabic language]. This makes more extensive use of Arabic typography, in quotations and examples. Here again we find incorrect letter-forms in places, e.g. ال ا for الا and البل اغة for البلاغة on p. 23 and إلي for إلى on p. 73, as well as spelling errors such as اهل الكتب for اهل الكتاب on p. 33. Persian words occur in one or two places, but the letter گ is replaced by ك. On pp. 64–66 are tables of verb paradigms, which have full vocalisation (*ḥarakāt*) – always a tricky feature of Arabic typography.

This book was published by the booksellers Kincaid and Bell, but printed by Robert Fleming and Patrick and Adam Neill. This was a temporary partnership between the two leading Edinburgh printers of the period: Patrick Neill retired in favour of his son Adam in 1769, although his name was at first retained; Robert Fleming had been a printer, bookseller, auctioneer and paper maker since 1748.[11] A history of the firm states that "the partnership did not long endure, which was unfortunate, for Fleming was one of the chief printers in Edinburgh ... Perhaps he was 'difficult', having had several partners in his career, which closed in 1779".[12] However that may be, during this brief period they managed to print this substantial scholarly work, again using Arabic types from the Caslon foundry.

It has not been possible to trace further uses by Neill of Caslon Arabic. The type specimens of Neill and Co in the 1840s contain no Arabic at all, although they were by then typefounders as well as printers.[13] Nor, as far as can be seen, were any other Arabic types used in Edinburgh in the 18th or early 19th centuries. The second edition of Robertson's *Grammatica Hebrææ*, edited by Dr Charles Wilson (Edinburgh, 1783), was printed by Robert Wilson, and used no Arabic types, although there were still remarks on Arabic in the preface. This may have been because Robert Wilson had no access to the types; or maybe because of the attitude of Charles Wilson, who in his own *Elements of Hebrew grammar* (Edinburgh: W. Creech, 1782), cast aspersions on the value of studying Arabic and Persian (p. iv).

Probably the most celebrated production of the Edinburgh press in the 18th century was the first edition of the *Encyclopædia Britannica* in 1771. This contained no Arabic – perhaps not surprising in view of its rather poor and ill-informed coverage of the Arab and Muslim world. Nor does Arabic script appear in the publications of the pioneer Edinburgh Arabist John Leyden. Not until the 1820s did Arabic make its reappearance (see below).

Meanwhile, a new field of activity for 'exotic' printing was opening up. The Edinburgh Missionary Society, like its counterparts in England and elsewhere, sought to use the

---

[11] *Scottish Book Trade Index* (Edinburgh: National Library of Scotland), online database, viewed 14 March 2011 http://www.nls.uk/media/63385/sbti-a-m.pdf>.

[12] M. McLaren (ed.), *The House of Neill* (Edinburgh, 1949), p. 8.

[13] Neill and Co, *Specimens of printing types from the foundry of Neill and Co*, 1: *Book and newspaper types* (Edinburgh, 1843); id., *Specimens of printing types by Neill and Co, printers, stereotypers, and typefounders* (Edinburgh, 1845).

printed word to make converts among heathens and Muslims in far-off places. One of their missionaries, Henry Brunton, prepared a number of books in the Susu language of Sierra Leone and Guinea, which were printed in Edinburgh by J. Ritchie in 1801–02. But although many Susu speakers were Muslims, the language was influenced by Arabic, and Brunton's *Grammar and vocabulary of the Susoo language* (Edinburgh, 1802) contained a catalogue of relevant Arabic books, no Arabic script was used, perhaps because of the lack of types available to Ritchie.

In April 1805 it was reported in the *Christian Observer*, referring to Brunton, by then a missionary in 'Tartary', that "An Arabic tract which he drew up, in order to expose the delusions of the Mohammedan superstition, is printing for distribution among the Mussulmen".[14] In August the same year, it was further reported that this tract had been printed at the expense of the "Mission Society to Africa and the East", i.e. the (English) Church Missionary Society, in conjunction with the Edinburgh Missionary Society, and that it was intended for distribution in Africa.[15] This was the 31-page booklet entitled خطاب من صديق لمسلمان [*Khiṭāb min ṣadīq li-Musulmān* (sic)], printed by A. Wilson in London, of which Schnurrer was extremely critical, both as to its bad Arabic and its offensiveness to Muslim susceptibilities.[16] It was also criticised "very unfavourably" by the Cambridge Orientalist Samuel Lee, who worked for the CMS.[17] Whether it was distributed in Africa is not known, but 750 copies were sent in May 1805 to Karass in the North Caucasus,[18] where Brunton was later said to have "dispersed it with success".[19] The Edinburgh Missionary Society also shipped from Leith at the same time a press with an Arabic fount[20] (of unknown origin).This was used mainly for publications in Turkish, notably the complete New Testament, translated by Brunton, in 1813; also Tatar and Persian. In 1817 an Arabic tract, consisting of Bible extracts, was printed in an edition of 800, as well as 2000 copies of a Bible history and catechism[21]. In 1822 or 1823, by which time they were known as the Scottish Missionary Society, they also published, in an edition of 500, an Arabic رسالة [*Risāla*] by Mīrzā Muḥammad ʿAlī Kāẓim Beg, a local convert to Christianity.[22] This was printed at Astrakhan, where they had established a new press in 1821, with Arabic types, different from the Karass fount and apparently from the London foundry of Richard Watts. With these they also printed a series of further books, mainly Bibles in Tatar, before the establishment was suspended in 1825 because of difficulties with the Russian authorities.[23]

---

[14] 'Religious intelligence: Tartary', *Christian Observer*, 4 (1805), p. 257.

[15] 'Religious intelligence: Mission Society to Africa and the East', *Christian Observer*, 4 (1805), pp. 506–507.

[16] C.F. Schnurrer, *Bibliotheca Arabica* (Halle, 1811), #314, pp. 332–335. Cf. M. Steinschneider, *Polemische und apologetische Literatur in arabischer Sprache* (Leipzig, 1877), p. 47, #28b.

[17] C. Hole, *The early history of the Church Missionary Society for Africa and the East to the end of A.D.1814* (London, 1896), p. 597.

[18] 'Religious intelligence: Edinburgh Missionary Society', *Christian Observer*, 4 (1805), p. 574.

[19] H. Pearson, *A dissertation on the propagation of Christianity in Asia* (Oxford, 1808), p. 63.

[20] 'Religious intelligence: Edinburgh Missionary Society', p. 574.

[21] *Missionary Register* (1817), p. 491.

[22] *Missionary Register* (1824), p. 552 and (1825), p. 44; A.D.H. Bivar, 'The portraits and career of Mohammed Ali, son of Kazem-Beg: Scottish missionaries and Russian Orientalism', *Bulletin of the School of Oriental and African Studies*, 57 (1994), p. 300.

[23] H. Kirimli, 'Crimean Tatars, Nogays, and Scottish missionaries', *Cahiers du Monde Russe*, 45

While this activity did not take place in Scotland, the involvement of Scottish organisations and personnel justifies its place in any account of Scottish Arabic printing, and it gains significance from the fact that it brought the first printed books in the Arabic script to a part of the Muslim world where they were previously unknown.

Back in Edinburgh, Charles Stewart took over as University Printer in 1809,[24] and in 1820 he printed at the University Press *An Arabic vocabulary and index for Richardson's Arabic grammar ... with tables of Oriental alphabets, points and affixes* by James Noble, 'teacher of languages in Edinburgh'. On the dedication page this work is proclaimed as 'being the first in Arabic ever printed in Scotland'. Since the 18th-century works of Robertson previously mentioned were primarily concerned with Hebrew, this is not strictly untrue, but it is a little misleading, especially as this too does not contain any substantial or continuous Arabic text. The table of alphabets is executed as a copper-plate engraving, but the vocabulary again uses Caslon Arabic types. They are, however, distinctly better set than in the Robertson books printed by Neill, and the use of higher-quality paper enabled a clearer impression.

In 1822 Stewart again used the Caslon Arabic types to print Professor Alexander Brunton's *Outlines of Persian grammar, with extracts*, which contained much more substantial passages of text, and can perhaps be regarded as the first Scottish book mainly printed in the Arabic script. The Persian letters پ, چ, ژ and ڭ appear, which were not in Caslon's original fount.

In Glasgow, meanwhile, the successors of the Foulis brothers tried to continue their high standards as scholarly printers to the University. In 1811 Andrew Duncan was appointed 'College Printer'. His forebear John Duncan had printed Charles Morthland's Hebrew and Aramaic grammar (*Brevis introductio ad grammaticam Hebraicam et Chaldaicam in usum Academicorum Glasgoviensium*) in 1721 and had also used Hebrew types in the *Spicilegia Antiquitatum Ægypti* (1720), a curious work of pre-Egyptology by William Jameson, Professor of History in the University of Glasgow. Andrew Duncan's printing office possessed Greek and Hebrew types: he too produced a number of Hebrew books with the latter.

At some stage he also acquired Arabic types. They are of a larger size than Caslon's and may be those cut by the London typographer Joseph Jackson (1733–92), an apprentice of Caslon, originally for John Richardson's massive *Dictionary, Persian, Arabic, and English* (Oxford, 1777).[25] The only Glasgow books in which they appear, as far as can be ascertained, are two volumes of polemical review articles. The first appeared in 1824 under the title *Critical researches in philology and geography*, and it was printed, not by Duncan, but by another Glasgow 'merchant printer',[26] James Curll: he must have borrowed the types for the purpose.

The author of this book is not named, but it is attributed to the Glasgow geographer and classical tutor James Bell (in collaboration with the unrelated John Bell, a student).[27] In it he followed an old and enduring tradition of Glaswegians by attacking what had recently come out of Edinburgh, in this case Noble's *Arabic vocabulary and index* (1820) and Brunton's

---

(2004), pp. 94–95

24 *Scottish Book Trade Index* online

25 G. Roper, 'Arabic Printing and Publishing in England', p. 21.

26 *Scottish Book Trade Index* online

27 British Library, *Integrated catalogue* online, record 003076906, shelfmark 622.h.26; E. Baigent, 'Bell, James (1770–1833)', *Oxford Dictionary of National Biography* (Oxford, 2004), online database, viewed 14 March 2011 <http://www.oxforddnb.com/view/article/2009>.

*Outlines of Persian grammar* (1822), mentioned above. Not content with being highly critical of their authors, he also asserts that "the typography, besides, confers no honour upon the Edinburgh University press". The Arabic typography in his own book, however, confers no greater honour on Glasgow printing, being confined to a few scattered letters and words in the disproportionately large types used.

The greater part of Bell's book, however, is devoted to an even more virulent attack on the English Orientalist Samuel Lee. To this Lee replied immediately in a letter to the *Asiatic Journal* in London, whereupon Bell published (still anonymously) his yet more venomous *Remarks on Professor Lee's vindication* in 1825. This was printed by Andrew and John M. Duncan, Printers to the University, and includes more words in their Arabic types.

The Duncans, however, eventually ran into severe financial difficulties, and the entire University printing establishment had to be put up for sale in 1826.[28] The inventory which was prepared for the sale reveals that it had not only numerous Greek and Hebrew founts, but also twelve pounds of Syriac types, and nineteen pounds of Arabic, with special cases for them.[29]

Most of these printing materials were bought in 1829 by John Blackie, another leading Glasgow printer. It was reported in 1931 that the firm of Blackie "still have some Greek and Arabic founts which belonged to Duncan",[30] but what they did with them (if anything) is unknown.

In the 1830s another Edinburgh printing-house entered the field of Arabic typography: the firm of Ballantyne and Company, which had acquired fame, and later notoriety, as printers of the works of Walter Scott.[31] Its interest in Muslim literature went back to 1812 when, under its founder, James Ballantyne (1772–1833), it published *Tales of the East*, comprising translations of the 1001 Nights and various Persian, Turkish and Tatar stories, but with no Arabic script involved. In 1838 James Ballantyne's nephew James Robert Ballantyne (1813–64), who had studied Indian languages at the East India College at Haileybury,[32] published his *Grammar of the Hindustani language*, and naturally turned to his uncle's old firm. In fact, the book itself credits the printing jointly to Robert Cox and Son, London, and Ballantyne and Company, Edinburgh, so it is not possible to be certain which of them is responsible for the Urdu content. The types used seem to be one of the small Arabic faces of the London Oriental type-founders Richard Watts, based on the designs originally produced by William Martin[33]. The extra Persian/Urdu letters are included.

---

[28] J. Maclehose, *The Glasgow University Press 1638–1931, with some notes on Scottish printing in the last three hundred years* (Glasgow, 1931), pp. 217–224.

[29] [A. Duncan], *The Glasgow University Printing Office in MDCCCXXVI* [reprint of the inventory of printing materials and a digest of the inventory of type from the sale catalogue of 1826, entitled *Specimens of Types, and inventory of printing materials, belonging to the University Printing Office of Glasgow*] (Cambridge, 1953), pp. 5 and 14.

[30] Maclehose, *The Glasgow University Press*, p. 225.

[31] *Scottish Book Trade Index* online; S.A. Ragaz, 'Ballantyne, James (1772–1833)', *Oxford Dictionary of National Biography* (Oxford, 2004), online database, viewed 29th January 2009 <http://www.oxforddnb.com/view/article/1228>

[32] R.S. Simpson, 'Ballantyne, James Robert (1813–1864)', *Oxford Dictionary of National Biography* (Oxford, 2004), online database, viewed 14 March 2011 <http://www.oxforddnb.com/view/article/1229>.

[33] G. Roper, 'Arabic Printing and Publishing in England', pp. 22–24.

James Robert Ballantyne went on to produce a long series of Urdu and Persian grammars and anthologies, intended for use at the Scottish Naval and Military Academy. These were nearly all co-published in London and Edinburgh, and were printed by Ballantyne and Company (sometimes Ballantyne and Hughes). In at least one case they are credited as sole printers, which presumably indicates their own use of the Arabic types (always the Watts face). In one or two of them, however, most of the Urdu or Persian is romanised, which may indicate either shortage of type or lack of qualified typesetters. There were also two editions (1839 and 1844) of *Principles of Persian caligraphy* [sic], in which the Persian texts are presented entirely on lithographic plates, and also his *Hindustani letters* (1840), in which the Urdu texts are likewise lithographed. The whole series came to an end in 1845, when J.R. Ballantyne went to India.

It was in that year, however, that Scottish Arabic-script printing reached its apogee, when much the most substantial text ever printed there made its appearance. This was the complete Bible in Persian, published by the United Associate Synod (the United Secession Church) of Scotland, supported by the British and Foreign Bible Society, and printed by the celebrated Edinburgh firm of Thomas Constable (later T.and A. Constable). The Old Testament had been translated by the Scottish missionary-scholar William Glen (1778–1849), who had previously served at the mission in Astrakhan (see above). It came out in four volumes in 1845. The New Testament, which appeared the following year, was a newly edited version of the well-known translation of Henry Martyn.[34] Both were set in small *naskh* types, apparently from the Watts foundry in London, and represent a considerable typographic achievement on the part of both printers and correctors. Constable retained the types, which appeared in their specimen of 1907.[35] But although they had become Printers to the University in 1859,[36] it is not clear what use, if any, they made of these types in the intervening period.

These Bibles were, it seems, aimed optimistically at Muslim readers: this is indicated by the use of Hijrī as well as Christian dates in the imprints. In 1847 Glen travelled to Iran to distribute copies, and was received by the Shah, who accepted a set.[37] How many others were distributed, and to whom, is not known.

We next encounter, in the 1850s, the curious figure of Robert Young (1822–88), a native of Edinburgh, who was both a printer and a self-taught Orientalist, as well as being a bookseller and publisher.[38] He compiled, printed and published, in his establishment at the Head of the Mound in Edinburgh, a long series of books containing texts, translations and lists in various, mainly Semitic languages, starting with the *Book of the Precepts* of Maimonides in

---

[34] T.H. Darlow and H.F. Moule, *Historical catalogue of the printed editions of Holy Scripture in the library of the British and Foreign Bible Society*, vol. II: *Polyglots and languages other than English* (London, 1911), p. 1206, #7341–7342.

[35] T. and A. Constable Limited, *Printing types in use at the Edinburgh University Press* (Edinburgh, 1907), p. 106.

[36] *Scottish Book Trade Index* online.

[37] G. Carter, 'Glen, William (1778–1849)', *Oxford Dictionary of National Biography* (Oxford, 2004), online database, viewed 14 March 2011 <http://www.oxforddnb.com/view/article/37460>

[38] D.S. Margoliouth, revd. R. Steer, 'Young, Robert (1822–1888)', *Oxford Dictionary of National Biography* (Oxford, 2004), online database, viewed 14 March 2011 http://www.oxforddnb.com/view/article/30279

1849. Several of these include Arabic, notably the *Hexaglot Pentateuch* (Hebrew, Hebrew-Samaritan, Aramaic-Samaritan, Aramaic, Syriac and Arabic) of 1851/52.[39] This contains, not the whole Pentateuch, but just the first five chapters of Genesis, with the six texts arranged interlinearly. The Arabic types are again the small *naskh* of Watts. Two separate folded sheets contain 'Comparative Tables of the Semitic Languages', which also feature Arabic types. The author's somewhat hazy notions of Arabic orthographical principles are revealed in his remarks that "Gezma [*jazma* = *sukūn*] shows that the letter on which it is placed is connected with the preceding syllable" and that "Hamza ء is another name and form for Alif."

Young produced at least two other polyglot Biblical extracts containing Arabic printed with the Watts types: *The Prophecy of Obadiah* (1853) and the *Biblia Polyglotta Edinensia: specimens, in all languages,of a new and uniform series of Bibles, so constructed as to interleave with each other* (1855). However, when he came to print a catechism entirely in Arabic, *כתאב תעלים לאולאד צגאר* (1854), he used only Hebrew types. It is not clear whether this was because it was aimed at Arabophone Jews, who normally wrote Arabic thus, or because he had insufficient Arabic types. Another reason might be his considerable eccentricity. He seems to have been obsessed with languages and linguistic erudition: he later extended his range to Gujarati and Finnish, and published a Finnish folk lyric with parallel translations in Hebrew, Samaritan, Aramaic and Syriac (*Song of a Finlandian country-girl*, Edinburgh 1854). Perhaps unsurprisingly, his application for the Professorship of Hebrew at St Andrews in 1871 was not successful.

In the 1850s two other books appeared in Edinburgh containing Arabic, both also apparently the work of eccentric individuals. In 1855 Hermann Philip, 'Doctor of Medicine, Surgeon, Accoucheur, and practical oculist; corresponding member of the Zoological Association, Dublin University, and missionary in northern Africa', published his *Arabic grammar*, printed for him by Schenk and M'Farlane of St James Square, Edinburgh. These were lithographic printers,[40] and the entire 82-page work, English and Arabic, is reproduced from handwriting, quite crude although legible.

Four years later, one George Washington Chasseaud (otherwise known as the author of a book on the Druzes) also planned to publish an Arabic grammar, but he only got as far as producing a fold-out broadsheet entitled *Arabic alphabetical table (with the vowels and accents)* (Edinburgh, 1859). This uses the Watts types, but it is not known who printed it. It was published by the firm of Sutherland and Knox, but they were booksellers,[41] not printers, and the printer's name is not stated.

After the 1850s, Arabic typography seems to have almost disappeared from Scotland for the rest of the 19th century. The Watts founts possessed by Constable in Edinburgh apparently lay idle, and in Glasgow the Jackson Arabic seems not to have been used after the 1820s and the forced sale of the Duncan establishment. The type specimen book of the Glasgow University Press issued by the University printers Robert Maclehose and Co in 1901 shows Greek and Hebrew (in three sizes), but no Arabic.[42]

---

[39] Darlow and Moule, *Historical catalogue*, II, p. 31, #1461.

[40] *Scottish Book Trade Index* online (under "Schenck"), viewed 14 March 2011 http://www.nls.uk/media/63386/sbti-n-z.pdf

[41] *Scottish Book Trade Index* online, viewed 14 March 2011 http://www.nls.uk/media/63386/sbti-n-z.pdf

[42] *Specimens of types used for the printing of books at the University Press Glasgow* (Glasgow, 1901).

In one notable work published in Glasgow one might have hoped to find some Arabic script. In 1876 Hay Nisbet brought out *Hafed, Prince of Persia: his experiences in Earth-life and Spirit-life, being spirit communications received through Mr. D. Duguid.* But unfortunately 'Hafed or Hafiz', despite being Prince of Persia, delivered his spirit communications only in Hebrew, Greek, English, Latin and German, not in Persian.

Glasgow, however, did make a significant, albeit very specialised, contribution to Arabic book production at the end of the 19th century. The firm of David Bryce and Sons specialised in miniature books, and has been described as "one of the most prolific and successful makers of [them] ... who sallied forth with great vigour and unusually modern marketing methods on making the best of the latest technological advances in the field of photo-lithography ... in the reduction of larger volumes to the smallest imaginable size by the use of electroplates".[43] Towards the end of the 1890s they decided to produce by this means a miniature version of the Arabic text of the Qur'ān, which came out around 1900. Measuring 25 × 19 mm, each copy was issued in a metal locket with inset magnifying glass.[44]

Bryce were not the first to print miniature Qur'āns: the earliest seems to have come from the Matbaa-i Osmaniye in Istanbul in 1888,[45] and other ones were published there and in Delhi in the 1890s. They were often used as amulets, and were carried into battle by soldiers on both sides in the First World War: the Istanbul ones by the Turks, and Delhi and Glasgow ones by Indian and other Muslims serving in the British forces.[46]

These miniatures were obviously not typeset. In late 19th-century Scotland, only in Aberdeen, hitherto absent from the world of Arabic printing, do Arabic types make a fleeting and exiguous appearance. In 1898 James Lindsay, Earl of Crawford (1847–1913), published privately a *Hand-list of Oriental manuscripts: Arabic, Persian, Turkish* in his own collection, the Bibliotheca Lindesiana (now in the John Rylands Library in Manchester). This was printed at the Aberdeen University Press. All the information in the catalogue entries (Arabic names, titles, etc.) is romanised, according to an elaborate system quite unlike any other, involving curious diacritics and Irish letters. But this is explained and tabulated in a section on the 'Mode of transliteration adopted' (pp. xxxix–xli), in which the full Arabic alphabet is given, albeit in the isolated forms only. The source of the types is not known.

What was the reason for the strange disappearance of Arabic typography from Scotland in the second half of the 19th century? We can only speculate; but one factor may have been the lack of local production of such types. As far as can be ascertained, no Scottish type-foundry ever cut or cast Arabic types. In the leading founders' specimens, such as those of Andrew and Alexander Wilson, William Miller, Duncan Sinclair and James Marr,[47] they

[43] L.W. Bondy, *Miniature books: their history from the beginnings to the present day* (Farnham, 1981, rp. 1994), p. 103.

[44] See illustration in Bondy, *Miniature books*, p. 112; also in E. Hanebutt-Benz, D. Glass and G. Roper (eds), *Middle Eastern languages and the print revolution: a cross-cultural encounter* (Westhofen, 2002), pl. 80.

[45] N. Kuran-Burçoğlu, 'Osman Zeki Bey and his printing office the *Matbaa-i Osmaniye*' in P. Sadgrove (ed.), *History of printing in the languages and countries of the Middle East* (Oxford, 2004), p. 50.

[46] Hanebutt-Benz, Glass and Roper (eds), *Middle Eastern languages and the print revolution*, p. 490; Bondy, *Miniature books*, p. 112.

[47] William Miller and Company, *Specimen of printing types* (Edinburgh, 1813 and subsequent

are conspicuous by their absence. Any which were required had therefore to be brought from England, at considerable expense, and there was generally insufficient demand to make it worthwhile for printers to do so. It made more sense to have Arabic texts printed in England, by the new breed of specialised 'Oriental' printers such as Watts and his successors in London or Stephen Austin in Hertford, who could do it more expertly and economically. This is indeed what happened in a number of cases.

This tendency was probably reinforced, paradoxically, by the rise and development of Arabic and Islamic studies in the Scottish universities. Such eminent scholars as William Muir and William Robertson Smith gained international reputations, which attracted English publishers, who used English printers. In this context, Scottish publishers and printers were inevitably handicapped by a 'provincial' stigma, aggravated by the unviability of any attempts to compete in the field of 'exotic' languages and scripts.

In the 20th century, which lies beyond the scope of this essay, Arabic did again make spasmodic appearances, mainly in catalogues and occasional publications of the University of Glasgow. But, there do not seem to have been any substantial productions of Arabic texts. In the latter part of the century typesetting and printing became increasingly separate operations, and publishers in Scotland, as elsewhere, entered a global market-place for both.

All the foregoing information, and the conclusions drawn from it, must be regarded as provisional and tentative, in the absence of a thorough typographical survey of the five hundred years of Scottish printed output. Future discoveries may well overturn some of these findings, and allow us to upgrade the Scottish contribution to Arabic printing history, the study of which in general is still in its infancy.

---

editions of 1814, 1822, 1834, 1838 and 1839); Duncan Sinclair and Sons, *Specimens of modern printing types, cast at the letter foundry of D. Sinclair and Sons* (Edinburgh, 1840); James Marr and Co, *Specimens of ancient and modern printing types* (Edinburgh [1870?]). The Glasgow Foundry of Andrew and Alexander Wilson in 1825 offered 'foreign and learned founts' (Greek, Hebrew, Saxon, etc.) but no Arabic, according to T.B. Reed, revd. A.F. Johnson, *A history of the old English letter foundries* (London, 1952), p. 263.

# 11

# 'The usual Leiden types' A compositor's personal account of Brill's Arabic printing in the late 19th and early 20th century

*Arnoud Vrolijk*

Marie Joseph Brusse (Amsterdam 1873–Alkmaar 1941) was a Dutch journalist who for many years contributed to the Rotterdam daily *Nieuwe Rotterdamsche Courant* (NRC). He is known for his true-to-life sketches of the red-light district of Rotterdam in the early years of the twentieth century.[1] At some point he went under cover and led the life of a tramp, publishing his adventures as 'Vagrancy: rambles of a journalist among poachers and vagabonds'.[2] His main achievement is his novel *Boefje* ('Little rascal', 1903), the record of his experiences with a materially and emotionally deprived boy from the slums of Rotterdam whom he had taken under his wing. His feeling for the adventurous and melodramatic, mixed with social engagement, won him immense popularity among his readership.

That he also chose more sedate subjects is shown by his series of more than twenty articles on the publishing business in the Netherlands. Between 24 November 1926 and 2 March 1927 he devoted three articles of these to the history of the firm of E.J. Brill in Leiden, well known for their many editions in Oriental languages.[3] The author, who was not intimately familiar with the subject, took the approach of the typical newspaperman. After interviewing the managing director Corneille Peltenburg and carefully jotting down the statistics and the official history of Brill, as might be expected, he immediately turned to

[1] M.J. Brusse, *Het rosse leven en sterven van de Zandstraat* ('Living and dying in the red-light district of the Zandstraat', Rotterdam, 1912).

[2] M.J. Brusse, *Landlooperij: zwerftocht van een dagbladschrijver onder stroopers en schooiers* (Rotterdam, 1906).

[3] I would like to express my thanks to Mr Steven Claeyssens, formerly of the Short Title Catalogue of the Netherlands project, who brought the articles to my attention in the summer of 2006. On the history of Brill now see S. van der Veen [et al.], *Brill: 325 years of scholarly publishing* (Leiden [etc.], 2008). Earlier histories of the company are *Tuta sub Aegide Pallas: E.J. Brill and the World of Learning. Published on the Occasion of the Company's Tercentenary* (Leiden, 1983), and [J.M. van Ophuijsen], *E.J. Brill: Three Centuries of Scholarly Publishing since 1683* (Leiden, [1994]); W.P. Wolters, 'De firma E.J. Brill in hare nieuwe woning', *Eigen Haard: Geïllustreerd volkstijdschrift* (1883), pp. 356–360.

the men on the production floor for a touch of 'real life', in this particular case the Chinese and Arabic typesetters.

The Arabic typesetter, whose interview was published in the morning edition of 7 January 1927, was a man named Kloos. His first names are not given, but they appear to be Willem Hendrik, born in Leiden on 23 June 1850.[4] More information on him should become available when the Brill archives, preserved at the Special Collections department of the library of the University of Amsterdam, are opened to the public.

At the moment of the interview he had 48 years of service behind him, which implies that he had started working for Brill around 1878. According to his own words his first book was R.P.A. Dozy's *Supplément aux dictionnaires arabes*, which came out in parts between 1877 and 1881.

The compositor related his experiences with Dutch and foreign Orientalists with relish and occasionally with painfully revealing insight, for instance when he commented on the clumsy, print-like Arabic handwriting of European scholars. Almost half a century of typesetting at Brill's was no doubt an admirable achievement, and even an interesting one in view of the languages that the man worked with, but Brusse nevertheless enhanced his article by introducing a number of *dramatis personae* of more than common interest.

To begin with, he cited from the memoirs of the Medinese scholar and bookseller Amīn b. Ḥasan al-Madanī,[5] who visited the World and Colonial Exhibition in Amsterdam in the summer of 1883, and the Sixth Congress of Orientalists convened later that year at Leiden. His lively account was translated into Dutch and published by the young Christiaan Snouck Hurgronje (1857–1936), who was to become the Netherlands' foremost scholar of Islam.[6]

Faced with financial troubles, al-Madanī had travelled from Cairo to Amsterdam in the hope of finding a market for a collection of nearly 700 Arabic manuscripts. During the summer months of the exhibition his hopes seemed dashed until he encountered an acquaintance, the Swedish orientalist Carlo Landberg (1848–1924). Landberg, later Count de Landberg when the king of Italy bestowed a peerage on him, was a private scholar who greatly appealed to the public taste. A gentleman of independent means through his marriage to a German heiress, he had the money and the leisure to travel in the Middle East, spending months among the Bedouins for his linguistic research. Landberg knew al-Madanī from Cairo and he introduced him to his publisher Brill. Landberg entertained al-Madanī as a guest during his stay in Leiden, mediated in the sale of his collection to Brill and also prepared a catalogue before hurrying back to the Bedouins.[7] During the following years Landberg and al-Madanī formed a fruitful relationship, selling three more collections of Oriental manuscripts to Brill, which subsequently found their way to Berlin (in 1885) and Princeton (in 1900 and 1904 respectively).[8]

---

[4] Regional Archives, Leiden, Marriage certificate No. 59 issued at Leiden on 28 March 1877.

[5] Khayr al-Dīn al-Ziriklī, *al-Aʿlām*, 4th edn. (Bayrūt, 1979), v. 2, pp. 15–16.

[6] C. Snouck Hurgronje, *Het Leidsche Orientalistencongres: Indrukken van een Arabisch Congreslid* (Leiden, 1883) (reprinted in *Verspreide Geschriften* (Bonn [etc.], 1923–1927) v. 6, pp. 240–272).

[7] *Catalogue de manuscrits arabes provenant d'une bibliothèque privée à el-Medina et appartenant à la Maison E.J. Brill* (Leide, 1883). In the catalogue, p. v, Landberg explains in a few words how he knew al-Madanī from Cairo. For his haste in preparing the catalogue see ibid.

[8] In 1885 Brill sold a collection of al-Madanī/Landberg manuscripts to the Royal Prussian Library,

With extra government funding raised by the Leiden Arabist Michael Jan de Goeje (1836–1909), the entire collection offered by Brill in 1883 was purchased by the library of Leiden University for the amount of 14,250 guilders. It carries the classmarks Or. 2363–Or. 3025 and Or. 8409.[9] The same M.J. de Goeje figures prominently in the history of Brill as the driving force behind its numerous Arabic text editions of the late 19th and early 20th century.

All these characters appear in M.J. Brusse's interview not only for a touch of drama, but also because each of them plays a distinctive role in Brill's typographical tradition. Al-Madanī's account is cited – sometimes almost literally – to portray the reaction of an astonished but interested outsider, who wonders at the miracles of Western Orientalist publishing performed by Brill and the Leiden Arabist De Goeje. It is De Goeje who takes the initiative to acquire a special fount from Beirut that will be attractive to Europeans and Orientals alike. In spite of prolonged efforts, this idea proves to be unsuccessful. Fortunately, Count de Landberg makes his appearance and finds an appropriate use for the Beirut fount.

Before addressing the question what this Beirut fount actually was and who designed it, one should first take a closer look at the broader context of Brill's typography in the period under survey. One should also take into consideration that Brill never had their own type-foundry and that they relied exclusively on types supplied by others. This implies that Brill never played a creative role in the development of Arabic typography as such, except in its application. However, because of both the quality and quantity of their Arabic publications, Brill's typography deserves more attention than it has had so far.

Like most commercial printers, Brill provided type specimens as a service to their customers. The samples that fall more or less within the time-span of this contribution date from c. 1883, 1931 and 1938.[10] Especially the first specimen is so handsomely made that it must have been intended as a celebratory gift and a showcase of their technical performance. Most likely, it was offered on the occasion of the World and Colonial Exhibition at Amsterdam and the 6th Congress of Orientalists of 1883.[11] Unfortunately, Brill never provided information

---

which was briefly described by W. Ahlwardt, *Kurzes Verzeichniss der Landberg'schen Sammlung arabischer Handschriften, Königliche Bibliothek, Berlin* (Berlin, 1885). For the second collection, brought together by Landberg and al-Madanī between 1886 and 1889 and acquired by Princeton University Library in 1900, and a third collection of the same provenance and also acquired by Princeton in 1904 see Ph.K. Hitti [et al.], *Descriptive Catalog of the Garrett Collection of Arabic Manuscripts in the Princeton University Library* (Princeton, 1938), p. iii; E. Littmann, 'Special Collections in American Libraries: The Garrett Collections of Arabic Manuscripts at Princeton University Library', *The Library Journal*, vol. 29 (1904), pp. 238–243.

[9] *Bulletin du Sixième Congrès international des Orientalistes, Leide, 1883*, no. 7 (15 Septembre). For the purchase see the archives of Leiden University, Archief College van Curatoren, AC3 (1878–1953), inv. no. 1524, pp. 208–209. For a highly critical assessment of the vendor and the purchase see D. v.d. Zande, *Martinus Th. Houtsma, 1851–1943* (diss. Utrecht, 1999), pp. 127, 162–164, 704–708. On M. J. de Goeje see, for instance, A.J.M. Vrolijk, 'De Goeje, Michaël Jan', *Encyclopedia Iranica*, v. 7, pp. 174–175, with literature.

[10] *Catalogue des caractères non-latins employées* [sic] *à l'imprimerie E.J. Brill* (Leiden, c. 1883); *Catalogue des caractères étrangers de l'imprimerie E.J. Brill* (Leyde, 1931); *Catalogue des caractères étrangers de l'imprimerie E.J. Brill: 1683–1938* (Leiden, 1938).

[11] Although the historical link between Luchtmans (established 1683) and Brill was mentioned in W.P. Wolters' 'De firma Brill in hare nieuwe woning' (1883), there was no actual mention of a

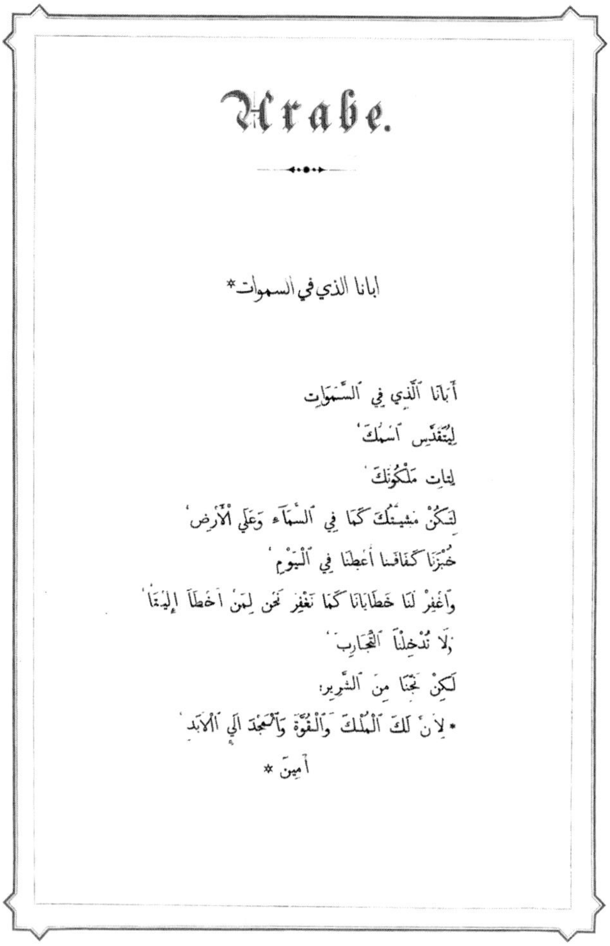
Arabe.

ابانا الذي في السموات *

أبانا الذي في السموات
ليتقدس اسمك
ليأت ملكوتك
لتكن مشيئتك كما في السماء وعلى الارض
خبزنا كفافنا اعطنا في اليوم
واغفر لنا خطايانا كما نغفر نحن لمن اخطا الينا
ولا تدخلنا التجارب
لكن نجنا من الشرير
لان لك الملك والقوة والمجد الى الابد
امين *

Figure 1. Brill type specimen pl. 12.

on the name or the origin of the founts in their specimens. It is equally unfortunate that the development of Arabic printing in Europe in the 19th century is not very well covered in scholarly research. Miroslav Krek gave an overview of examples of Arabic typography arranged according to country in his exhibition catalogue *Typographia Arabica* (Waltham, 1971), but the descriptions, or rather captions, are very brief.[12] Josée Balagna's *L'imprimerie arabe en occident* (Paris, 1984) stops at the end of the eighteenth century, and in a more recent study by Huda Smitshuijzen AbiFarès entitled *Arabic Typography: A Comprehensive Sourcebook* (London, 2001), 19th-century Europe is passed over altogether. An exception is Hartmut Bobzin's study of the printing history of the Qur'an, which does include 19th-

bicentenary and there is nothing to show that the year 1883 was perceived as such.

[12] M. Krek, *Typographia Arabica: The Development of Arabic Printing as Illustrated by Arabic Type Specimens. Exhibition held at the Rapaporte Treasure Hall* (Waltham, 1971).

century Europe.[13] Another exception is the involvement of European missionary societies in the printing history of the Middle East in the 19th century, which has been studied by scholars like Père Joseph Nasrallah, Geoffrey Roper and Dagmar Glass.[14]

## BRILL'S 'BERLIN TYPES'

Brill's most widely used Arabic fount of the 19th century has a square and spidery appearance with some characteristics of the Maghribī script. The upward and downward strokes are very restrained, which allows for very dense typesetting, no doubt an economical advantage. Characteristic is the box of the final *nūn*, which slopes heavily to the right. In his *Typographia Arabica* Miroslav Krek identifies the typeface only as a "vocalized, small font frequently used by this publishing house [i.e. Brill]," without giving additional information.[15]

The fount gained renown by virtue of M.J. de Goeje's many Brill editions from the late 19th century, and the largest single project in which it was ever used is his 10,000-page edition of the *Annales* of al-Ṭabarī, published between 1879 and 1901. However, it is much older than that, the earliest instance being an Arabic thesis by the young Leiden Orientalist H.E. Weyers (1805–1844), which was published in 1831. This book was printed by Johannes Brill (1767–1859) for the firm of S. and J. Luchtmans, the predecessor of E.J. Brill.[16] In all likelihood it was Weyers's supervisor H.A. Hamaker (1789–1835) who suggested the introduction of the fount to Johannes Brill.

Where did this fount come from? The Haarlem type-foundry of Johan Enschedé en Zonen, who carried it from 1907,[17] was quite positive about its country of origin:

---

[13] H. Bobzin, 'Von Venedig nach Kairo: Zur Geschichte arabischer Korandrucke, 16. bis frühes 20. Jahrhundert = From Venice to Cairo: On the History of Arabic Editions of the Koran, 16th-early 20th Century', in E. Hanebutt-Benz, D. Glass, G. Roper [et al.] (eds) *Sprachen des Nahen Ostens und die Druckrevolution: Eine interkulturelle Begegnung = Middle Eastern Languages and the Print Revolution: A Cross-Cultural Encounter* (Westhofen, 2002), pp. 151–176.

[14] J. Nasrallah, *L'imprimerie au Liban* (Harissa, 1948); D. Glass, 'Die *nahḍa* und ihre Technik im 19. Jahrhundert: Arabische Druckereien in Ägypten und Syrien', in U. Marzolph (ed.), *Das gedruckte Buch im Vorderen Orient* (Dortmund, 2002), pp. 59–64; Id. and G. Roper, 'Arabischer Buchdruck in der arabischen Welt = The Printing of Arabic books in the Arab World', in Hanebutt-Benz [et al.], *Sprachen des Nahen Ostens und die Druckrevolution = Middle Eastern languages and the print revolution*, pp. 190–192

[15] Krek, *Typographia Arabica*, p. 19.

[16] H.E. Weyers, *Specimen criticum: Exhibens locos Ibn Khacanis de Ibn Zeidouno, ex mss. codicibus Bibliothecae Lugd. Bat. et Gothanae editos* (Lugd. Bat., 1831). Johannes Brill combined his business as printer with the role of manager of the Leiden publisher Luchtmans, established in 1683. In 1848 his son Evert Jan Brill (1812–1871) took over the firm of Luchtmans and continued it under the name of E.J. Brill. See Van der Veen [et al.], *Brill*, pp. 34–37, 45–52.

[17] *Letterproef van Oostersche schriften uit de lettergieterij van Joh. Enschedé and Zonen te Haarlem* (Haarlem, [1907]), pp. 7–8. Their fount no. 4304 Text (16p) matches the typeface used in M.J. de Goeje's edition of the *Futūḥ al-Buldān* by al-Balādhurī (*Liber expugnationis regionum*, Lugd. Bat., 1866), while the smaller fount No. 4303 Augustijn (12p) corresponds with the typeface used in the *Annales* of al-Ṭabarī.

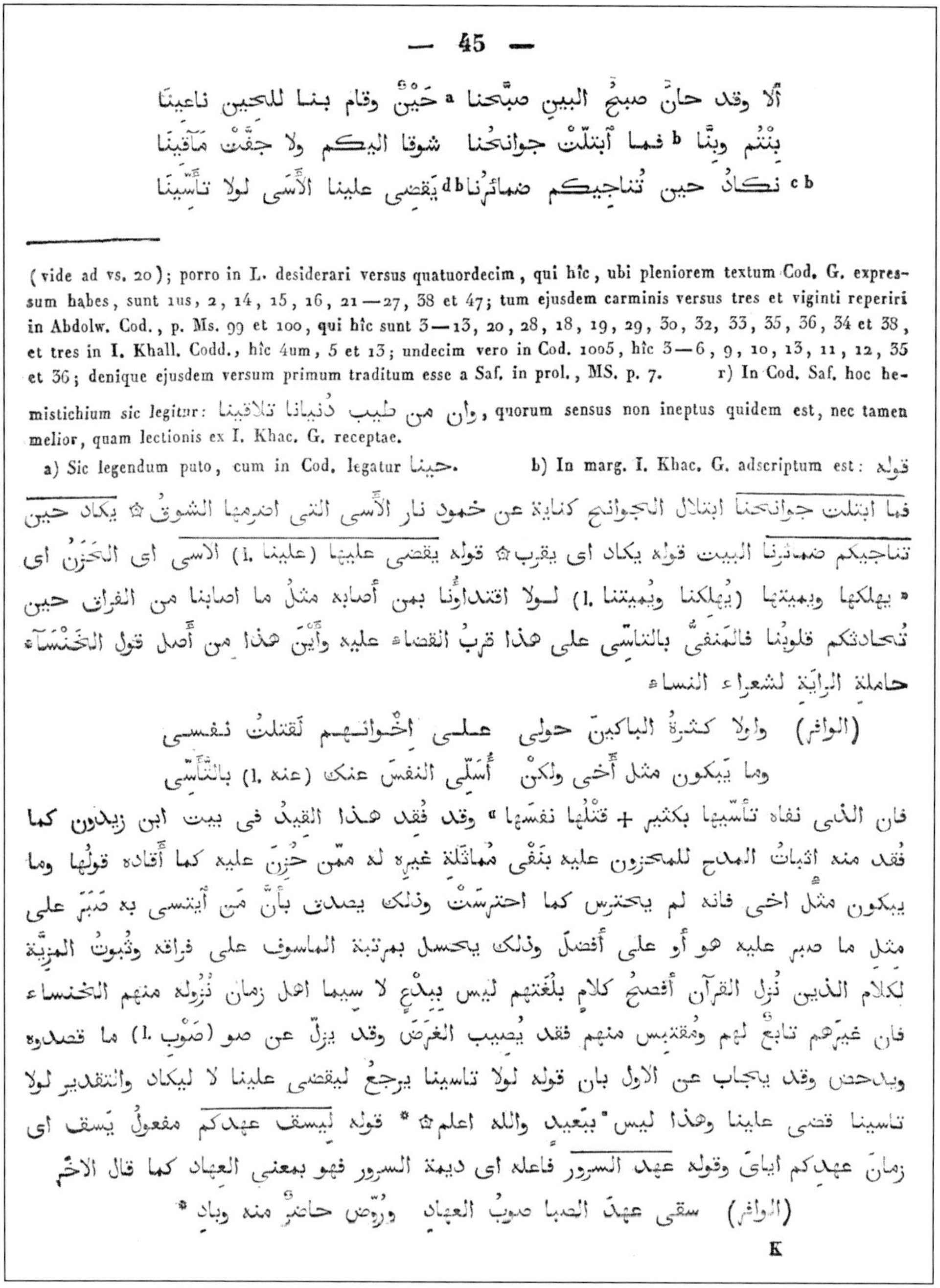

— 45 —

ألا وقد حانَ صبحُ البينِ صبّحنا a حَيْنٌ وقام بنا للحين ناعينا

بِنْتُم وبِنّا b فما ابتلّتْ جوانحُنا شوقا اليكم ولا جفّتْ مآقينا

c b نكادُ حين تُناجيكم ضمائرُنا d b يَقضِي علينا الأسَى لولا تأسّينا

(vide ad vs. 20); porro in L. desiderari versus quatuordecim, qui hîc, ubi pleniorem textum Cod. G. expressum habes, sunt 1us, 2, 14, 15, 16, 21—27, 38 et 47; tum ejusdem carminis versus tres et viginti reperiri in Abdolw. Cod., p. Ms. 99 et 100, qui hîc sunt 3—13, 20, 28, 18, 19, 29, 30, 32, 33, 35, 36, 34 et 38, et tres in I. Khall. Codd., hîc 4um, 5 et 13; undecim vero in Cod. 1005, hîc 3—6, 9, 10, 13, 11, 12, 35 et 36; denique ejusdem versum primum traditum esse a Saf. in prol., MS. p. 7. r) In Cod. Saf. hoc hemistichium sic legitur: وان من طيب دُنيانا تلاقينا, quorum sensus non ineptus quidem est, nec tamen melior, quam lectionis ex I. Khac. G. receptae.

a) Sic legendum puto, cum in Cod. legatur حينا. b) In marg. I. Khac. G. adscriptum est: قوله فما ابتلت جوانحنا ابتلال الجوانح كناية عن خمود نار الأسى التى اضرمها الشوقُ ☆ يكاد حين تناجيكم ضمائرنا البيت قوله يكاد اى يقرب ☆ قوله يقضى عليها (علينا .l) الاسى اى الحَزَنُ اى * يهلكها ويميتها (يُهلكنا ويُميتنا .l) لولا اقتداؤُنا بمن أصابه مثلُ ما اصابنا من الفراق حين تُحادثكم قلوبُنا فالمَنفيُّ بالتأسّي على هذا قربُ القضاء عليه وأيّنَ هذا من أصل قول الخنساء حاملة الراية لشعراء النساء

(الوافر) ولولا كثرةُ الباكينَ حولى على اِخْوانهم لَقتلتُ نفسى

وما يَبكون مثل أخى ولكنْ أُسَلّى النفسَ عنك (عنه .l) بالتأسّى

فان الذى نفاه تأسّيها بكثير + قتْلُها نفسَها " وقد فُقِد هذا القيدُ فى بيت ابن زيدون كما فُقد منه اثباتُ المدح للمحزون عليه بنَفْى مُماثلة غيرِه له ممّن حُزِنَ عليه كما أفاده قولُها وما يبكون مثلَ اخى فانه لم يحترس كما احترسَتْ وذلك يصدق بأنّ مَن أيتسى به صَبَرَ على مثلِ ما صبر عليه هو أو على أفضلَ وذلك يحسل بمرتبة الماسوف على فراقه وثُبوتُ المزيّة لكلام الذين نُزل القرآن أفصحُ كلامٍ بلُغتهم ليس ببِدْعٍ لا سيما اهل زمان نُزوله منهم الخنساء فان غيرَهم تابعٌ لهم ومُقتبِس منهم فقد يُصيب الغرَضَ وقد يزلّ عن صو (صَوْب .l) ما قصدوه ويدحض وقد يجاب عن الاول بان قوله لولا تاسينا يرجعُ ليقضى علينا لا ليكاد والتقدير لولا تاسينا قضى علينا وهذا ليس ببَعيدٍ والله اعلم ☆ * قوله ليسق عهدكم مفعولُ يَسق اى زمانَ عهدِكم اياىَ وقوله عهد السرور فاعله اى ديمة السرور فهو بمعنى العهاد كما قال الاخر

(الوافر) سقى عهدَ الصبا صوبُ العهادِ وروّض حاضرٌ منه وبادِ *

K

Figure 2. Weyers Specimen p. 4.

> [It] is of German origin. Who the punchcutter was is unknown to us, but the clear legibility of the scripts and the great regularity of the types certainly provide the evidence that the cutting of the punches was left in able hands.[18]

A very general survey shows that these 'able hands' produced the staple typeface of 19th and early 20th-century Arabic editions from Germany, churned out by a great variety of printers. One should only mention classics like G.W. Freytag's *Lexicon Arabico-Latinum* (Halis Saxonum: apud C.A. Schwetschke et filium, 1830–1837), H.R. Fleischer's *Kleinere Schriften* (Leipzig: Hirzel, printed by Breitkopf and Härtel, 1885–1888), and H. Reckendorf's *Arabische Syntax* (Heidelberg: Winter, 1921).

Rijk Smitskamp identified Berlin as the source of the typeface,[19] more specifically the Prussian Government printing office.[20] Until 1877 this was not a state-run establishment but a private company, the Deckersche Geheime Ober-Hofbuchdruckerei.[21] Unfortunately, little is known about Decker's typefoundry and the Oriental typefaces that were developed there in the nineteenth century. In 1988 Fritz Lendenmann concluded that the business archive was lost.[22] Part of the Decker archive appears to be preserved at the Staatsbibliothek in Berlin but there is nothing, unfortunately, on the firm's Oriental typefaces.[23] A reconstruction can therefore only be tentative.

In its earliest stage the 'Berlin' typeface appears to have been used in Bonn, which was then part of the kingdom of Prussia. A very early example that predates the first Luchtmans publication in this fount by almost a decade is *Amrulkeisi Moallakah. Cum scholiis Zuzenii e codicibus Parisiensibus* ed. Ern. Guil. Hengstenberg (Bonnae, typis regiis in Officina Thormanniana, 1823). In the preface, dated 20 December 1822, Hengstenberg explicitly mentioned the "new Arabic types, donated to the University of Bonn by the munificence of the King."[24] This implies that the 'Berlin types' were already available in 1822, if not before that. Another early example is Maximilian Habicht's Arabic edition of the Arabian Nights, *Tausend und eine Nacht*, which was published in the Prussian city of Breslau (now Wrocław, Poland) from 1824 by "Dār Ṭibāʿat al-Madrasa al-Brislāwiyya," and typeset with the "Royal types" by a certain Johann Theophil Langner.

---

18 Ibid., p. viii.

19 [R. Smitskamp], Het Oosters Antiquarium, catalogue 621 no. 646 (al-Suyūṭī) and catalogue 642 no. 2149 (Roorda), where the founts are described as the 'Berlin types'.

20 Rijk Smitskamp, personal communication, 23 May 2008.

21 On the Prussian Government Printing Office in general see F. Lendenmann, *Deckersche kleine Verlagsgeschichte* (Heidelberg, 1988); R. Schmidt, *Deutsche Buchhändler. Deutsche Buchdrucker. Beiträge zu einer Firmengeschichte des deutschen Buchgewerbes* (Berlin, 1902–1908), v. I, p. 169, viewed 21st May 2012, <http://www.zeno.org/Schmidt-1902/A/Decker,+Familie>.

22 Lendenmann, *Deckersche Verlagsgeschichte*, pp. 68–69.

23 Personal communications from Ralf Breslau and Michaela Scheibe of the Staatsbibliothek in Berlin, whose generous help is hereby gratefully acknowledged.

24 E.G. Hengstenberg, ibid., p. [iv]: "Quum interim munificentia Regia novi Academiae Rhenanae typi Arabici dati essent…".

## THE FLUEGEL/TAUCHNITZ FOUNT

The second fount used by Brill is a boldface with almost vertical downward strokes of the *rāʾ*, *zayn* and *wāw*. It is identical with a fount that was especially developed by the Leipzig firm of Carl Tauchnitz for Gustav Fluegel's stereotyped edition of the Qurʾān (Leipzig, 1834). It was designed by Anton von Hammer with the help and advice of his relative, the famous Austrian Orientalist Joseph von Hammer-Purgstall. Although Fluegel maintained that Von Hammer-Purgstall's calligraphic samples sent from Istanbul had been instrumental in designing the fount, it is difficult to see the resemblance between genuine Ottoman calligraphy and this product.[25]

The foundry of Tauchnitz was taken over in 1868 by the firm of W. Drugulin, also of Leipzig, who continued to use the typeface for their own publications.[26] This does not necessarily mean that Brill imported the types directly from Germany, as they were readily available from a Dutch type-foundry like Lettergieterij 'Amsterdam', formerly N. Tetterode of Amsterdam, who also cast Chinese types for Brill.[27] Brill used the typeface for publications in modern European languages with only a limited amount of Arabic text, such as citations of book titles, fragments of poetry or proverbs. It appears in works by Carlo de Landberg, for instance his catalogue of the al-Madanī collection (1883), and his *Proverbes et dictons du peuple arabe*, also dated 1883.

### *The types employed at Beyroot*

When M.J. de Goeje was making his preparations for the publication of the Annales of al-Ṭabarī, he felt that the old-fashioned Brill typefaces might not be suitable for a project that in his eyes would transcend the boundaries of European Orientalism. In March 1876 he circulated a 'notice', explaining among other things the choice of a new typeface:

> As it seems probable that the Annals will be in some demand in Moslem countries, we resolved to try whether we could find types agreeable both to European and Oriental taste. Our choice fell upon those employed at Beyroot.[28]

The 'types employed at Beyroot' occur for the first time in the *Catalogue des caractères non-latins employées* [sic] *à l'imprimerie E.J. Brill*, which was published in 1883. In a variety of Oriental scripts and languages it gives the text of the Lord's Prayer.[29] The Arabic specimen in plate [12], starting with the familiar incantation '*Abānā lladhī fī l-samāwāt...*', appears

[25] *Corani textus Arabicus* [...] recensuit [...] Gustavus Fluegel (Lipsiae, 1834), p. v. See Bobzin, 'Von Venedig nach Kairo = From Venice to Cairo', p. 169.

[26] See, for instance, H. Gies, *al-Funūn al-sabʿa: Ein Beitrag zur Kenntniss sieben neuerer arabischer Versarten* (Leipzig, 1879).

[27] *Proeven van Oostersche schriften: Lettergieterij 'Amsterdam' voorheen N. Tetterode* (Amsterdam, [c. 1912–1913]), pp. 37, 39.

[28] M.J. de Goeje, *Annales quos scripsit Abu Djafar Mohammed Ibn Djarir at-Tabari*, Introductio (Leiden, 1901), p. xxxiv, cited in J. Brugman, 'Arabic and Islamic studies', p. 37.

[29] The Lord's Prayer as a sample text already occurred in an 1855 type specimen from Brill, *Het gebed des Heeren in veertien talen: Strekkende tot proeve van letters, van het gewoon Europeesch karakter afwijkende, aanwezig in de Boekdrukkerij van E.J. Brill* (Leiden, 1855).

to be identical with a typeface designed by the American missionary Eli Smith (1801–1857) and cut by the punchcutter Homan Hallock (1803–1894) for the press of the American Board of Commissioners for Foreign Missions (ABCFM) in Beirut. The types were cast by the Leipzig firm of Carl Tauchnitz, the same who had printed the Fluegel Qur'an, and they were introduced in Beirut in 1841. In Beirut it was known as the 'American' typeface, to distinguish it from the 'Stambouli' type of the Imprimerie catholique.[30] It was most prominently used for the vocalised Arabic translation of the Bible by the same Eli Smith and his successor Cornelius van Dyck, which was published between 1860 and 1865.[31] Photomechanical reprints of this translation are still widely available.[32]

It is likely that this fount, originally cast by Tauchnitz, was also acquired by W. Drugulin when they took over the Tauchnitz type-foundry in 1868. A large and very well-made example of a work set in Germany in the ABCFM typeface is, for instance, F. Schwally's edition of Ibrāhīm b. Muḥammad al-Bayhaqī's *Kitāb al-maḥāsin wa-al-masawī*, published in Giessen by Ricker in 1902 but printed by Drugulin.

As it happened, the Beirut fount was never used for the Ṭabarī edition. In a second notice issued three years later in March 1879, De Goeje had to announce that the types had indeed been acquired, but that Brill had encountered difficulties in using them. Instead, the printers had reverted to the old familiar 'Brill' typeface:

> In a former notice I stated that we had selected for our edition the types employed at Beyroot. Accordingly Messrs Brill procured these types, and the compositors tried hard, and not without success, to master their many difficulties. However, partly the troublesome correction which we foresaw, but still more the fear lest the types should wear very soon, made us change our plan and determine to employ the usual Leiden types, which are favourably known for their clearness and neatness, although they may be inferior to some other types in elegance.[33]

Brill's fear that the types would "wear very soon" sounds like an excuse of questionable validity, for the American Mission Press at Beirut used it for years on end, apparently without any problems of the kind. However, it can be speculated that Brill had to work with a limited amount of type which had to be redistributed and re-used over and over again, in the long run a serious problem for an edition as large as the *Annales*. The article by M.J. Brusse throws more light on what actually happened: the complexity of the fount with its eight or nine hundred combinations and its unfamiliar method of inserting vowels simply proved too much for Brill.

As mentioned above, it was Count de Landberg who some years later found an alternative use for the typeface in his work *Primeurs arabes*, a collective volume of Arabic texts published by Brill in two fascicles between 1886 and 1889. This time, Brill hired a Syrian compositor

---

[30] See *L'Imprimerie catholique de Beyrouth et son oeuvre en Orient: 1853–1903* (Bruxelles, 1903), p. 34; Nasrallah, *L'imprimerie au Liban*, p. 138.

[31] On the typeface of the ABCFM Press see Glass, 'Die *nahḍa* und ihre Technik im 19. Jahrhundert', pp. 60–62; Id. and Roper, 'Arabischer Buchdruck in der arabischen Welt = The printing of Arabic books in the Arab World', pp. 190–192.

[32] Leiden University Library holds a reprint [no place], Dār al-Kitāb al-Muqaddas fī l-Sharq al-Awsaṭ, 1993.

[33] De Goeje, *Annales*, Introductio, p. xxxvi; Brugman, 'Arabic and Islamic Studies', p. 37.

to handle the material and train the Dutch typesetters, apparently with success. Nothing is known about the identity of this Syrian typesetter as yet, but no doubt the Brill archives at Amsterdam will yield more information when they become accessible.

Much later the Beirut fount would be truly revived in another ambitious Brill project, A.J. Wensinck's *Concordance et indices de la tradition musulmane* (Leiden: E.J. Brill, 1936–1988). Typically, this edition also aimed at a market in the Muslim world and accordingly required a typographical design that would be 'agreeable' to Muslim readers. Only the first three volumes, published between 1936 and 1955, were actually set in this fount; several of the later volumes were typeset in a different fount and printed abroad by ad-Dar ul-Qayyima of Bhiwandi, India. Nevertheless, there is some irony in the fact that Brill used a Protestant Bible fount for a concordance of the *ḥadīth*, the most sacred Islamic text corpus after the Qur'an. Possibly, few if any Muslims were aware of its origin. In any case the *Concordance* achieved great popularity in the Middle East, giving rise to many pirated editions.[34]

A few years after the interview with M.J. Brusse Kloos retired. Interestingly, the last book he made in his long career was *Introduction to the Jawámiʿu ʾl-ḥikáyát* by Muḥammad Niẓámu ʾd-Dín, printed in 1929 for the R.J.W. Gibb Memorial Series and also featuring the Beirut fount.[35]

As a conclusion one may say that Brill, though gaining pre-eminence as a publisher of Arabic texts, always relied heavily on German typographical products. The 'Berlin types' and the Fluegel/Tauchnitz fount were purely German in origin, and the 'types from Beyroot', although designed and developed by American missionaries, were cast by Carl Tauchnitz, also a German company. However, this reliance on foreign products must not necessarily be regarded as a sign of weakness of Brill alone. Until well into the 20th century almost all branches of industry in the Netherlands used the technology of more advanced countries like Great Britain and Germany. Secondly, by borrowing German technology Brill showed that they wanted to work on a truly international scale, an ambition that is still the hallmark of the firm.

Below, the reader will find the translated text of M.J. Brusse's interview with typesetter Kloos. Understandably, Brusse made mistakes in his text because of his lack of familiarity with the printing business, and after half a century the memory of the elderly typesetter was no longer what it once must have been. Where possible, the errors have been corrected in the footnotes.

## *The Interview*

> *Kloos, the Arabic compositor. Sheikh Amin with his manuscripts and his impressions of Leiden. The Arabic typesetter from Damascus. Arabic scholars proficient in the language, but not in the composition of types.*

Kloos, the oldest Arabic compositor at the printing press of E.J. Brill's at Leiden, related to me that when he first started working here forty-eight years ago, he was immediately put

[34] Van der Veen [et al.], *Brill*, pp. 130–131.

[35] Muḥammad Niẓámu ʾd-Dín, *Introduction to the Jawámiʿu ʾl-ḥikáyát wa Lawámiʿu ʾr-riwáyát of Sadídu ʾd-Dín Muḥammad al-ʿAwfī* (Leiden: Brill, 1929). (also published London: Luzac and Co.; 'E.J.W. Gibb Memorial' New Series; v. 8).

to work on Dozy's *Supplément aux dictionnaires arabes*. For three years [?] he worked on this edition, which is now sold out.

'When I entered the service of Brill,' so the sympathetic typesetter went on, 'I had already learned to set Greek at other printers. At Brill's I was employed at the Arabic cases with the old and new Syriac types.[36] I set out to examine the accompanying charts. Fortunately, there were some colleagues working there who were familiar with these types and gave me some directions. I started searching for the types right away. It is very convenient that you can immediately recognise the types from the handwriting of European Arabists, because it is very similar to print. On the other hand, the handwriting of real Arabs is much more difficult to decipher for a typesetter. Just as in Hebrew, European typesetters always add the vowels above and under each line, invariably resulting in three lines of type. However, those who speak Arabic as their mother-tongue and use it with fluency, so to speak, have no need for the marking of consonants. One line is quite enough for them, and they insert a few vowels here and there between the other letters.'[37]

In later years Kloos did typesetting work for Professor De Goeje's *magnum opus*, at-Tabari, *Annales quos scripsit Abu Djafar Mohammed Ibn Djarir at-Tabari*, in thirteen volumes with Introduction, Glossary, Addenda and Emendanda, and Indexes. This work is now also sold out.

The professor wanted this edition to be set in Beirut types. Since the Leiden printer did not possess this material, it was acquired for the purpose in three sizes: large, text letter and a smaller size for the notes. Professor De Goeje appeared to think that a European compositor could handle this material as a matter of course. However, it turned out that this particular fount consists of about eight or nine hundred different types. Such a large number is indispensable to make the printed text resemble the handwriting of Arabs as much as possible. For a Dutch typesetter, however much familiar with Arabic, it was quite impossible to execute this work to satisfaction. Eventually it was decided to revert to the well-tested American system which is also current in Europe.[38] As a result, this costly pile of Beirut material remained unused until an alternative application could be found for it at a later stage.

At the 1883 World Exhibition in Amsterdam an Arab made his appearance, the learned Amin ibn Hasan [al-]Holwani al-Madani al-Hanafi. He was accompanied by a collection of valuable Arabic manuscripts. His legs crossed, the decorative sheikh remained seated among his manuscripts in the maelstrom of countless Western visitors, practically without exciting anybody's interest in all this Arabic beauty and wisdom at all.

The same year, 1883, professor Snouck Hurgronje published an amusing booklet on the subject at Brill's.[39] Later that year the learned Arab, himself 'Professor at the Pristine Garden',[40] was brought into contact with various scholars who introduced him to the

---

[36] Obviously a mistake. It is quite possible, however, that Kloos also composed Syriac type.

[37] In all probability Kloos refers to the Beirut fount, which he appears to regard as indigenous. In the ABCFM fount the vowel signs are inserted in slots, which allows for typesetting in one single line, see also below.

[38] The journalist is mistaken here: the Beirut fount, which was of American origin, was abandoned in favour of the usual European typeface.

[39] Snouck Hurgronje, *Het Leidsche Orientalistencongres*.

[40] Snouck Hurgronje, *Het Leidsche Orientalistencongres* , pp. 3–4: 'Pristine Garden' ('Gereinigde Lusthof') is Snouck Hurgronje's rendering of *al-Rawḍa al-sharīfa*, the burial place of the Prophet

Sixth International Congress of Orientalists convened at Leiden. The Sheikh reported his impressions to one of the newspapers appearing in Cairo, the Borhan. These remarkable essays, written by an Oriental about a gathering of Western scholars dedicated to the study of the Arabic sciences – all of them Europeans whom he had previously taken for haters or despisers of the Mohammedans – were duly translated by Professor Hurgronje and provided with an introduction.

In his translation, Professor Hurgronje explains that Amin had understood that in Europe he would be able to make more money from his manuscripts than in the East: 'Quite a stranger to Western languages and customs, he thought that the World Exhibition would offer him the best chance of finding a buyer. Thus he betook himself to the city on the Amstel [i.e. Amsterdam]. Here, bitter disappointment awaited him: only the curious few, who saw our worthy sheikh immersed motionless in the perusal of his manuscripts in the Egyptian stand right behind the well-known Arab perfumer Mustapha, wondered whether it was a statue sitting there or a human being. For the rest no one took much notice of him. In this way he spent two long months without seeing anybody but his fellow stand-holder, the above-mentioned perfume merchant. Moreover, this period of solitude happened to coincide with the Mohammedan month of Ramadan, during which the believers abstain from all food and drink. Amin, whose conscience suffered no transaction on this point, faithfully lived up to Allah's injunction.'[41]

This Sheikh, who was not only a man of learning in his own country, but also a travelling bookseller, repeatedly gave vent to his astonishment – though not entirely without misgivings – about the knowledge extant in Europe of the history, language, arts and sciences of the Egyptian people, all of which hails from an era when the world was still groping in the darkness of ignorance:

> 'It should also be pointed out with some emphasis that we in the East know much too little about the doings of the peoples of Europe, the sciences they dedicate themselves to and the books they publish on the religions and sciences of the Orient.'

And with genuine amazement he cites examples of the familiarity of the Orientalists gathered here with the most arcane aspects of Oriental wisdom: 'Nay, one of them confided to me that every day he recites one of the thirty parts of the Exalted Qur'an from memory!'

Consequently, the professor at the Pristine Garden comes to the following conclusion: 'Even with disregard to the intentions of the Franks (i.e. the Europeans) in printing all these Oriental books, the question arises where they will sell them, given the fact that they usually print at least 500 copies of each title. I myself, who have applied myself to the book trade for a great number of years, have hardly ever seen these European imprints in the East, nor had I ever heard that they were printed in Europe.'

'Truly, if this European fervour should last I fear that camels will be saddled from all parts (i.e. in our countries) to take everything away from us, eventually even the fruits of our own Mohammedan jurisprudence. For if the Franks dedicate themselves to a branch of

---

Muḥammad and several of his followers in the Ḥaram mosque of Medina, probably a *pars pro toto* referring to the city as a whole. According to Snouck Hurgronje al-Madanī taught 'Mohammedan sciences' in his birthplace Medina.

[41] Snouck Hurgronje, *Het Leidsche Orientalistencongres*, pp. 8–9. 'Mustapha' is the Paris-based perfumer Muṣṭafā al-Dīb.

knowledge they never give it up again, but dive into its seas and harvest the pearls from the bottom…'[42]

Among the many visitors to the World Exhibition at Amsterdam there appeared a certain Dr C. Landberg, a Swedish Arabist. Later he preferred to be called Count de Landberg. Occasionally, he returned to the West unexpectedly after having spent long periods in Egypt, where he lived like a sheikh among the nomadic tribes.

Dr Landberg discovered Amin al-Madani in Amsterdam together with his manuscripts, and soon realised their great value. Quite naturally for an Arabist, he took his discovery to the firm of Brill at Leiden and suggested to them that they purchase this exquisite collection of manuscripts from the mosques. Which is exactly what happened. A large part was sold on to the University Library at Leiden and another part to the Royal Library of Berlin.[43] This helped the firm to establish a closer relationship with Landberg, and until two years ago they published a whole series of his works, mostly on the proverbs and sayings of the Arabs, on dialects and so forth, all of it in Arabic. He had been unable to find a publisher for them in Germany.

For the use of the Beirut types the firm temporarily engaged a real Arab compositor from Damascus. Under the rule of the Turks this man had apparently helped to disseminate revolutionary pamphlets through his own little press, which had caused him to flee. For a certain time he had been working at the Imprimerie Nationale in Paris before making his appearance in Leiden. Typesetter Kloos distinctly remembers that the Arab always referred to the Turks as *filoux*, 'scoundrels'. He started systematically to organise the cases with the Beirut types and then began to set Landberg's book: *Proverbes et dictons du peuple arabe.*[44] After having worked there for about a year Kloos was to take over from him. In the meantime, Kloos had learned the ins and outs of this fount, although the Arab had claimed that no Dutchman could ever learn it, for even his own countrymen needed a whole year to become proficient in setting the Beirut types. Yet, after only three months Kloos was working alongside with him, typesetting just as quickly, and when the Arab left Kloos was able to finish the last six sheets of the book on his own. Although he does not really understand what he is typesetting, he usually gets the drift of it, and more often than not they appear to be religious subjects. All the same, he prefers Arabic typesetting to Dutch.

He has dedicated his exceptional professional expertise to the works of Professor De Goeje and many other Arabists, including foreign scholars, for example Ibn Saad's *Biographien Muhammeds*, published in 14 volumes by various Arabists under the chief editorship of professor Ed. Sachau.[45] Presently Kloos is busy typesetting *Jawami* for the E.J.W. Gibb Memorial Fund, most probably his last work before he will retire to enjoy his well-deserved rest.

Generally, the learned authors make but few corrections to his proofs. 'Of course,' so he remarked with a twinkle in his eye, 'the learned gentlemen are very good at the Arabic

[42] Snouck Hurgronje, *Het Leidsche Orientalistencongres*, pp. 51–54.

[43] See Ahlwardt, *Kurzes Verzeichniss der Landberg'schen Sammlung arabischer Handschriften.*

[44] Brusse and Kloos are mistaken here. It was Landberg's *Primeurs arabes* (Leiden, 1886–1889) that was set in the Beirut types. For his *Proverbes et dictons arabes* (Lugd. Bat., 1883) the Flügel/Tauchnitz fount was used, see above.

[45] The *Kitāb al-ṭabaqāt al-kabīr* of Abū ʿAbd Allāh Ibn Saʿd (784–845 CE), published by Eduard Sachau [et al.] as *Biographien Muhammeds, seiner Gefährten und der späteren Träger des Islams bis zum Jahre 230 der Flucht*, 9 pts. In 16 v. (Leiden, 1912–1940).

مقدّمة المؤلّف

بسم الله الرحمن الرحيم

الحمد لله وحده والصلاة والسلام على من صارت بواسطته
العربيّة لذّة للعالم اما بعد فاقول وانا العبد الفقير الراجي
صفح النبلاء عن سهوه وقصوره كرلو لانْدبرج الاسوجي انه
هدتني الافكار و جرّتني الاقدار للتوجّه الى بلاد العرب واشتغلت
مدّة طويلة بلغتها الشريفة التي هي لسان الادب. ولمّا عرفت
معناها وفهمت مبناها تحقّق لي انها احسن اللغات. كيف
لا وبها نزلت الايات البيّنات و قد جاء فى السنّة انها لسان
اهل الجنّة. ثم لا يخفى على كلّ ذي بصيرة وفكرة منيرة ان
علماء العرب اشتغلوا باللغة العربيّة الفصحى خاصّةً دون غيرها
واهملوا تدوين اللغة الدارجة التي كانوا يتكلّمون بها في المؤالفة
اليوميّة حيث كانت القواعد والاصول تقرّرت في القرآن المجيد
وفي كتب السنّة بالكيفيّة التي بها يتحرّر انشاء اللغة العربيّة
الادبيّة فامست اللغة الدارجة في غاية الاستحقار والازدراء
عند اهل العلم منذ ان هاجر المسلمون من اراضي الحجاز
المقدّسة لاجل انتشارهم بين امم مختلفة ولغات غير متخالفة.
ويتّضح جليّا ان امّة الاسلام التي فتحت البلاد التزمت بان
تغيّر لغتها الحجازيّة بعض الغيار وتسلك في معاشرة امم تلك الاقطار
ومكالمتهم بحسب طبيعتهم الغريزيّة. وسهل علينا ان نبرهن بانّ
اللغة الدارجة كانت مستعملة فى القرن الاوّل من الهجرة بل
ويمكن ايراد ادلّة كافية و بيّنات شافية بانها كانت سائرة

Figure 3. Landberg Proverbs p. 3.

language, but sometimes they appear to be much less at home with the composition of types.' Once he had seen a page of Arabic print at an exhibition. As a typographer he had understood immediately that it was complete gibberish, and after reporting his findings to Professor De Goeje he had set the page all over again. The main difficulty with the Beirut types is that you have to insert the vowels in special incisions, because this fount uses only one line instead of three.[46] In the past, Kloos has trained a number of apprentices. Somc have given up, but others have become his close collaborators. They will take over from him on the day he bids a wistful farewell to the intellectual world of the Arabs, whose knowledge he has helped to disseminate around the world without actually fathoming its meaning.'

[46] This is the second time Brusse refers to the difference between 'ordinary' European Arabic type and the 'Beirut types' in the handling of vowel signs, see above n. 35.

# 12

# L'organisation des collections orientales à la Bibliothèque nationale de France

*Sara Yontan Musnik*

En 1995, nous avions, ensemble avec ma collègue Annie Vernay-Nouri, présenté une communication commune à la Bibliothèque universitaire de Leyde qui réunissait la 17e rencontre annuelle du MELCom International, l'association européenne des bibliothécaires du Moyen-Orient. Nous étions toutes les deux chargées des collections imprimées, elle à la Division orientale du département des Manuscrits et moi-même au service turc du département des Entrées étrangères. Nous avions alors titré notre présentation à deux voix, 'L'organisation des collections orientales à la nouvelle Nationale', collections dont on appréhendait l'avenir.

Qu'en est-il aujourd'hui de la 'nouvelle' Nationale qui a mis en œuvre cette organisation depuis plus de dix ans ? Pour mieux apprécier la situation actuelle, il convient d'esquisser le passé, de s'arrêter brièvement sur les années qui ont précédé ce changement, en se concentrant ensuite sur le cas du turc, secteur dont le fonctionnement nous est particulièrement familier.

## 1. ESQUISSE HISTORIQUE: LES 'LIVRES ORIENTAUX' À LA BIBLIOTHÈQUE

Toutes les histoires de la genèse des collections orientales à la BnF commencent par citer les deux *libri arabici* qui se trouvaient déjà dans la bibliothèque de François Ier lors de l'inventaire de 1518. Une présence plus importante est remarquée à la Bibliothèque royale au siècle suivant, fruit de l'impulsion du ministre français Colbert. La volonté de collecter des manuscrits, puis des imprimés en langues étrangères, y compris orientales, s'officialise en 1669 puis s'accentue, grâce à l'ouverture d'esprit du bibliothécaire du Roi, l'abbé Bignon, qui y exerça de 1719 à 1741. Pour les livres arabes, hébreux, grecs, etc., il dira qu'ils "sont ceux dont nous devons être le plus curieux".[1] Les collections continueront de croître tout au long du XVIIIe siècle, arrivant d'abord du Proche-Orient puis de l'Extrême-Orient et de l'Asie du Sud-est.

Au cours du XVIIe siècle, le nombre des imprimés ayant égalé puis rapidement dépassé de façon spectaculaire celui des manuscrits, un nouveau département est inauguré en 1721 pour accueillir les 'livres imprimés'. Au fils des siècles, ce département devenu trop important numériquement, il en engendre un autre en 1942, réservé aux entrées des livres étrangers. Ce dernier se voit à son tour très rapidement augmenté d'une section spécifique pour les imprimés orientaux, grâce à la décision de Julien Cain, alors administrateur général de la Bibliothèque nationale (BN). Cependant, les livres chinois et japonais et, dans une moindre mesure, les ouvrages coréens bénéficient d'une situation spécifique où manuscrits, estampages, imprimés anciens et modernes restent réunis dans un même ensemble, celui conservé par le département des Manuscrits.[2]

Si le Service des langues slaves et orientales (SLSO), fédérant tous les 'services par langues' émergeant avec le russe dès 1945 n'a vu le jour officiellement qu'en décembre 1986, le fonds d'imprimés orientaux, nous l'avons vu plus haut, s'est véritablement constitué depuis le XVIIIe siècle. Jusqu'en 1995, c'est à dire avant la naissance de la Bibliothèque nationale de France (BnF),[3] le SLSO regroupait les langues suivantes, avec un ou plusieurs spécialistes qui se chargeaient des entrées et du traitement des ouvrages dans tous les domaines du savoir privilégiés par la BN, et ce, dans le cadre d' une de ses missions, *l'encyclopédisme* : arabe, arménien, bulgare, chinois, coréen, hébreu et yiddish, langues de l'Inde, japonais, persan, polonais, roumain, russe, serbo-croate, tchèque, turc, vietnamien.

De son côté, au département des Manuscrits, et sous l'impulsion de Marie-Roberte Guignard, une salle de lecture fut aménagée en 1961. Réservée aux orientalistes, le cabinet oriental offrait, outre la consultation des documents en 82 langues différentes non européennes, une collection d'imprimés, indépendante de celle enrichie par le département des Entrées. De nature essentiellement documentaire, l'objectif de cette collection était de permettre aux lecteurs et au personnel de travailler sur les manuscrits. Depuis lors, elle compte environ 150 000 volumes, toutes langues confondues.

Pour ce qui est du nombre de volumes imprimés en langues orientales dans l'ensemble de la BnF, il est très difficile d'avancer un chiffre précis notamment pour les langues écrites en caractères latins dont les collections n'ont pas bénéficié de catalogues spécifiques. Un rapport établi en 2002[4] a néanmoins avancé le nombre de 730 000 volumes de monographies

[1] Cité dans Simone Balayé, *La Bibliothèque nationale, des origines à 1800.* (Genève, 1988), p. 212

[2] Juilien Cain, *Les Transformations de la Bibliothèque nationale de 1936 à 1959* (Paris, 1960), p. 3: "Par suite d'une longue tradition qu'expliquent les caractères particulières de l'imprimerie de l'Extrême-Orient, les collections d'imprimés de ces pays ne sont pas conservées au département des Imprimés". Ce n'est qu'en 1976 avec la création du service Asie aux Entrées que les acquisitions furent partagées avec le département des Manuscrits, les ouvrages traitant des périodes postérieures à 1850 gagnant le fonds d'imprimés.

[3] BnF: fusion de la Bibliothèque nationale et de l'Etablissement public de la Bibliothèque de France qui menait le projet d'une 'bibliothèque de type entièrement nouveau' annoncé par le Président de la République française, François Mitterrand en juillet 1988.

[4] "Langues et civilisations du monde à la Bibliothèque nationale de France. Carte documentaire

et de 3500 titres de périodiques, les entrées annuelles présentant alors un accroissement entre 12 000 et 15 000 volumes.

Selon les langues, les époques et les compétences disponibles, les autres départements spécialisés de l'ex-BN[5] ont fait appel au SLSO pour leurs ressources imprimées qui comprennent également des ouvrages en langues orientales. Cette fonction transversale continue dans la nouvelle organisation de la BnF aussi bien pour les départements spécialisés que pour les départements thématiques de la direction des Collections.[6] Elle concerne surtout des compétences relevant du catalogage (translittération ou saisie des écritures non latines, établissement des notices d'autorités personnes physiques, collectivités, titres uniformes ou encore sujets) et parfois des connaissances relatives à la veille documentaire. Pour ce qui est des acquisitions proprement dites, les départements spécialisés qui comptent de documents 'orientaux' sur divers supports et des collections d'imprimés plus modestes, demeurent seuls juges de leur opportunité.

Aujourd'hui et depuis la réorganisation de 1995, si le service des Littératures orientales (SLO) est rattaché au département Littérature et art (LLA), les collections dont il a la charge, allant du japonais à l'est jusqu'au tchèque à l'ouest, ont été reparties dans l'ensemble des quatre départements thématiques qu'il enrichit de façon très variable. Le caractère de 'service ressource' du SLO est ainsi confirmé; il continue à assurer la sélection et le traitement des imprimés orientaux arrivant par échanges. Quant aux acquisitions onéreuses, le service assume essentiellement les achats dans les disciplines de son propre département et du département Philosophie, histoire, sciences sociales (PHS) qui est le seul à lui déléguer des crédits spécifiques. Cependant les chargés de collections du SLO bénéficient depuis peu de conditions administratives et financières nécessaires pour jouer leur rôle scientifique, qui consiste à proposer une veille documentaire transverse pour les autres départements thématiques. Ce travail se fait pour les ouvrages dans les langues dites orientales qui comprennent dix-huit groupes linguistiques.[7] Si ce principe est acquis, la consigne reste néanmoins souple et sa mise en œuvre dépend des paysages éditoriaux de chaque pays qui sont évalués et valorisés par le personnel en exercice.

---

des collections imprimées en caractères non latins et latins étendus à la BnF". Document réalisé par S Yontan Musnik sous la direction de Denis Bruckmann, septembre 2002.

[5] Par département spécialisé on comprend ceux dont les supports de leurs collections ne sont pas des imprimés. Il s'agit des départements suivants: Manuscrits, Estampes et photographies, Musique, Cartes et plans, Monnaies et médailles, Opéra, Arts du spectacle.

[6] Les quatre départements thématiques sont: 1, Philosophie, histoire, sciences sociales (PHS); 2, Droit, économie, sciences politiques (DEP); 3, Sciences et Techniques (SCT) et 4, Littérature et art (LLA). Un nouveau département crée à la BnF et qui se distingue par la nature des formats de ses collections est celui de l'audiovisuel (DAV)

[7] A savoir: l'arabe, arménien, le bulgare, le chinois, le coréen, le grec moderne, l'hébreu, le yiddish et les autres langues juives, le hongrois, le japonais, le maltais, le polonais, le russe et l'ukrainien, le tchèque et le slovaque, le turc, le vietnamien, les langues de l'ex-Yougoslavie, les langues de l'Inde, les langues baltiques. A noter que contrairement à la situation de l'ex-BN, le roumain ne fait plus partie de ce groupe, alors que le grec moderne, le hongrois et les langues baltiques s'y sont ajoutées. Par ailleurs, le poste du persan est à pouvoir depuis le départ à la retraite de la chargée des collections en 1999.

## 2. GROS PLAN SUR LE TURC

Le Service turc de la Bibliothèque nationale a été créé à la fin de l'année 1970,[8] trois siècles après l'entrée à la Bibliothèque du Roi des premiers volumes en langue turque par l'acquisition de la bibliothèque de Mazarin et de celle de Gilbert Gaulmin qui, à elles deux, contenaient cent cinquante volumes en cette langue. Par la suite, il y a eu les achats faits au Levant sur instructions royales.[9] La constitution du fonds fut ainsi 'légitimée'. Plus tard, les collections d'imprimés ont continué à l'alimenter assez régulièrement, depuis l'arrivée du premier ouvrage turc sorti frêchement des presses de Müteferrika[10] à Constantinople, suivi de tous les autres "incunables turcs" par accord conclu entre l'abbé Bignon et Said Aga,[11] le jeune fils de l'Ambassadeur Mehmed Effendi qui accompagna son père dans son voyage officiel en France en 1721.

En effet, on apprend par une *Note concernant le traitement et la remise en ordre des fonds imprimés turcs et iraniens de la Bibliothèque nationale* datée du 20 avril 1956 que Mr. Rodinson[12] aurait assuré, entre 1946 et 1955 "le traitement des ouvrages imprimés arabes, persans et turcs entrant à la Bibliothèque, tant au Département des Imprimés qu'au Département des Manuscrits (Usuels du Cabinet Oriental)". Cette même note propose la poursuite des travaux pour le turc et le persan par un bibliothécaire en exercice "qui connaît ces deux langues" et qui "continuerait à apporter son aide pour le hongrois et autres langues rares de son ressort". Cependant, le Conservateur en chef des Entrées ne peut pas suivre ces recommandations et suggère que le bibliothécaire en question, Monsieur Pierre Barkan, ne dédie que "2 jours par semaines au service oriental et l'inventaire général et 4 jours par semaine au Catalogue où son temps sera, ... consacré uniquement au traitement des ouvrages en langues étrangères relevant de ses compétences" c'est-à-dire en "néerlandais, scandinaves, hongrois, espagnol, portugais et roumain"!

---

[8] Une lettre de Louis Bazin, professeur de turc à l'Inalco et à l'EPHE, directeur de l'Institut d'études turques, à l'administrateur général de la BN, Georges Le Rider Réf BN 13 DEC 78–82554 laisserait croire que la création du service date de 1978: "J'ai été très heureux d'apprendre que vous aviez créé un Service Turc (regroupant les publications des diverses langues du monde turcophone) à la Bibliothèque Nationale." Or le service en tant que tel a existé depuis juillet 1970 alors qu'un conservateur n'a eu sa charge exclusive qu'en décembre 1977 pour permettre son développement. La lettre fait sans doute référence à cette affectation.

[9] Annie Berthier, 'Le fonds turc du département des Manuscrits' *Revue de la Bibliothèque nationale*, no. 2 (1981), pp. 78–95. Voir aussi par le même auteur sa contribution sur le turc dans *Manuscrits, xylographes, estampages: les collections orientales du département des Manuscrits: guide* (Paris, 2000) p. 54.

[10] Ibrahim Müteferrika (1670?–1747?) le premier éditeur et imprimeur turc d'origine hongroise, conseillé de la Sublime Porte.

[11] Saïd à Bignon (BnF N.a.f 8972 f 235–236) (ma traduction): "dorénavant nous vous enverrons à vous notre ami un [ou] deux exemplaires de tous les livres soit en turc soit en arabe soit en persan qui seront imprimés dans notre imprimerie". Voir aussi la notice manuscrite de *Tarih-i Naima* reproduite dans *Topkapi à Versailles: trésors de la cour ottomane*: [exposition] Versailles, 4 mai–15 août 1999. Paris: AFAA-RMN, 1999, p. 326–327: 'Donné à la Bibliothèque du Roy par Saïd Pacha, Ambassadeur de la Porte. L'année 1742 Mr Bignon intendant de Soissons étant Bibliothéquaire [sic]. Signé Selliers'.

[12] Il s'agit du savant islamologue Maxime Rodinson. En général dans le passé, les mêmes personnes étaient chargées d'acquérir et de cataloguer les collections dans les langues arabe, persane et turque.

Sept ans plus tard, en 1963, le même Conservateur en Chef des Entrées demande à son subordonné polyglotte d'établir un rapport sur l'état actuel du fonds turc dont les conclusions tirées attestent qu'il est riche tant en quantité (15 000 ouvrages dont un millier de doubles au Cabinet Oriental des Manuscrits) qu'en qualité, pour ce qui est du passé. La description fait état d'un fonds très représentatif, allant "de l'incunable [...] en passant par les premiers récits des voyageurs [...] les premiers éditions des textes [...] les premières grammaires et les premiers thésaurus, jusqu'aux rapports d'expéditions scientifiques et aux éditions de textes plus solidement étayées des orientalistes occidentaux [...et de ceux] des orientalistes turcs [...]".[13] Cependant, l'activité de la BN dans ce domaine serait "entrée en sommeil depuis 1914".[14] Ce constat indique que les entrées turques auraient bénéficié d'un dynamisme certain pendant le XIXe siècle, époque où l'orientalisme – dont la turcologie – est affirmé par l'érudition. En effet lors du recatalogage des imprimés turcs en caractères arabes parus entre 1728 et 1928, nous avons remarqué que la majorité du fonds "osmanli", comptant près de 800 volumes, était constituée d'impressions achevées pendant la seconde moitié du XIX siècle. Seule une partie, minoritaire mais non négligeable, était entrée par acquisition, témoignant ainsi d'une démarche volontaire de la part de la Bibliothèque.

Pour revenir au rapport de 1963 mentionné plus haut, le responsable qui le rédige conclut qu'il est d'un "très réel intérêt national de combler l'essentiel des lacunes et d'entretenir ... le fonds [turc]".

Cependant, c'est en 1966 que 'le fonds turc' commence à avoir l'appellation du 'service turc du catalogue' dont le rapport d'activité pour l'année précédente fait état "d'un lot d'environ 7000 fiches [...] en vue d'alimenter les premiers fichiers d'un futur service turc". Un an plus tard, on lit en conclusion d'un mémoire, le souhait de M Barkan de pouvoir se consacrer "[après avoir accompli plusieurs projets qu'il cite] au fonctionnement d'un véritable 'Service turc' parallèle aux Services 'arabe' et 'persan' [...]". Les rapports sur le turc se succèdent assez régulièrement mais celui établi pour l'année 1971 démarre avec la phrase "Etant donné que ce service a réellement commencé son activité au cours du 4e trimestre de 1970, ...": le service turc voit donc le jour officiellement le 11 septembre 1970 et il est maintenu jusqu'à la cession d'activité de son titulaire en mai 1976. Son remplacement, cette fois par une personne exclusivement chargée de ce fonds, ne se fait pas avant le 5 janvier 1977.[15]

Il n'existe aucun travail à notre connaissance sur les registres d'entrées d'imprimés turcs à la Bibliothèque durant la période allant du début du XIXe jusqu'à la première moitié du XXe siècles. En revanche, un rapport de Monsieur Pierre Barkan daté de mars 1950 et adressé à l'Administrateur général de la BN sur les échanges de publications avec la Turquie pour les années précédentes exprime la générosité de nombreuses institutions officielles et scientifiques notamment à Ankara. Les mémoires d'activités des années 1970 qui traitent de plusieurs fonds, font état d'entrées plus maigres pour le turc sans préciser ni la provenance, ni le contenu. C'est alors que l'on fait allusion à deux fournisseurs de livres en Turquie et

[13] 'Les fonds imprimés turcs et persans à la Bibliothèque Nationale' de Pierre Barkan, Conservateur au Service étranger du Catalogue, Paris, le 3 avril 1963.

[14] Nous savons que le régime d'*Union et progrès* et les guerres successives n'ont certainement pas été propices à l'activité éditoriale en Turquie.

[15] Mileva Božič, 'Le fonds imprimé turc de la Bibliothèque nationale. Les débuts de l'imprimerie ottomane' *Revue de la Bibliothèque nationale*, no.1 (1981), p. 8–16 et no. 2 (1981), no. 2, p. 70–79.

à deux autres librairies orientalistes à Paris, plutôt comme projets de contact. Cependant, il paraît y avoir des incertitudes quant au budget de la Bibliothèque. La volonté de développer les acquisitions n'est suivie d'effet qu'en 1981. Auparavant, les entrées semblent se limiter aux dons "dont la valeur est exceptionnelle" ou "des ouvrages rares et intéressants" venant de l'Ambassade de Turquie ou, individuellement, des auteurs turcs. Enfin, ce n'est qu'en 1987, après dix ans d'efforts portés sur l'établissement des relations avec la Milli Kütüphane (la Nationale d'Ankara) que reprend l'accroissement par échanges internationaux.

Les rapports rédigés pour cette période sont moins portés sur les chiffres et les découpages thématiques; ils sont plus narratifs. Cela change dramatiquement en 1990 avec des grilles de statistiques où l'on exige de distinguer le nombre de titres commandés, entrés et traités. Grâce aux précisions apportées sur les disciplines d'ouvrages catalogués, on remarque que la littérature (histoire et critique mais aussi textes) occupe déjà une place importante dans les collections turques.

En 1991, après environ 14 ans de fonction, lors du départ à la retraite de son titulaire, le Service turc s'était redressé, moyennant une continuité d'efforts qui lui étaient réservés. Il figurait désormais sur l'organigramme aux côtés des autres langues slaves et orientales.

L'attribution du poste vacant à un spécialiste s'est fait ensuite en septembre 1992. La consigne pour les acquisitions à cette époque était d'assurer une couverture entre 5% et 10 % de la production éditoriale du pays pour les disciplines privilégiées par la BN, que l'on peut résumer étant les publications en langues originales d'études académiques en sciences humaines et de textes littéraires d'œuvres confirmées.

Cependant, la situation en Turquie ne permettait pas la mise en pratique d'une instruction aussi nette: la seule source pour une veille documentaire fiable, qu'était la bibliographie nationale, arrivait en retard. De plus, elle était lacunaire, malgré la loi de dépôt légal en application dans le pays depuis 1934. Nonobstant cette contrainte majeure, les collections d'imprimés turques s'enrichissaient régulièrement grâce à un choix opéré sur des catalogues de fournisseurs et sur des propositions d'échange d'ouvrages proposés par la BN d'Ankara et par quelques autres institutions scientifiques.

Avec davantage de moyens budgétaires alloués aux achats et des rapports d'échanges internationaux désormais bien établis, il était aisé de continuer le travail de développement des collections turques entamé par les prédécesseurs; il fut même possible de le consolider avec un goût personnel prononcé pour les littératures contemporaine et populaire, jusqu'alors considérées mineures.

Très vite cependant, ce départ en élan fut réorienté vers le nouveau projet d'une bibliothèque dont les collections d'imprimés devaient se repartir par thème. Le rattachement des langues orientales au département Littérature et art, accompagné de la priorité à constituer – sans toucher aux ouvrages conservés dans les magasins – deux niveaux de libre accès, l'un consacré à l'étude et l'autre à la recherche, a mis en veille la couverture pluridisciplinaire pendant quelques temps. En revanche, les lacunes en littérature et en linguistique ont été comblées, et des ouvrages de références, souvent très peu représentés en salles de lecture, ont pu être mis à la disposition des usagers. Les crédits d'acquisitions, dont bénéficiait ce projet de réorganisation, ont ainsi permis d'assurer des entrées à la hauteur des ambitions.

Néanmoins, c'est à cette époque de transition que les inquiétudes concernant la continuité des fonds en magasins pour les autres disciplines que celles de littérature et linguistique se sont fait sentir. Alors que l'offre documentaire en libre accès atteignait son objectif, les réunions entre les acquéreurs des départements thématiques se multipliaient et le retour à un rythme de croisière semblait possible pour les chargés des collections orientales. Ces derniers réclamaient leur fonction transversale sans pour autant bousculer le schéma organisationnel de l'établissement. L'appareil administratif de la Bibliothèque a fini par permettre une souplesse: les acquisitions pluridisciplinaires furent à nouveau reprises par les secteurs du service des Littératures orientales depuis 2004. Un travail rétrospectif fut engagé alors pour combler les lacunes de la décennie précédente dans la mesure du possible.

Compte tenu du nombre assez modeste de volumes que le secteur turc devait mettre en accès libre, l'objectif de rattrapage fut relativement rapidement atteint. Avec le retour progressif aux acquisitions de publications turques pour les magasins, notamment pour renforcer le collections en littératures et langues turques, il était possible de compléter la couverture d'usuels, de bibliographies, d'ouvrages sur l'histoire du livre et sur l'art. Par conséquent, on peut affirmer l'existence à la BnF d'un fonds turc assez riche dans ces disciplines. Il n'est cependant que documentaire et représentatif pour l'histoire et les sciences sociales. Enfin, il reflète peu ou pas les domaines des autres départements comme l'économie, le droit ou les sciences. En revanche, les chargés de collections thématiques, tous sujets confondus, sauf langue et littérature, commandent des publications européennes et nord américaines relatives à la turcologie, dans le cadre de la politique documentaire de la bibliothèque et selon leurs appréciations et leurs budgets,. Ceci est complété par la production éditoriale française qui arrive à la BnF par voie de Dépôt légal.

Si les achats de monographies turques et les abonnements au périodiques ont considérablement augmenté depuis, les entrées par échanges ont elles diminué de façon remarquable. Les raisons à l'abandon progressif et irréversible de ce mode d'entrée peuvent s'expliquer aisément; ce phénomène est commun à toutes les bibliothèques. Aujourd'hui, les échanges représentent moins de 5% des entrées turques. En revanche, les dons, bien que variables par définition, sont encore fructueux de part la notoriété dont bénéficie l'existence continue du service auprès des institutions et des réseaux d'auteurs constitués : c'est un mode d'accroissement qui compte parfois jusque 30 % des volumes entrés annuellement.

## 3. EN GUISE D'UN BILAN PROVISOIRE

Ainsi, alors que les départements et les acquisitions à la BnF sont organisés par thèmes, les secteurs du service des Littératures orientales sont, eux, toujours organisés par langues. Pour des raisons de division de travail, les chargés de ces collections sont considérés comme des spécialistes de langue. La connaissance du paysage éditorial, l'établissement des rapports étroits avec les libraires qui saisissent bien le profil du fonds et qui font des propositions d'une acquisition opportune, le tissage des liens utiles pour mobiliser des recherches sur place ou pour susciter des dons de tirages limités, la constitution des réseaux pour pister les éditions hors commerce et les ouvrages épuisés... tels sont les avantages non négligeables de ce fonctionnement.

Quant aux craintes ressenties par le personnel concerné au moment des transformations, elles étaient certainement fondées à l'époque de la réorganisation; mais grâce à la volonté de poursuivre la mission encyclopédique, la Bibliothèque nationale de France a su trouver un nouvel ajustement en matière de développement des collections en faveur du maintien des fonds orientaux dont le turc.

Depuis la rédaction de cet article, deux changements majeurs ont eu lieu quant à l'organisation des collections d'imprimés orientaux en général et du turc en particulier : (1) à partir du 1er janvier 2014, le service des littératures orientales (SLO) a fusionné avec celui des littératures étrangères, donnant naissance au Service des littératures du monde (SLM) ; (2) après le départ à la retraite du conservateur chargé du catalogue des manuscrits turcs, et dès 2011, un seul conservateur est désormais responsable pour l'ensemble du fonds turc, imprimés et manuscrits.

# 13

# Some Arabic Textbooks from Kerala

*Jan Just Witkam*

## INTRODUCTION[1]

The small collection of five Arabic volumes from Kerala (South India), printed in the late 1970s and early 1980s, which is the subject of the present research, was purchased by me in the course of 2000, when I was on an acquisition trip in India on behalf of ISIM, the Leiden based International Institute for the Study of Islam in the Modern World. I found a small cache of books from Kerala tucked away, and apparently impossible to sell, in the storage of one of the Islamic bookshops on Muhammad Ali Road in Mumbai. It took me little hesitation to purchase everything, including all doubles, as I had so far been unaware of the existence of such materials. That was, of course, mainly due to my insufficient knowledge of Islamic presence in South-West India. I was struck by the peculiar script used in the books, and decided to devote more attention to it later. Writing about it for my old friend Paul Auchterlonie seemed to me the perfect occasion to do what I had been postponing for so long.

All texts in the booklets are in Arabic, but there are a few features in Malayalam as well, where the publisher refers to himself. In order to understand such notes in Malayalam in Arabic script I used the alphabet table provided by Asher and Karassery.[2] As a modern primary source for the Arabic writing system as applied to Malayalam I refer to the educational materials in use in Kerala, in particular those published by the Samastha Kerala Sunni Vidyabhyasa Board in Calicut.[3] Another source for the transliteration of Malayalam in Arabic script is the table for 'Moplah', the somewhat antiquated term for the language

---

[1] I gratefully acknowledge the help I received from Dr Herman Tieken (Leiden) and Dr Torsten Tschacher (Heidelberg) while I was trying to find my way in South-Indian Islamic literature.

[2] R.E. Asher and M.N. Karassery, art. 'Malayalam', in K. Versteegh (ed.), *Encyclopedia of Arabic language and linguistics*, vol. 3 (Leiden, etc., 2008), pp. 128–135 (with the table on p. 130).

[3] *Tafhīm al-Qirā'a. Al-Ğuz' al-Thānī, lil-Ṣaff al-Awwal. Al-Ṭab'a al-Sādisa: 1423 H /002 M*, published by the Hay'at al-Taʿlīm al-Sunniyya bi-ʿUmūm Kīrālā, al-Hind (All Kerala Sunni Education Board. India). This booklet is designed to teach students the Arabic script, but also includes a few pages (pp. 44–48) on writing Malayalam using Arabic letters (communication and images from Dr. Tschacher).

of the Mapillas, the Muslims of Malabar, which can be found in the 1997 edition of the *ALA-LC Romanization Tables*, and which is also on-line available in the website of the Library of Congress.[4] The system of transliteration of Malayalam words in Arabic script in Asher & Karassery is identical to that in the Library of Congress tables, but the *y* and *m* have been shifted in Asher and Karassery, apparently by mistake.

I will here only give a survey of the content of the five volumes. Later, and elsewhere, I will try to reconstruct an intellectual or educational context for the texts described. That research would involve a further identification of most of the texts involved, especially of the local authorship, and an attempt to see where these texts come from, and where they may have gone.[5] With the data presently supplied others can work now on these subjects as well. The present collection is too limited to thoroughly study still discernible scribal practices, but it is immediately evident that the books can be characterized as 'printed manuscripts', with which term I mean to say that the text was not typeset but instead first written by a copyist, and then somehow photographically reproduced. In two cases (nos 1, 4) stereotype blocks were made, possibly by way of zincography after the handwritten original, and these were mounted and printed in a book press, not in offset. The other three volumes (nos 2, 3, 5) are printed in offset, which in the technical sense is the direct successor to lithography. It may suffice here to call to mind that reproducing handwritten texts in book form has been, ever since the introduction of lithography in the Muslim world, a favourite way of printing in many regions, firstly because the technical requirements for lithography were much less sophisticated than the necessities for typography, and secondly because the final result for the reproduction of the cursive Arabic script was esthetically much more agreeable than any result obtained from typography. The present descriptions with the accompanying reproductions constitute a first attempt to signal and to describe some modern Mapilla scribal practices.

The five volumes with their thirty-five Arabic texts described below are all registered in Leiden University Library, but belong to the ever increasing backlog of that institution. The present descriptions are based on the doubles of the same volumes which I purchased for my private library. I herewith express the hope that the present contribution to Arabic bibliography may serve as the preparatory work for the inclusion of the texts in the Leiden catalogue, which is long overdue.

---

[4] *ALA-LC Romanization Tables. Transliteration Schemes for Non-Roman Scripts.* 1997 edition. Approved by the Library of Congress and the American Library Association. Tables compiled and edited by Randall K. Barry. Washington (Library of Congress) 1997, pp. 134–137, in scanned form on-line available in http://www.loc.gov/catdir/cpso/roman.html (last accessed June 2014).

[5] Would they have travelled further East, as far as the Malay world? What to think, e.g. of the occurrence of the title *ʿIshrūn Ṣifa* (volume 2, text 3)?

# A SURVEY OF THE CONTENT OF FIVE ARABIC TEXTBOOK VOLUMES FROM KERALA

## 1

A collective volume with texts on Arabic morphology and Arabic syntax. Title-page and text printed on the cover are identical.

The title page reads (see Figure 1):

> *Hādhihi Kutubun Mağmūʿatun min al-Tisʿa Khamsa fil-Ṣarf wa-Arbaʿa fil-Naḥw*. Mīzān (1) wa-Ağnas (2) wa-Ağnas al-Kubra (3) wa-Zanğan (4) wa-ʿAwamil (5) wa-Taqwim al-Līsān (6) wa-Tuḥfa (7) wa-Qaṭr al-Nadā (8) wa-Shawāhid al-Qaṭr.

C.H. Printing Works, Unniyūr, 300 pp., 19.5 cm, half-cloth binding with pasted boards (red paper with imprint). On the back cover the name of the publisher set in a floral ornament: C.H. Printing Works | Unniyūr, Kerala (see Figure 1).

The imprint 'Unniyūr, Kerala' is in so far problematic because the only locality with the name Unniyūr could be found on any map is in Central Tamil Nadu. However, in volume no. 4, below, the imprint is also Unniyūr, Kerala, but here is added Malapuram as the district.

Collective volume said on the title-page to contain nine texts (in fact ten, if one counts, as I have done, the final *Shawāhid* list which is derived from the penultimate text, as a separate bibliographical entity) in Arabic on Arabic grammar, five on morphology, four (in fact five) on syntax. Texts nos 1–6, 8 and 10 start right away, and usually have the title as given on the title-page of the volume repeated on top of the text, or in the margin, next to the initial words. Texts nos 7, 9 have a title-page of their own (pp. 129, 189). On p. 300 is a printer's colophon for the entire volume. This reads:

> Qad tamma Ṭabʿ hādhā al-Kitāb bi-ʿAwn Allāh al-Malik al-Wahhāb. Hiğra 1402 Dhī al-Ḥiğğa No. 3 ʿĪsawiyya 1982 September No. 21 tīt Unniyūral sthā patmāy C.H. Printing Worksal adkapadat. Katabahu Pūkar wa-Kač Muḥammad ghafara Allāh la-humā Amīn. C.H. Printing Works, Unniyūr. 21-9-82.

(1) pp. 2–26. *Mīzān*. An anonymous paradigm of the morphology of the Arabic verb (*faʿala*), usually written in three columns and five rows on each page. The derivations of *faʿala* are written in a large and bold script, the grammatical categories are written above each derivation, in a smaller script, upside down and in an oblique writing direction. Occasionally the columns are interrupted by headings in very small script, or by short remarks in small script (see Figure 2).

Beginning (p. 2):

> (بسمله) الحمد لله رب العالمين والعاقبة للمتقين ... وبعد فان الافعال على اربعة اقسام ما من مثل
> فعل وضرب ومستقبل مثل يفعل ويضرب

First explained word (p. 2):

> **فعل**: صيغة وحدان مذكر غائب از اثبات فعل ماضي معروف ضمير درو هو .

From the occurrence of two Persian words (*az*, *darū*) in the explanation of *faʿala* a Persian origin of the interlinear commentary may be assumed (see Figure 2).

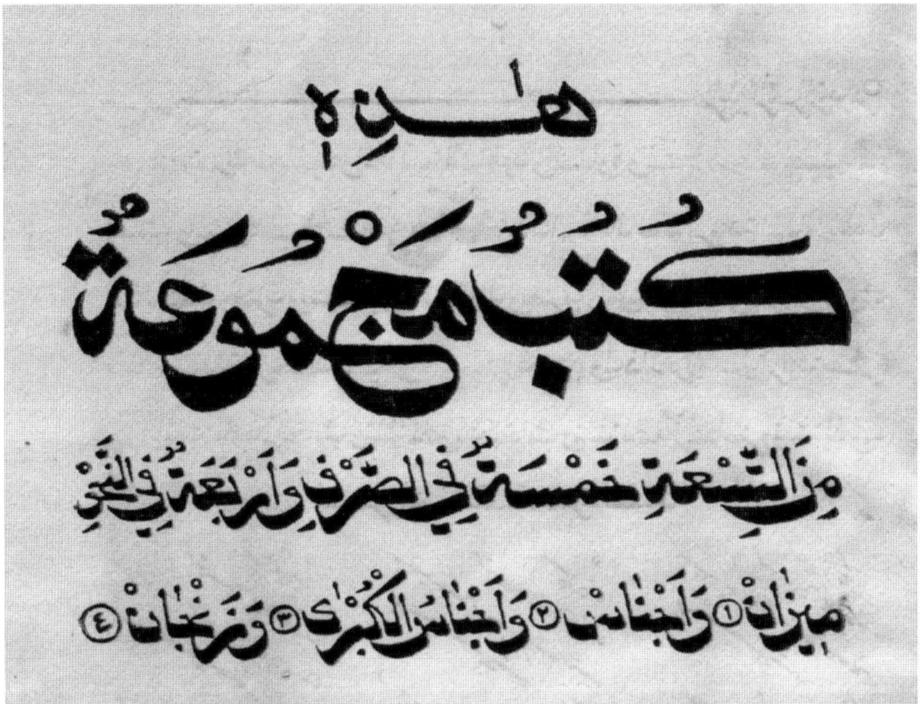
هذه
كتب مجموعة
من التسعة خمسة في الصرف واربعة في النحو
ميزان ① واجناس ② واجناس الكبرى ③ وزنجان ④
وعوامل ⑤ وتقويم اللسان ⑥ وتحفة ⑦
وقطر الندى ⑧ وشواهد
القطر ⑨

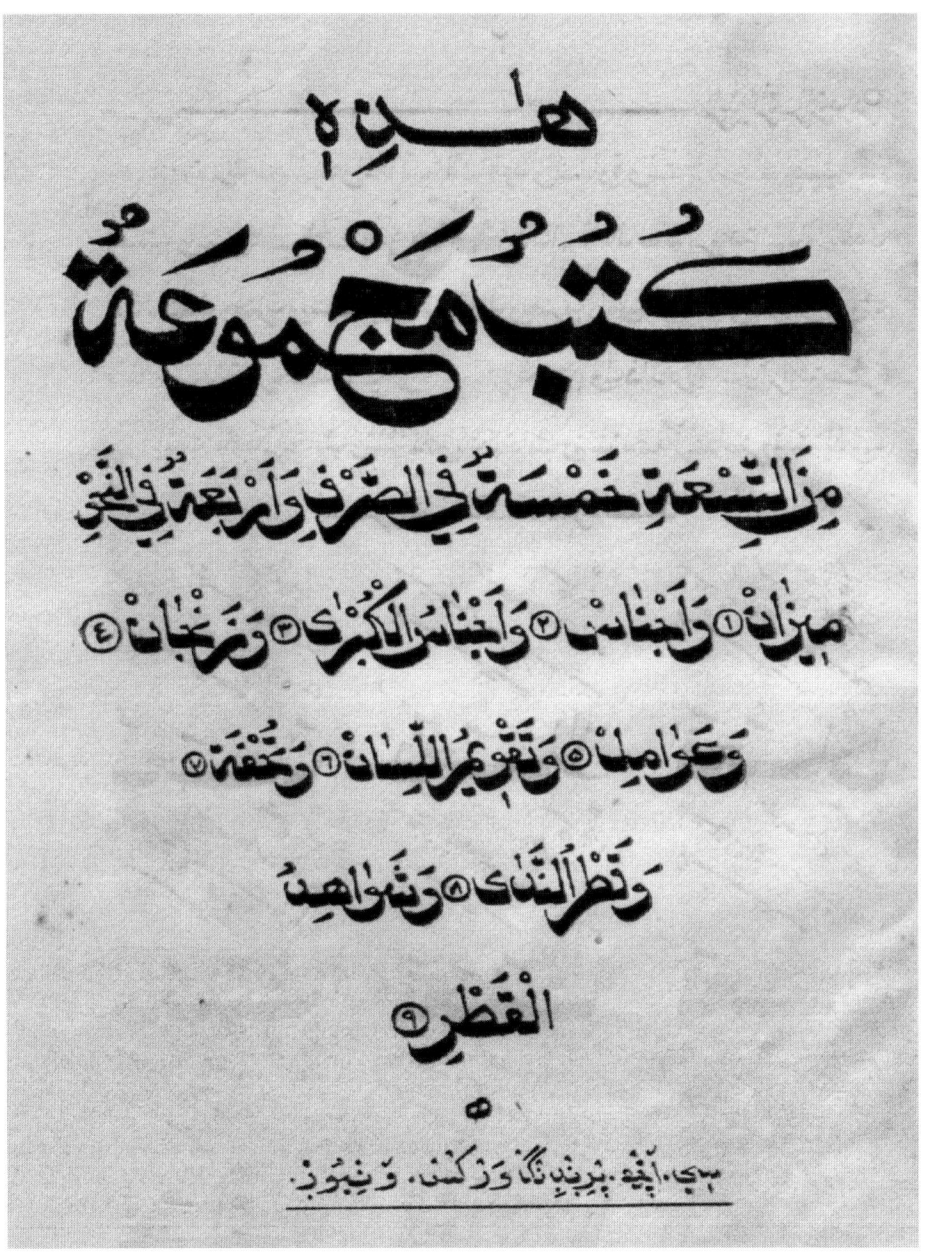

Figure 1. Hādhihi Kutubun Majmūʿatun min al-Tisʿa Khomsa fīl-Ṣarf wa-Arbaʿa fīl-naḥw. Unniyūr 1982. No. 1, collective title page.

The last explained word (p. 26) is *mafʿūlātun*, which is followed by a short list of nominal categories: ism al-āla, ism al-zamān wal-makān, ism al-ḥala, ism al-marra, etc. Final words (p. 26):

تم الكتاب بعون الله الملك الوهاب برحمتك يا ارحم الراحمين

(2) pp. 27–31. *Faṣl fī Ağnās al-Afʿāl.* Title in the margin (p. 27): *Ağnās al-Ṣughrā.* A short anonymous prose text on the morphology of the Arabic verb. Small script, written over 18 lines to the page. Headings and titles in larger and bold script. Beginning (p. 27):

(بسمله) وبه نستعين، فصل في اجناس الافعال **اعلم** ان الافعال، اما ثلاثي واما رباعي وكل واحد
منهما اما مجرد او مزيد فيه واما الثلاثي المجرد فخمسة ابواب الباب **الاول** فعل يفعل فعلا ...

Final words (p. 31):

... وفرّ يفرّ فرّا فهو فارّ وفرّ يفرّ فرّا وهو مفرور الامر منه فرّ والنهي لا تفرّ وفك الادغام افرر
ولا تفرر، تمت الكتاب بعون الله الملك الوهاب،

(3) pp. 32–41. *Ağnās al-Kubrā* (title only in margin of p. 32). A short anonymous prose text on the morphology of the Arabic verb (*awzān al-afʿāl*, p. 41). It seems to be an expanded version of *Ağnās al-Ṣughrā*, the previously described text. The author is not mentioned but he occasionally refers to himself in the first person singular (*qultu*, *lī*, both on p. 41). Small script, written over 18 lines to the page. Headings and titles in larger and bold script. Beginning (p. 32):

(بسمله) وبه نستعين، الحمد لله رب العالمين والعاقبة للمتقين والصلوة والسلام على سيّدنا ... **وبعد**
فاعلم يا اخي اسعدك الله تعالى وايّانا في الدارين ان الافعال من حيث المعنى نوعان لازم ومتعدّ
فاللازم ما لا يتجاوز الفاعل الى المفعول فلا يبنى منه المجهول ...

Author's colophon and final words of the text (p. 41):

تمت فهذه آخر ما تيسر الله تعالى لي ايراده على اوزان الافعال والمرجو من فضله ان يجعله من
مصالح الاعمال والمسئول ممن اطلع فيه على خلل ان يصلحه بالفضل، تم الكتاب بعون الملك
الوهاب، برحمتك يا ارحم الراحمين، وصلى الله على خير خلقه سيدنا محمد وآله وصحبه اجمعين،
والحمد لله ربّ العالمين،

(4) pp. 42–85. *Zanğān* (title in margin of p. 42). This is in fact the elementary textbook on Arabic morphology, *al-Taṣrīf al-ʿIzzī* by ʿIzz al-Dīn ʿAbd al-Wahhāb b. Ibrāhīm al-Zanğānī (fl. 655/1257), GAL G I, 283, but he is not mentioned in the text. A shortened version of his *nisba*, referring to the North-West Persian town of Zanğān, has apparently changed into the title of the work. Large and bold script throughout, written in 9 lines to the page, headings in an even slightly larger script. Occasional interlinear explanatory etymological notes in Arabic (often introduced by *aṣluhu*) in tiny script, written upside down. Beginning (p. 42):

(بسمله) الحمد لله رب العالمين، والصلوة والسلام على سيدنا محمد وآله وصحبه اجمعين، اعلم ان
التصريف في اللغة التغيير وفي الصناعة تحويل الاصل الواحد الى امثلة مختلفة لمعان مقصودة ...

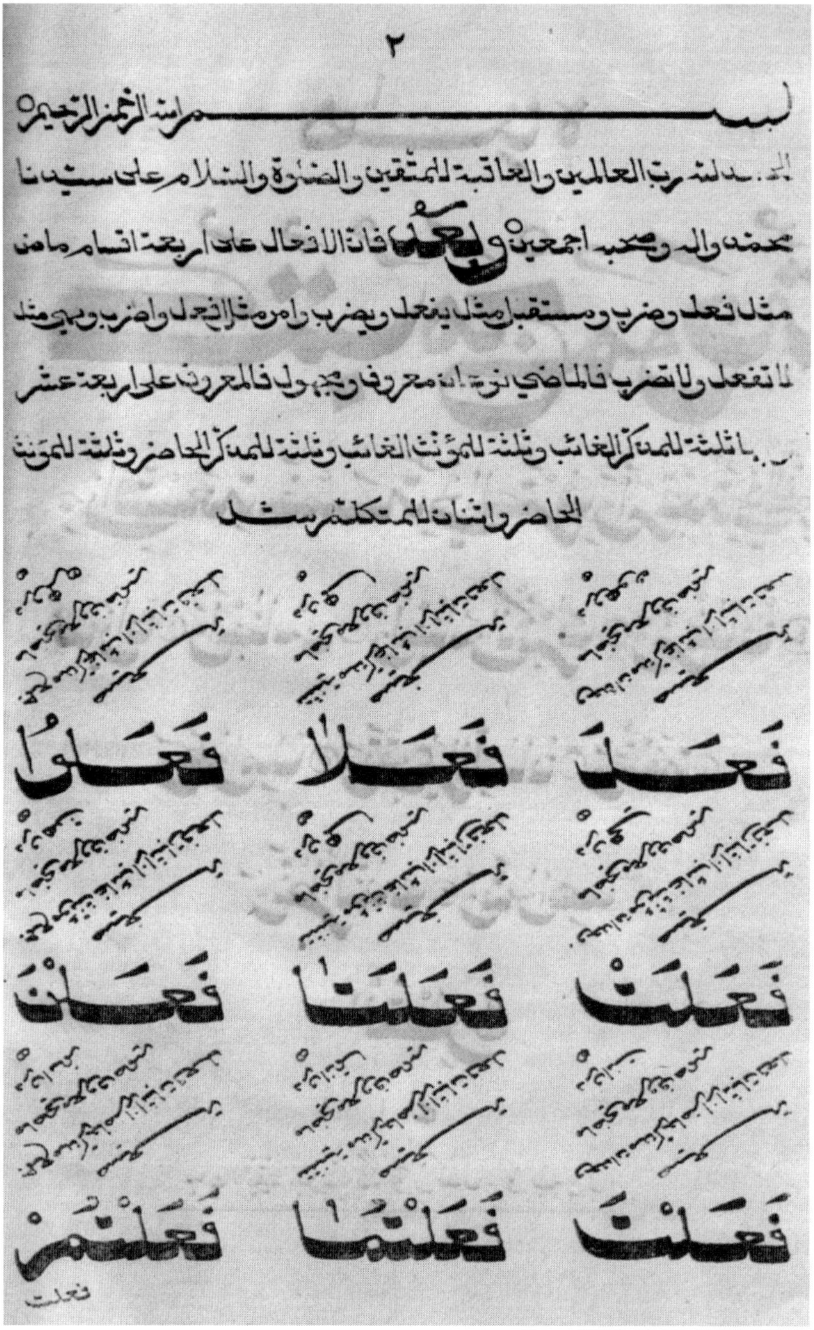


Figure 2. Mīzān. An anonymous paradigm of the morphology of the Arabic verb. No. 1, p. 2.

Final words (p. 85):

... والفعلة بالكسر للنوع من الفعل تقول هو حسن الطعمة والجلسة، تم الكتاب بعون الله الملك
الوهاب، برحمتك يا ارحم الرامين،

(5) pp. 86–93. *ʿAwāmil* (title in margin only of p. 86). This is in fact *Kitāb al-ʿAwāmil al-Miʾa* by ʿAbd al-Qāhir b. ʿAbd al-Raḥmān al-Ğurğānī (d. 471/1078), GAL G I, 287, a short prose work on Arabic syntax, on the one hundred *regentia*. Large and bold script throughout, written in 9 lines to the page, headings in an even slightly larger script. Frequent interlinear explanatory notes in Arabic, written upside down in oblique direction in a smaller script. Beginning (p. 86):

(بسمله) الحمد لله رب العالمين وافضل الصلوة والتسليم على سيدنا محمد واله وصحبه اجمعيم **وبعد**
فاعلم يا اخي وفقك الله وايانا لمرضاته ان النحو علم باصول يعرف بها احوال اواخر الكلم والكلمات
ثلثة انواع اسم كزيد وشجر وفعل كضرب يضرب وحرف كهل وبل وقد وسوف ...

Final words (p. 93):

... نحو جاءنى زيد وعمرو ورأيت عمروا وبكرا ومررت ببكر وخالد، تمت الكتاب بعون الله الملك
الوهاب، برحمتك يا ارحم الرامين،

(6) pp. 94–128. *Taqwīm al-Lisān* (title in margin of p. 94, and also in the beginning of the text). It is an anonymous prose work on Arabic syntax. The author refers to himself in the first person singular (*allaftuhu bi-shawāhid al-Qurʾān*, p. 94). On p. 128, after the end of the text, is a distich (*Muṣannif Taqwīm al-Lisān Mulaqqabun * wa-Ṣāḥib Kashshāfin sammāhu ʾl-Zamakhsharī*) in which the authorship of the text seems to be given to Maḥmūd b. ʿUmar al-Zamakhsharī (d. 538/1144), GAL G I, 292, the author of the *Kashshāf.* Small script, written over 18 lines to the page. Headings and titles in larger and bold script. Beginning (p. 94):

(بسمله) الحمد لله رب العالمين والصلوة والسلام على سيدنا محمد واله وصحبه اجمعين **وبعد** فهذا
كتاب البداية في تقويم اللسان الفته بشواهد القران ليقرب على المتناول ويتقرر في طبع الطالب معناه
ولفظه وبالله التوفيق فاول ذلك باب الكلمة والكلام كلها على ثلثة اضرب اسم وفعل وحرف فالاسم ما
سميت به مسمى ...

Final words (p. 128):

... وان قلت من ابو بكر فهو على الابتدآء والخبر، تمت الكتاب بعون الله الملك الوهاب، برحمتك يا
ارحم الرامين، وصلى الله على خير خلقه سيدنا محمد واله وصحبه اجمعين، والحمد لله رب
العالمين، آمين،

(7) pp. 129–181. Title-page: *Hādhihi al-Tuḥfa al-Wardiyya wa-Sharḥ hādhihi al-Tuḥfa al-Wardiyya li-Mawlānā al-Kabīr Zayn al-Dīn al-Makhdūm al-Awwal al-Fanānī Ibn ʿAlī Aḥmad al-Maʿbarī raḥimahum Allāh taʿālā wa-nafaʿanā bihim fī al-Dārayn Amīn wal-Matn li-ʿUmar b. al-Wardī raḥimahum Allāh taʿālā Amīn bi-Raḥmatak yā Arḥam al-Rāḥimīn.*

The *Tuḥfa* was written by Abū Ḥafṣ ʿUmar Ibn al-Wardī Sirāğ al-Dīn (c. 850/1446), GAL G II, 131. It is an *Urğūza* on Arabic syntax. Beginning (p. 130–131):

(بسمله)
قال الفقير عمر بن الوردي * لله شكري ابدا وحمدي
مصليا علي الرسول العربي * والآل والصحب وتباع النبي
وبعد فالجاهل بالنحو احتقر * اذ كل علم فاليه يفتقر

The commentary is by Zayn al-Dīn b. ʿAlī b. Aḥmad al-Maʿbarī al-Malībārī, who died in Fanān in 928/1522 (GAL G II, 221; S II, 311–312). It consists of interlinear notes only. The lay-out of the work is very wide, as only three lines of the original poem are given on each page. Such a lay-out gives ample space for notes and explanatory remarks. The commentator comments on the *basmala* as follows (p. 130):

الباء متعلق بمحذوف تقديره بسم الله ابتدئ ولا محل لمجموع الجار والمجرور لانه ظرف لغو والظرف اللغو ما كان متعلقة مذكورا نحو مررت بزيد او في حكم المذكور نحو بسم الله ولكن محل المجرور نسب علي المفعولية لانه تعدّي الفعل بحرف الجر ولم تكتب الالف لكثرة الاستعمال وطوّلت الباء عوضا عنها،

Final distich of the *Tuḥfa* (p. 181):

حامدا لله مصليا علي * محمد والال والصحب ولا

To this the commentator adds (p. 181):

حال من اليآء في نظمي ويجيئ الحال من المضاف اليه اذ كان المضاف عاملا في الحال كقوله تعالي الي الله مرجعكم جميعا او كان جزء ما اضيف اليه كقوله تعالي ونزعنا ما في صدورهم من غل اخوانا وكان مثل جزته في صحة الاستغناء عنه بالمضاف اليه كقوله تعالي فاتبعوا ملة ابراهيم حنيفا فانه لو قيل في غير القرأن فاتبعوا ابراهيم حنيفا صح،

Final words (p. 181):

تم الكتاب بعون الله الملك الوهاب، برحمتك يا ارحم الرامين، والحمد لله رب العالمين،

(8) pp. 182–188. *Shawāhid al-Tuḥfa al-Wardiyya* (given title on the basis of information on p. 188: *tamma Kitāb al-Tuḥfa al-Wardiyya maʿa Shawāhidihā wa-yalīhi Sharḥ Qaṭr al-Nadā*). Survey of the lines of illustrative poetry in *al-Tuḥfa al-Wardiyya*. As the end of *al-Tuḥfa al-Wardiyya* was on p. 131, the lines of poetry cannot but be the *Shawāhid* to *al-Tuḥfa al-Wardiyya*. On most words there is an interlinear note in Arabic in small script indicating the syntactical function. The distichs are written in a medium-size script, with 11 lines to the page. Beginning (p. 182):

(بسمله)
ان اباها وابا اباها * قد بلغا في المجد غايتاها
رأيت الوليد بن اليزيد مباركا * شديد ابا عباء الخلافة كاهله

Final words (p. 188):

يا اقرع بن حابس يا اقرع * انك ان يصرع اخوك تصرع
وان اتاه خليل يوم مسئلة * يقول لا غائب مالي ولا حرم
برحمتك يا ارحم الرامين، وصلي الله علي خير خلقه سيدنا محمد واله وصحبه اجمعين، والحمد لله رب العالمين،
تم كتاب التحفة الوردية مع شواهدها ويليها شرح قطر الندي،

(9) pp. 189–293. Title-page (p. 189):

> *Hādhā Kitāb ʿAyn al-Hudā bi-Sharḥ Qaṭr al-Nadā wal-Sharḥ lil-ʿĀlim al-ʿAllāma al-Shaykh ʿUthmān al-Madfūn fī Wasaṭ Ṭaraf Ǧihat al-Shamāl min Maqbarat al-Masǧid al-Ǧāmiʿ al-Fanānī yuzāru baʿd al-Ṣalawāt al-Khams dāʾiman wal-Matn li-Ibn Hishām raḥimahumā Allāh taʿāla wa-raḥimanā maʿahum fil-Dunyā wal-Ākhira wa-ʿĀfānā Allāh min Ǧamīʿ Balāʾ al-Dunyā wa-Maʿībātihā wa-ʿAdhāb al-Ākhira wa-tawaffanā Muslimīn wa-alḥaqanā bil-ʿāliʾīn, bi-Raḥmatak yā Arḥam al-Rāḥimīn.*

*Qaṭr al-Nadā* is *Qaṭr al-Nadā wa-Ball al-Ṣadā*, the work on Arabic syntax by ʿAbdallāh b. Yūsuf Ibn Hishām (d. 761/1360), GAL G II, 23. The commentary *ʿAyn al-Hudā* was written by al-Shaykh ʿUthmān, who is buried in the central part of the North side of the cemetery of Friday mosque of Fanān (which is possibly identical with present-day Ponnani). It is apparently a locally written commentary and does not seem to be known in the bibliographical literature. The commentary is a running commentary, wherein the *matn* is written in large and bold script, whereas the sharḥ is written in a smaller script, in 18 lines to the page. Beginning of the commentary, with the matn in bold script (p. 190):

(بسمله) الحمد لله موجه من يشاء نحو الهدى والصلوة والسلام على سيدنا محمد ارفع من نصب
لخفض العدى **وبعد** فهذا ما احتاج اليه المتعلمون ذوو الابتداء المتعطشون الى التروى بقطر الندى
للشيخ العالم العلامة ابي عبدالله جمال الدين محمد بن يوسف بن هشام الانصاري ... **الكلمة** في اللغة
تطلق على الجمل المفيدة كقوله تعالى كلا انها كلمة هو قائلها وفي الاصطلاح **قول مفرد** ...

Final words (p. 293):

... **كما بقي** اي كما يجب الكسر في الباقي من الفعل الماضي المتجاوز اربعة احرف وامره
ومصدره والاسماء الاعشرة المتقدمة، هذا اخر ما تيسر ايراده علي هذه المتقدمة المرجو من فضل
الله تعالي ان يجعله من صالح الاعمال المتقدمة والمسئول ممن اطلع فيه علي خلل ان يصلحه
بالمكرمة، والحمد لله الذي هدينا لهذا وما كنا لنهتدي لولا ان هدينا الله ولا حول ولا قوة الا بالله
العلي العظيم، وصلي الله علي خير خلقه سيدنا محمد واله وصحبه اجمعين، والحمد لله رب
العالمين،

(10) pp. 293–300. *Shawāhid al-Qaṭr* (title on p. 293). A survey of the illustrative poetical quotations occurring in the *Qaṭr al-Nadā wa-Ball al-Ṣadā* by Ibn Hishām. The names of the chapters of the Qaṭr al-Nadā are written in the margins. First line (p. 293):

اذا قالت حذام فصد قوها * فانا القول ما قالت حذام

The last line (p. 300) reads as a copyist verse:

لكاتبه سعادات تدوم * من الرحمن ما طلعت نجوم

## 2

A collective volume with texts in Arabic on Islamic dogmatics and Islamic law.

Title-page (identical with front cover):

> *Sabʿat Kutub.* Minhāğ al-Ṣaghīr (see Figure 3), Sharḥ Āmantu billāh, ʿIshrūn Ṣifa, Sanūsī, Fatḥ al-Raḥmān, Qayd al-Ğāmiʿ, Iḥyā Narṣawm. Ighin Ayž Kitābukāḍ. ʿĀmir al-Islām Power Press, Tirūrangādi, 121 + [1] pp, 19.8 cm.

Colophon on p. 121:

> *Hiğra 1403 Shawwāl 19, ʿĪssawiyya 1983 July 30. Tirūrangadi. C.H. Muḥammad Ānrsans ʿĀmiru al-Islām Power Press & Company. Kāna Allāh li-man khaṭṭa hādhihi al-Kutub wa-liman ishtaghala fī Ṭabʿihā wa-ʾāḥib al-Maṭābiʿ fil-Dīn wal-Dunyā wal-Ākhira.*

On the unnumbered reverse of p. 121 is a list of books published by the same producer. On the back of the end cover the press is called: C.H. Muḥammad Ānrsans ʿĀmiru al-Islām Litho Power Press, Tirūrangādi. The same print is on the back cover of volume no. 3, below. Tirurangadi is a small town in the Malapuram district of Kerala. It is located 30 km south of Calicut.

(1) pp. 2–42. *Mukhtaṣar al-Minhāğ lil-Ghazzālī* (title and author so on p. 2; on the title page: *Minhāğ al-Ṣaghīr*). An anonymous compendium of the *Minhāğ al-ʿĀbidīn ilā Manāzil al-Muttaqīn* by Abū Ḥāmid Muḥammad b. Muḥammad al-Ghazzālī (d. 505/1111), GAL G I, 423. Small script, with headers in bolder and larger script, written in 19 lines to the page (see Figure 4).

Beginning (p. 2):

> (بسملة) وبه نستعين، الحمد لله الذي ارشد المومنين الى منهاج العابدين، والصلوة والسلام على من
> ارسله رحمة للعالمين، وعلى اله وصحبه الذين شيّدوا الدين، وبعد فهذا مختصر المنهاج للغزالي
> سيد المصنفين رحمه الله وسائر الصالحين موسوم بارشاد المريدين الى منهاج العابدين والمسئول
> من قاضي الحاجات ان يوفقني للعمل به والاقتداء بالمهتدين ويتوقاني مسلما ويلحقني بالصالحين وقد
> نظمت العقبات السبع سردا في ابيات وهي هذه ...

After the versification of the seven *ʿUqba* (p. 2), the author of the compendium from p. 3 onwards proceeds to comment on each *ʿUqba.* Final words (p. 42):

> ... ان الله لغني عن العالمين، استغفر الله من كل ما زلّ به القدم وجر به القلم ونسأله ان يجعلنا
> واياكم علينا عاملين واوجهه به من يدين وان لا يجعله وبالا علينا وان نضعه في ميزان الصالحات
> اذ اوزنت اعمالنا امة جواد كريم، تمت الكتاب بعون الله الملك الوهاب، وصلى الله على محمد وآله
> وصحبه اجمعين،

(2) pp. 43–52. *Sharḥ Āmantu billāh* (title on p. 43). Anonymous commentary on the *Arkān al-Īmān*, the pillars of the Islamic creed. Small script, with headers in bolder and larger script, written in 19 lines to the page. Beginning (p. 43):

> شرح آمنت بالله
> (بسملة) الحمد لله رب العالمين والصلوة والسلام على سيدنا محمد واله وصحبة اجمعين **اما بعد**
> فاول ما يجب على العاقل البالغ الايمان وبؤمر بقلبه ويقر بلسانه بان يقول **امنت بالله** اي بالله
> صبحانه وتعالى واحد لا شريك له حي ازلي لا بداية لازليته ابدي ...

Figure 3. Sabʿat Kutub. Title page of a collective volume with religious texts. Tirūrangādī 1983. No. 2, p. 1.

Figure 4. Opening page of *Mukhtaṣar al-Minhāǧ lil-Ghazzālī*, Tirūrangādi 1983. No. 2 (1), p. 2.

Final words (p. 52):

... لئلا يقع فيه الجهل والسهو او النسيان فاذا اصدر عنه ذلك حكم بارتداده والعياذ بالله منه آمين،
تمت الكتاب بعون الله الماجد المنان الرؤف الرحيم رب تمم بالخير والسعادة وارجمنا معهم برحمتك
يا ارحم الراحمين، وصلى الله على خير خلقه سيدنا محمد وآله وصحبه اجمعين، والحمد لله رب
العالمين،

(3) pp. 52–57. *ʿIshrūn Ṣifa* (title and author on p. 52). This is in fact the work known as *Umm al-Barāhīn*, or ʿAqīdat Ahl al-Tawḥīd al-Ṣughrā, the shorter creed by Abū ʿAbdallāh Muḥammad b. Yūsuf al-Sanūsī (d. 892/1486), GAL G II, 250, treating the twenty divine attributes. The title *ʿIshrūn Ṣifa* is the Arabic version of the title under which this text has become known in the Malay world, *Sipat duapuluh*. Small script, with headers in bolder and larger script, written in 19 lines to the page. Beginning (p. 52):

عشرون صفة
(بسملة) قال ابو عبدالله محمد بن يوسف السنوسي رحمه الله تعالى الحمد لله رب العالمين والصلوة
والسلام علىرسول الله اعلم ان الحكم العقلي ينحصر على ثلثة اقسام الوجوب والاستحالة والجواز
...

Final words (p. 57):

... وسلام على جميع الانبياء والمرسلين والحمد لله رب العالمين تمت هذه العقائد المجموعة بصفات
مولانا عز وجل وصلى الله على خير خلقه سيدنا محمد وعلى اله وصحبه اجمعين،

(4) pp. 57–93. *Hādhā Kitāb al-Sanūsī* (titles and authors on p. 57). The running commentary by Muḥammad b. ʿUmar b. Ibrāhīm al-Malānī *thumma* al-Tilimsānī (lived 897/1492, see Voorhoeve, *Handlist*, pp. 387–388) on *Umm al-Barāhīn*, the creed by Abū ʿAbdallāh Muḥammad b. Yūsuf al-Sanūsī (d. 892/1486), GAL G II, 250 (see previously described text). Brockelmann, GAL II, 251, refers for a copy of this commentary to MSS Berlin, Ahlwardt nos 2015–2016, and has as date of life of al-Tilimsānī c. 1000/1591. He also has the *nisbā* al-Mallālī ('from Melilla'), whereas the Kerala imprint described here clearly has al-Malānī. In *GAL* S II, 354, Brockelmann has further references to manuscripts and also a title for the commentary: *Fatḥ al-Mubīn*. The *sharḥ* is written in small script, with the *matn* in bolder and larger script, in 19 lines to the page. Beginning (p. 57):

هذا كتاب السنوسي،
(بسملة) وبه نستعين، رب يسر ولا تعسر يا كريم هو حي ونعم الوكيل يقول العبد الفقير محمد بن
عمر بن ابراهيم الملاقي ثم التلمساني غفر الله له ولوالديه بمنه وكرمه ... وبعد فقد سألني بعض
المحبين شرح الله قلبي وقلبه بانوار اليقين وجعلني واياه من العلماء العاملين المخلصين ان اصنع له
شرحا مختصرا مفيدا يستعين به هو وغيره من المبتدئين على فهم عقيدة الشيخ الامام ... سيدى ابي
عبدالله محمد بن يوسف السنوسي الحسني ...

Final words (pp. 92–93):

... وبالله التوفيق لا رب غيره ولا يخفى عليك حسن مناسبة دعاء الشيخ لنفسه ولاجئته بالختم على
اكمل الحالات وذلك بالنطق بها واستحضار العلم بها وليكن هذا اخر ما قصرته من هذا الشرح
المبارك المفيد فسنسأله سبحانه ان ينفع به دنيا واخرى كل من اعتقد به من اخواننا المؤمنين وان
يجمعنا بفضله مع الشيخ وسائر الاحبة في اعلى عليين || بجاه سيد الاولين والآخرين سيدنا ونبينا
ومولانا محمد صلى الله عليه وسلم وعلى اله وصحبه اجمعين وسلم على جميع الانبياء والمرسلين
والحمد لله رب العالمين وعلى عباده الذين اصطفى اللهم صل وسلم على سيدنا محمد واله صلوة
تحل العقد وتفرج الكرب يا رب العالمين والحمد لله رب العالمين،

(5) pp. 93–97. *Hādhā Kitāb Fatḥ al-Raḥmān fīl-Islām wal-Īmān taṣnīf al-Shaykh al-Imām al-ʿĀlim al-ʿAllāma Muḥammad b. Ziyād al-Ṣanāǧī raḥimahu Allāh* (title and author on p. 93). This is a short treatise on the pillars of Islam and the pillars of *Īmān*, which are here summarized as coming from the mouth of Ǧibrīl. There are several elementary works on these pillars with the title *Fatḥ al-Raḥmān* (see Voorhoeve, *Handlist*, p. 80). Small script, with headers in bolder and larger script, written in 19 lines to the page. Beginning (p. 93):

**هذا كتاب فتح الرحمن في الاسلام والايمان** تصنيف الشيخ الامام العالم العلامة محمد بن زياد
الصناجي رحمه الله،
(بسملة) وبه نستعين، الحمد لله الملك العلام والصلوة والسلام على سيدنا محمد افضل الانام وعلى
اله الكرام وصحابته الاعلام **وبعد** فهذا كتاب في الايمان والاسلام المدين رتب الله على وجودهما
الخلود في دار السلام وعلى فقدهما الخلود في دار الانتقام ...

Final words (p. 97):

... فنسأل الله التوفيق والهداية والحماية والرعاية تقوم بمأمورات خالقنا ونجتنب منهيات بارئنا
فتكون من المتقين الفائزين يا الله يا الله ارحم الراحمين وصلى الله على خير خلقه سيدنا محمد واله
وصحبه وسلم،

(6) pp. 97–113. *Kitāb Qayd al-Ǧāmiʿ*, by Ḥusayn b. Aḥmad (title and author on p. 97). The text is a *Mukhtaṣar* on the subject of *Arkān al-Nikāḥ*, marriage according to Islamic law. Small script, with headers in bolder and larger script, written in 19 lines to the page.

Beginning (pp. 97–98):

**كتاب قيد الجامع**
(بسملة) وبه نستعين، الحمد لله الديّان الرحمن الرحيم وصلى الله وسلم على خير من تزوج وامر به
لتحصين الفروع اي احصان وعلى اله وصحبه الموفين بالعمود والايمان وعلى من يتبعهم باحسان
**اما بعد** فقد قال الفقيه حسين بن احمد ارضاه الله بالجنة سألني بعض احبّائي حفظهم الله تعالى || ان
اصنف لهم كتابا مختصرا نافعا في اركان النكاح واحكامه ومعرفة ما يحل منه وما يحرم منه
فاجبتهم الى ذلك طالبا للثواب وراغبا الى الله سبحانه وتعالى في الصواب وهو حسبي وعليه توكلت
واليه المأب كتاب النكاح اعلم ارشدك الله وايانا بتوفيق منه ان الله عز وجل رغب في النكاح في
محكم كتابه العزيز فقال وهو اصدق القائلين فانكحوا ما طاب لكم من النساء مثنى وثلث ورباع فان
خفتم ...

Final words (p. 113):

... ويباح له منها جميع فنون الاستمتاع بها التي لا ضرر بها الا الاتيان في الدبر والوطء في حال
الحيض فانهما محرمان عليهما تحريما مؤكدا لقوله صلى الله عليه وسلم من اتى امرأته في حيضها
او في دبرها فان محمدا صلى الله عليه وسلم برئ منه والله وجميع الملئكة برئ منه نعوذ بالله منها
تمت الكتاب بعون الله الملك الوهاب برحمتك يا ارحم الراحمين،

(7) pp. 114–121. *Iḥyānrūṣawm.* Anonymous treatise on the principles of fasting (*Ṣawm*). The title (p. 114) is in a combination of Malayalam and Arabic, but the text is entirely in Arabic. The text is divided into an introduction, three sections (*faṣl*) and an epilogue. Small script, with headers in bolder and larger script, written in 19 lines to the page. Beginning (p. 114):

**احيانرصوم**
(بسملة) الحمد لله الذي اعظم على عباده المنة بما دفع عنهم كيد الشيطان وفنه ... والصلوة والسلام
على سيدنا محمد قائد الخلق وممهد السنة وعلى اله وصحبه ذوي الاراء الثاقبة والعقول المرجحة
وسلم تسليما كثيرا **اما بعد** فان الصوم ربع الايمان بمقتضى قوله صلى الله عليه وسلم الصوم نصف
الصبر وبمقتضى قوله صلى الله عليه وسلم الصبر نصف الايمان ...

Final words (p. 121):

... وذكروا ان ذلك يقسي القلب ويولمه ردئ العادات ويفتح ابواب الشهوات ولعمرى هو كذلك في
اكثر الخلق لا سيما من ان يأكل في اليوم والليلة مرتين فهذا ما اردنا ذكره من ترتيب المطوع به
والله سبحانه وتعالى اعلم تم الكتاب بحمد الله ومنه وحسن توفيقه برحمتك يا ارحم الراحمين، آمين،

This being the last text in the volume, there follows the printer's colophon for all texts.

## 3

An interlinear commentary by two Malabarese authors on *al-Alfiyya*, the textbook of Arabic syntax by Muḥammad b. ʿAbdallāh Ibn Mālik al-Ṭāʾī (d. 672/1274), GAL G I, 298. The first commentator is Zayn al-Dīn al-Makhdūm al-Maʿbarī (d. 928/1522), the second commentator his son ʿAbd al-ʿAzīz (d. 994/1586). Neither commentator seems to be mentioned by Brockelmann. Whether or not there is a family connection between either of these two grammatical scholars and the Ponnani historian Shaykh Zayn al-Dīn al-Maʿbarī (d. 987/1579), GAL G II, 416, the author of the *Tuḥfat al-Muǧāhidīn*, is not clear.[6]

Title-page (p. 1, see Figure 5):

> *Sharḥ al-Khulāṣa al-Alfiyya. Kitāb al-Shāriḥayn al-Imām al-Baḥr al-Ḥabr al-Niḥrīr Mawlānā wa-Mawlā al-Ǧahābidha al-Shaykh Zayn al-Dīn al-Makhdūm al-Maʿbarī wa-Ibn al-Shaykh al-Fāḍil al-ʿAllāma ʿAbd al-ʿAzīz ʿalā Alfiyyat al-Imām al-Aʿẓam al-ʿĀrif billāh taʿālā Abī ʿAbdallāh b. Mālik al-Ṭāʾī fil-Naḥw raḥimahum Allāh wa-nafaʿanā bihim wa-Sāʾir al-Muslimīn fil-Dārayn Āmīn wa-sayaʾtī fī Ākhir al-Kitāb Abḥāth al-Shāriḥayn in shāʾa Allāh taʿālā fal-yataʾammal.* [*dūbayt*]. *Al-Ṭabʿ wal-Nashr: C.H. Muḥammad Ānrsans, Tirūrangādī, Kerala.* 363 pp., 19.6 cm.

[6] Asher and Karassery spell 'Makhdūm' in the historian's name as Maqdoom.

# شرح الخلاصة الالفية

كتاب الشارحين الامام البحر الحبر النحرير مولانا ومولى الجهابذة
الشيخ زين الدين المخدوم المعبري وابن الشيخ الفاضل
العلامة عبد العزيز على الفية الامام الاعظم العارف
بالله تعالى ابى عبد الله بن مالك الطائي في النحو
رحمهم الله ونفعنا بهم وسائر المسلمين في الدارين
آمين وسيأتي في اخر الكتاب ابحاث الشارحين
ان شاء الله تعالى فليتأمل

كثرت شروحهم على الألفية　　اضواؤها كالأنجم الدرية
لكنها لما تجلت شمسها　　بالطبع والأضواء اذن مخفية

الطبع والنشر:— سي. اجهه. محمد آنر سنس
ترورنگاڈی، کیرلہ

Figure 5. Title page of the commentary by two Malabrese scholarson the *Alfiyya* by Ibn Mālik. Tirūrangādī n.d. (c. 1983?). No. 3.

On p. 336 is a biographical note on the author of the two commentators of the *Alfiyya*: The first commentator, from the land of Ponnāni died 57 or 56 years old after midnight on Friday 16 Shaʿbān 928 (1522). The second commentator, the son of the first commentator, died early in the morning on 16 Ramaḍān 994 (1586). On pp. 337–361: Hādhihi Shawāhid al-Alfiyya. On p. 361 is also the printer's colophon: *Faqad tamma Ṭabʿ Kitāb al-Alfiyya li-Ibn Mālik raḥimahu Allāh wa-nafaʿanā bi-ʿUlūmihi Āmīn. ʿĀmir al-Islām Litho Power Press, Tirūrangādī, Kerala.* This text is repeated on the pasted back cover, the same as on the back cover of volume no. 2, above. On pp. 363–363: *Fihrist al-Alfiyya*, the table of contents of the *matn*. The lay-out of the main part of the work is made very wide, with only three lines of the *matn* in fully vocalized bold script on each page, so that there is ample space for the interlineary *sharḥ*. Title-page (p. 1):

شرح الخلاصة الالفية، كتاب الشارحين الامام البحر الحبر النحرير مولانا ومولى الجهابذة الشيخ
زين الدين المخدوم المعبرىّ وابن الشيخ الفاضل العلامة عبد العزيز على الفيّة الامام الاعظم
العارف بالله تعالى ابى عبدالله بن مالك الطائي فى النحورحمهم الله ونفعنا بهم وسائر المسلمين فى
الدارين آمين وسيأتى فى اخر الكتاب ابحاث الشارحين ان شاء الله تعالى فليتأمل،
كثرت شروحهم على الألفية * اضواؤها كالأنجم الدرية
لكنها لما تجلت شمسها * بالطبع فالأضوا إذن مخفية،
الطبع والنشر: سى. اچهّ. محمد آنرسنس، ترورنگاڈی، كيرله

Beginning of the *Alfiyya* (p. 2, see Figure 6):

(بسملة) وبه نستعين
قال محمد هو ابن مالك * احمد ربى الله خير مالك
مصليا على الرسول المصطفى * واله المستكملين الشرفا

Beginning of the commentary, here of the respective words of the *basmala* (p. 2):

الباء متعلق بمحذوف تقديره بسمالله ابتداء ولا محل لمجموع الجار والمجرورلانه ظرف لغو
والظرف اللغو ما كان متعلقه مذكورا نحو مررت بزيد او في حكم المذكور نحو بسم الله ولكن محلّ
المجرورتضب علي المفعولية لانه تعد الفعل بحرف الجر ولمن يكتب الالف لكثرة الاستعمال
وطوّلت الباء عوضا عنها، الي المؤمنين خاصة بالمغفرةودخول الجنة وهما اسما بنيا للمبالغة من
رحم، المحسن الي البر والفاجر بالرزق ودفع الافات، اسم الموجود الحق الجامع للصفات الاليهية
ولاشبه انه جار مجري الاعلام،

On p. 326 is the end of the *matn*, with some commentary, and this followed by a historical note on the two Malabarese authors:

وآله الغر الكرام البررة * وصحبه المنتخبين الخيرة
تمت قصيدة الالفية لابن مالك الاندلسي رحمه الله ونفعنا بعلمه في الدارين امين،
ترجمة الشارحين علي الالفية رحمهما الله تعالى، توفي الشيخ الشارح الاول من بلد فنّان وهو ابن
سبع او ست وخمسين بعد نصف ليلة الجمعة السادسة عشر من شهر شعبان سنة ٩٢٨ ثمان
وعشرين وتسعمائة من الهجرة النبوية وتوفي ايضا ابنه الشارح الثاني وقت الضحي السادس عشر
من رمضان سنه ٩٩٤ تسعمائة وتسعين واربعة من هجرة خير الانام، صلي الله عليه وسلم وعلي
اله بالدوام، نسئل الله الحسن عند الختام، برحمتك يا ارحم الراحمين،

بسم الله الرحمن الرحيم

(٢) قال محمد هو ابن مالك أحمد ربي الله خير مالك

مصليا على الرسول المصطفى وآله المستكملين الشرفا

Figure 6. Beginning of the *Alfiyya* by Ibn Mālik with interlineary commentary by two Malabrese scholars. Tirūrangādī n.d. (c. 1983?). No. 3, p. 2.

On pp. 337–361 the *Shawāhid*, the poetical quotations and references, of the *Alfiyya* are given, in order of occurrence in the *matn*, in small script of 19 lines to the page. Beginning:

**هذه شواهد الالفية،**
الكلام وما يتألف منه
اقلي اللوم عاذل والعتابن * وقولي ان اصبت لقد اصابن

On p. 361 is the end of the *Shawāhid*:

الادغام
فعض الطرف انك من نمير * فلا كعبا بلغت ولا كلابا

There follows the printer's colophon, the first line written in what would seem to be a local variant of *thuluth* script:

فقد تم طبع كتاب الالفية لابن مالك رحمه الله ونفعنا بعلومه آمين، عامر الاسلام لتّو پور پرس،
ترورنگاڈی، كيرله

On pp. 362–363 is the table of contents of the chapters of the Alfiyya, headed by *Fihrist al-Alfiyya.*

## 4

A compendium of Shāfiʿite *fiqh*.

> *Kitāb ʿUmdat al-Sālik wa-ʿUddat al-Nāsik lil-Imām al-Hammām Shaykh al-Islām wa-Qudwat al-Anām al-Shaykh Shihāb al-Dīn Abī al-ʿAbbās Aḥmad b. al-Naqīb al-Miṣrī taghammadahu Allāh bi-Ghufrānihi wa-ʿammahu bi-Riḍwānihi wa-ḥaqqāhu bi-Nawālihi Āmīn. C.H. Printing Works, Unniyūr, Dari Wāḷaguḷam (Malapuram ğil) Kerala.* 131 + [1] pp., 19 cm.

The author of this compendium on Islamic law is Shihāb al-Dīn Aḥmad b. Luʾluʾ Ibn al-Naqīb al-Rūmī al-Miṣrī (d. 769/1368), GAL S II, 104. His sources are (see introduction on p. 2) the works by al-Rāfiʿī (d. 623/1226, probably his work *al-Muḥarrar*), and by al-Nawawī (d. 676/1278), whose *Minhāğ al-Ṭālibīn* is in fact a reworked compendium of al-Rāfiʿī's *al-Muḥarrar.*[7]

On p. 131 is the printer's colophon: Hiğra 1397 Ramaḍān 20 ʿĪsawiyya 1977 September 4, Unniyūr, Parampil Staha Pač C.H. Printing Works tin Aččadī Kappadat, katabahu Pukkar b. Kačpūkkar al-Pānančīr ghafara Allāh lahumā Āmīn.

Small script with bolder script for headings, written over 18 lines to the page. Chapter heading also in bold script in the margins. Title-page (p. 1, see Figure 7):

**كتاب عمدة السالك وعدّة الناسك**، للامام الهمام شيخ الاسلام وقدوة الانام الشيخ شهاب الدين ابي
العباس احمد بن النقيب المصري تغمده الله بغفرانه وعمّه برضوانه وحقاه بنواله آمين، سي. اچهـ.
پرندنگ وركس، ونّيور، درّ – واصكصم، (ملپرم جل) كيرله

[7] See for a still very useful survey of works on Islamic law with indications of how these are interrelated, Th.W. Juynboll, *Handleiding tot de kennis van de Mohammedaansche Wet volgens de leer der Shâfiʿitische school.* Leiden (E.J. Brill) 1930, pp. 373–378.

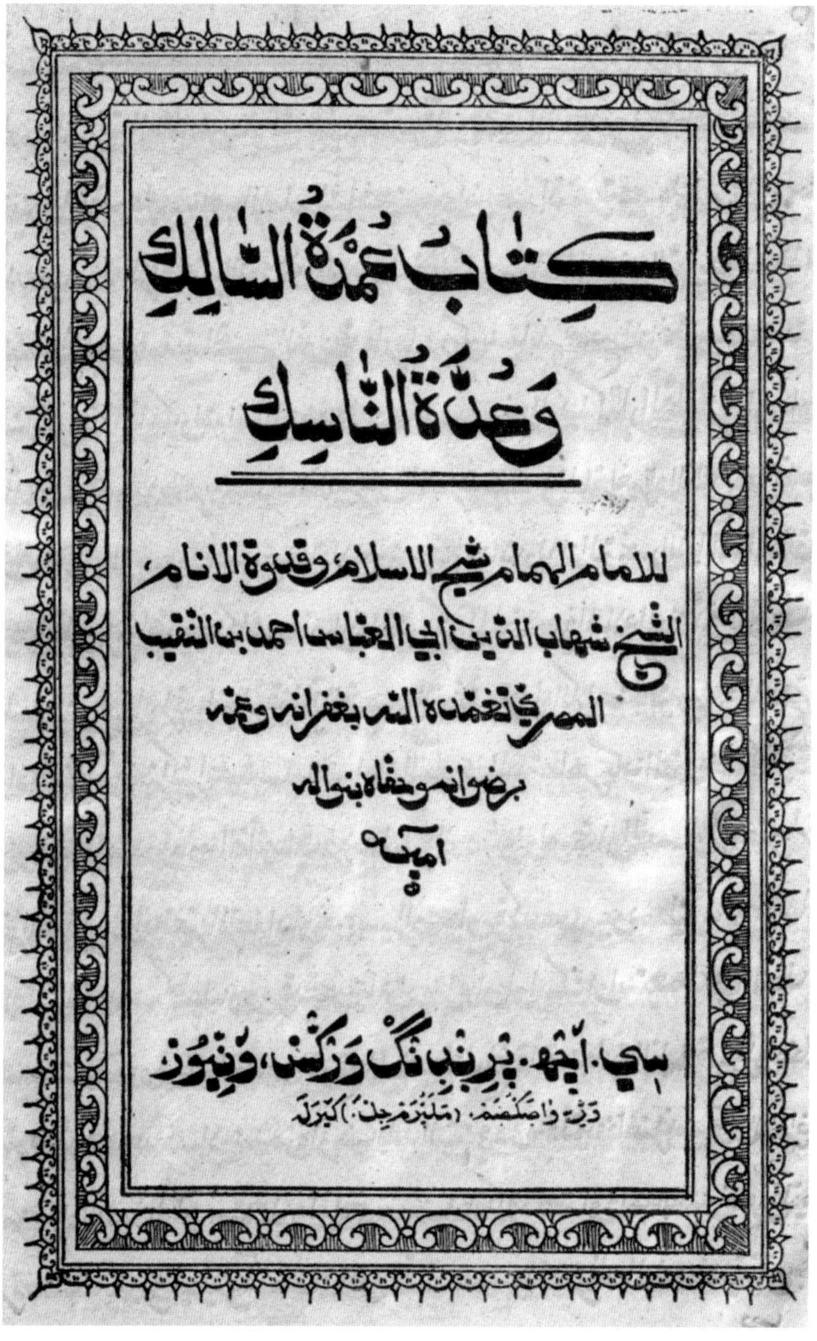

كتاب عمدة السالك

وعدة الناسك

للامام الهمام شيخ الاسلام وقدوة الانام

الشيخ شهاب الدين ابي العباس احمد بن النقيب

المصري تغمده الله بغفرانه وعمه

برضوانه وشفاه بنواله

امين

سي. اچه. برنبنگ ورکشن، ونيون

درر- واصکمنم. (ملبرم جل.) کيرله

Figure 7. Title page of *ʿUmdat al-Sālik wa-l-ʿUddat al-Nāsik*, the law compendium by Ibn al-Naqīb, Umiyūr 1977. No. 4.

Beginning (p. 2, see Figure 8):

(بسملة) وبه نستعين، الحمد لله رب العالمين وصلي الله علي محمد وآله وصحبه اجمعين **وبعد** هذا
مختصر الفته في الفقه علي مذهب الامام الشافعي رضي الله عنه اقتصرت فيه على ذكر الصحيح
من المذهب عند الرافعي والنووي او احدهما وقد اذكر فيه خلافا في بعض الصور وذلك اذا ...
كتاب الطهارة باب المياه ...

End (p. 131), the last chapter being the *Kitāb al-Shahāda*:

اما عيوب الوجه والكفين من النساء فانه لا يقبل فيها الا الرجال وقد تقدم في باب صوم رمضان
ثبوته بواحد والله اعلم، بالصواب وحسن التوفيق تمت الكتاب بعون الله الملك، الوهاب، الكريم المنان،
رب يسر ولا تعسر يا كريم، برحمتك يا ارحم الراحمين، والحمد لله اولا واخرا وظاهرا وباطنا
وصلي الله علي محمد وآله وصحبه وسلم امين،

Here follows the printer's colophon:

**تمت**، هجرة ١٣٩٧ رمضان ٢٠ عيسوية ١٩٧٧ سپتمپر ٤ تيّت ونيور پرمپل ستها پچ سي.
اچهـ. برندنگ ورکسل تن اچد کپدت، کتبه پوکر بن کچپوکر الپانچیر غفر الله لهما آمين،

On the unnumbered page ([132]) is an ornamented imprint by the printer, which is repeated on the back cover, just as is the case with volume no. 1, above.

## 5

A collective volume with twelve pieces of religious poetry (eleven *Qaṣāʾid* and a short fragment, see Figure 9).

> *Hādhihi Mağmūʿat kutub min Qaṣīdāt Shams al-Īmān* 1 *wa-Qaṣīda Ukhrā fil-Masāʾil al-Iʿtiqādiyya* 2 *Adhkiyā* 3 *Razzāna* 4 *Ṣalāḥ al-Dīn* 5 *Badʾ al-Amāl* 6 *Kifāyat al-ʿAwāmm* 7 *Nafāʾis al-Durar* 8 *Zubad* 9 *Bānat Suʿād* 10 *Dhakhr al-Maʿād* 11 *lil-Imām al-Būṣīrī raḥimahu Allāh taʿālā wa-nafaʿanā bi-ʿUlūmihi fil-Dārayn Āmīn. ʿĀmir al-Islām Litho Power Press, Tīrurangādī, Kerala.* 148 pp., 19.5 cm.

On p. 148 is a list of books published by the publisher of the present volume. Small script of 18 lines to the page, with occasionally headers in bold writing.
Title-page (p. 1):

هذه مجموعة كتب من قصيدات شمس الايمان ١ وقصيدة اخرى في المسائل الاعتقادية ٢ اذكيا ٣
رزانة ٤ صلاح الدين ٥ بدأ الامال ٦كفاية العوام ٧ نفائس الدرر ٨زبد ٩ بانت سعاد ١٠ ذخر
المعاد ١١ للامام البوصيري رحمه الله تعالى ونفعنا بعلومه في الدارين آمين،
عامر الاسلام لتّو پور پرسّ، ترورنگاڈی، کيرله

(1) pp. 2–11. *Qaṣīdat Shams al-Īmān fī Tawḥīd al-Raḥmān wa-ʿAqīdat Ahl al-Ḥaqq wal-Itqān* … which is said to be the first *qaṣīda* in the work *al-Durar*, a collection of poetry by ʿAbdallāh b. Asʿad (text has Saʿd) b. ʿAlī al-Yāfiʿī al-Yamanī al-Shāfiʿī *Nazīl al-Ḥaramayn al-Sharīfayn* (title and author on p. 2). The author is ʿAbdallāh b. Asʿad b. ʿAlī al-Yāfiʿī (d. 768/1367), GAL G II, 176–177. GAL G II, 177, No. 2 refers to MS Berlin, Ahlwardt No. 2000. It is possible that with the *Kitāb al-Durar* his work *al-Durr al-Naẓīm fī Khawāṣṣ al-*

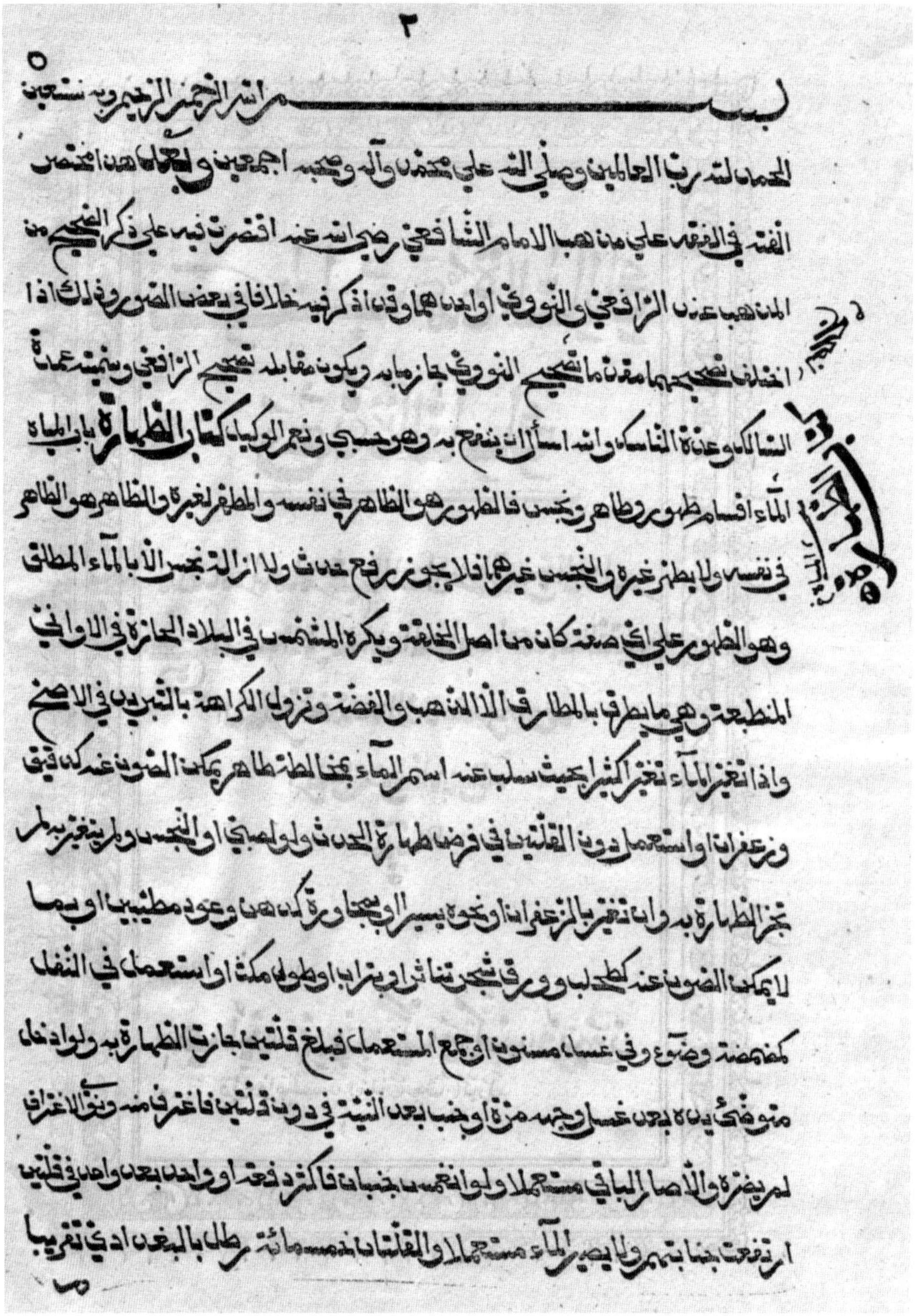

Figure 8. Beginning of ʿUmdat al-Sālik wa-l-ʿUddat al-Nāsik, the law compendium by Ibn al-Naqīb, Umiyūr 1977. No. 4, p. 2.

٢

بسم الله الرحمن الرحيم

الحمد لله حق حمده وصلى الله على سيدنا محمد وآله وصحبه اجمعين

هذه القصيدة المسماة بشمس الايمان في توحيد الرحمن وعقيدة اهل الحق

والايقان والتشويق الى الجنان والحور الحسان والتخويف من النيران ووعظ الغافلين

وهي الاولى من قصائد كتاب الدر من نظم العبد المسكين الحقير الفقير

الى الله الغني الكريم سبحانه وتعالى عبد الله بن اسعد بن علي اليافعي اليمني

الشافعي نزيل الحرمين الشريفين رحمه الله تعالى حلية الايمان ونور قلبه بنور العرفان ورفع

درجته وسلمه من النيران ووالديه واحبابه والمسلمين والاخوان الملك الوهاب المنان آمين

تبارك من شكر الورى عنه يقصر ... لكون ايادي جوده ليس تحصر

وشاكرها محتاج شكر لشكرها ... كذا ان شكر الشكر محتاج يشكر

ففي كل شكر نعمة بعد نعمة ... بغير تناه دونها الشكر يصغر

فمن رام يقضي حق واجب شكرها ... تحمل ضمن الشكر ما هو اكبر

فسبحان من لا قط يبلغ مدحه ... بليغ ومن عنه الثنا متعذر

ففي الفعل منه لاعن جميل صفاته ... وعن ذاته كل البرايا تحيروا

تسبحه الحيتان في الما وفي الفلا ... وحوش وطير في الهواء مسخر

وفي الفلك الافلاك كل مسبح ... نهار وليلا دائما ليس يفتر

تسبح كل الكائنات بحمده ... سماء وارض والجبال والبحر

جميعا وغربين والكل خاضع ... لهيبته العظمى ولا يتكبر

Figure 9. Beginning of Qaṣīdat Shams al-Imān by al-Yāfiʿī. Tirūrangādī 1981. No. 5 (1), p.2.

*Qur'ān al-ʿAḷīm* is meant. Title and author on p. 2. Beginning of the introduction in prose (p. 2, see Figure 10):

( بسملة) الحمد لله حق حمده وصلى الله على سيدنا محمد وآله وصحبه اجمعين، هذه القصيدة المسماة بشمس الايمان في توحيد الرحمن وعقيدة اهل الحق والاتقان والتشويق الى الجنان والحور الحسان والتخويف من النيران ووعظ الاخوان وهي الاولى من كتاب الدرر من النظم العبيد المسكين الحقير الفقير الى الله ... عبدالله بن سعد بن علي اليافعي اليمني الشافعي نزيل الحرمين الشريفين ...

First line of the *qaṣīda* of 160 distichs, rhyming in *rā'* (p. 2):

تبارك من شكر تاورى عنه يقصر * لكون ايادي جوده ليس تحصر

Last line of the *qaṣīda* (p. 11):

وتمت وفاح الحمد لله ختمها * شدى دونه في العرف مسك وعنبر

Colophon (p. 11):

تمت القصيدة المسماة بشمس الايمان في توحيد الرحمن وتتلوها قصيدة اخرى وهي مشتملة على المسائل الاعتقادية الضرورية وهي هذه

(2) pp. 11–16. *Qaṣīda Ukhrā wa-hiya Mushtamila ʿalā al-Masā'il al-Iʿtiqādiyya al-Ḍarūriyya* (title on p. 11), or al-Qaṣīda fil-Masā'il al-Iʿtiqādiyya (title on p. 16). Anonymous *qaṣīda dāliyya* of 83 distichs. First line of the *qaṣīda* (p. 11):

(بسملة) وبه ثقتي،
ساحمد ربي طاعة وتعبدا * وانظم عقدا في العقيدة اوحدا

Last line of the *qaṣīda* (p. 16):

كذاك سلام الله ثم رضاؤه * على الال والازواج والصحب سرمدا
تمت القصيدة في المسائل الاعتقادية

(3) pp. 16–28. *Qaṣīdat al-Adhkiyā'* (title on p. 28), or just *Adhkiyā'* (title in the margin of p. 16). A *qaṣīda lāmiyya* of 188 distichs, of mostly ethical content, arranged by subject (number of distichs between brackets), introduction (16), al-Tawba (6), al-Qināʿa (2), al-Zuhd (6), Taʿlīm al-Sharʿī (2), al-Muḥāfaẓa ʿalā al-Sunan (9), al-Tawakkul (3), al-Ikhlāṣ (8), al-ʿAzla (9), Ḥifẓ al-Awqāt (12), Ṣalāt al-Ishrāq (4), Ādāb al-Tālī (12), Ṣalāt al-Ḍuḥā (9), Taṣḥīḥ al-Niyya bil-ʿIlm (9), ʿAlāmat man yaqṣud al-Taʿallum (6), ʿAlāmat ʿUlamā' al-Ākhira (21), Ādāb al-Mutaʿallim (12), Ādāb al-Akl (4), Istiʿdād Ṣalāt al-Ẓuhr (5), Ādāb al-Nawm (2), al-Tahağğud (5), Muʿīn al-Tahağğud (9), Muhimma (4), Muğāhada (5), Mushāhada (8). On p. 25 the student is advised to study the *Iḥyā'* by al-Ghazzālī. On p. 27 al-Imām al-Suhrawardi is mentioned.

First line of the *qaṣīda* (p. 16):

(بسملة) وبه نستعين،
الحمد لله الموفق للعلى * حمدا يوافي برّه المتكاملا

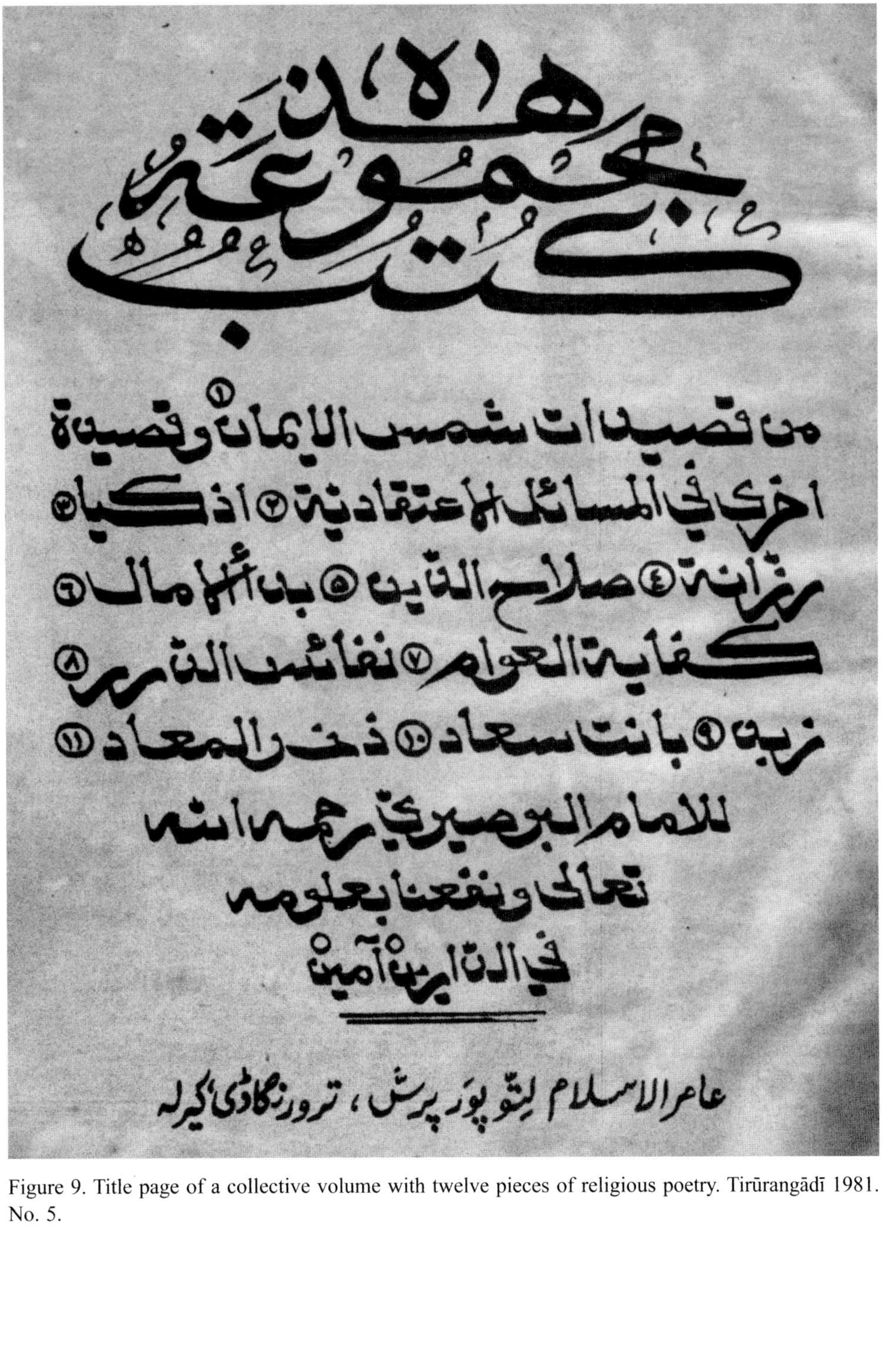
هذه مجموعة كتب

من قصيدات شمس الإيمان ① وقصيدة أخرى في المسائل الاعتقادية ② أذكيا ③ رزانة ④ صلاح الدين ⑤ بدء الأمال ⑥ كفاية العوام ⑦ نفائس الدرر ⑧ زبد ⑨ بانت سعاد ⑩ ذخر المعاد ⑪

للإمام البوصيري رحمه الله تعالى ونفعنا بعلومه في الدارين آمين

عامر الاسلام لیتھو پریس، ترورنگادی، کیرلہ

Figure 9. Title page of a collective volume with twelve pieces of religious poetry. Tirūrangādī 1981. No. 5.

Last line of the *qaṣīda* (pp. 27–28):

والحمد لله الباقي الرؤف مصليا * اعلى الصلاة على الرسول محوقلا ||
تمت قصيدة الاذكياء وتليها قصيدة رزانة

(4) pp. 28–39. *Qaṣīda Razzāna* (title on p. 28) or simply *Razzāna* (margin of p. 28). The title is derived from the first line. The *qaṣida* is a poem of changing rhyme, consisting in all of 205 distichs. First line of the *qaṣīda* (p. 28):

(بسملة) وبه نستعين،
رزانة العلم من كانت تثقله * يمشي بها خاضعا مقدارا تقال

Last line of the *qaṣīda* (p. 39):

مثل الاوزّ ولا درّ وغربال * كن يا فتى عند تعليم الاساتيذ
تمت قصيدة المباركة بعون الله الملك الوهاب

(5) pp. 39–46. *Qaṣīdat Ṣalāḥ al-Dīn* (title on p. 46, author's name in the first line: Ṣalāḥ al-Dīn b. Dāwud), short title *Ṣalāḥ al-Dīn* in the margin of p. 39. A *qaṣīda mīmiyya* of 132 distichs. First line of the *qaṣīda* (p. 39):

(بسملة) وبه نستعين،
يقول من بصلاح الدين قد وسما * ابوه باسم ابن داود فشا وسما

Last line of the *qaṣīda* (p. 46):

وآله العظما وصحبه الكرما * ما حركت عنما قمرية نعما
تمت قصيدة صلاح الدين بعون الله مالك يوم الدين

(6) pp. 47–51. *Badʾ al-Amālī.* This is *al-Qaṣīda al-Lāmiyya fīl-Tawḥīd* (or: *Badʾ al-Amālī* as written in the margin of p. 47, or: *Qaṣīdat yaqūl al-ʿAbd*), by ʿAlī b. ʿUthmān al-Ūshī (c. 569/1173), GAL G I, 429. The *qaṣīda lāmiyya* counts 98 distichs. First line of the *qaṣīda* (p. 47):

(بسملة) وبه نستعين،
يقول العبد في بدأ الامالي * بتوحيد بنظم كالألي

Last line of the *qaṣīda* (p. 51):

وصحبته الكرام ذوي عفاف * بعدد القطر والترب الرمال
تمت الكتاب بعون الله الملك الوهاب برحمتك يا ارحم الراحمين،

(7) pp. 51–55. *Qaṣīdat Kifāyat al-ʿAwāmm* (title on p. 55), or shortly *Kifāyat al-ʿAwāmm* (margin of p. 51). Anonymous *qaṣīda* of varying rhymes, containing 69 distichs. First line of the *qaṣīda* (p. 51):

(بسملة) وبه نستعين،
ابدأ بسم الله والرحمن * وبالرحيم دائم الاحسان

Last line of the *qaṣīda* (p. 55):

عامله الله بلطفه الخفي * وخفه بخير سره الوفي
تمت قصيدة كفاية العوام

(8) pp. 55–66. A *qaṣīda rāʾiyya* taken from a work (or *dīwān*?) entitled *Kitāb Nafāʾis al-Durar fī Tawḥīd al-Malik al-Muqtadar wa-Madḥ Sayyidinā Muḥammad Khayr al-Bashar* (title on p. 55, short title *Nafāʾis al-Durar* in the margin of p. 56). The *qaṣīda* consists of 150 distichs and is divided into two parts, first *ʿaqāʾid*, then *madḥ*. The part on *ʿaqāʾid* consists of the answer (*ǧawāb*) to nine questions. The part on *madḥ* (*al-nabī*) seems to have been taken from another *qaṣīda rāʾiyya* (with the name *al-Durar*, see the *khātima* on p. 65) and is divided into different subjects. Beginning of the prose introduction (p. 55):

(بسملة)
الحمد لله رب العالمين، والصلوة والسلام على سيد المرسلين، وعلى اله وصحبه اجمعين، **وبعد** فمن
كتاب نفائس الدرر، في توحيد الملك المقتدر، ومدح سيدنا محمد خير البشر ... قصيدة ابياتها مائة
وخمسون كلها مستويات الاعاريض والضروب، ...

First line of the *qaṣīda* (p. 56):

(بسملة)
حمدلت حمدا وافيا حق الشكر * اهل الثنا آلاؤه لا تنخصر

Last line of the *qaṣīda* (pp. 65–66):

تمت بعون الله اذ هان العسر * حمدلت حمدا وافيا حق الشكر
الحمد لله رب العالمين اولا واخرا وظاهرا وباطنا وعلانية وسرا وصلى الله || على خير خلقه سيدنا
محمد وآله وصحبه اجمعين برحمتك يا ارحم الراحمين، آمين،

(9) pp. 66–131. *Zubad* (title in the margin of p. 66). This *Urǧūza* on matters of Islamic law according to the Shafiʿite *madhhab* is the work known as *Ṣafwat al-Zubad* by Abū al-ʿAbbās Aḥmad b. Raslān al-Bārizī (d. 738/1337), GAL G II, 96. The arrangement of the material is as usual with works on *furūʿ*, although here (p. 66) the chapter on *ṭahāra* is preceded by an introductory chapter entitled *muqaddima fī ʿilm al-uṣūl*. First line of the *urǧūza* (p. 66):

(بسملة)
الحمد للاله ذي الجلال * وشارع الحرام والحلال

Last line of the *urǧūza* (p. 131):

والآل والصحب ومن لهم قفا * وحسبنا الله تعالى وكفى
تم الكتاب بعون الله الملك الوهاب برحمتك يا ارحم الراحمين وصلى الله على خير خلقه سيدنا محمد
واله وصحبه اجمعين،

(10) pp. 131–135. *Qaṣīdat Kaʿb b. Zuhayr al-Sulamī* (title and author on p. 131). This is the *Qaṣīdat al-Burda* by Kaʿb b. Zuhayr (1st cent. AH), GAL G I, 39. First line of the *qaṣīda lāmiyya* (p. 131):

هذه قصيدة كعب بن زهير السلمي رضي الله عنه
(بسملة)
بانت سعاد فقلبي اليوم متبول * متيّم اثرها لم يفد مكبول

Last line of the *qaṣīda* (pp. 134–135):

والآل والصحب هم بهم وبهلول * والتابعين لهم ما لالا اللولو ||
تمت القصيدة بعون الله الملك المنان،

(11) pp. 135–146. *Qaṣīdat Dhakhr al-Maʿād*, by al-Būṣūrī (title and author's name on p. 135). The title has been read as *Dhakhr*. The author is possibly the same as Muḥammad b. Saʿīd al-Būṣīrī (d. 694/1294), GAL G I, 264. The *qaṣīda lāmiyya* contains 204 distichs. First line of the *qaṣīda* (p. 135):

هذه قصيدة مسماة بدخر المعاد للامام الفاضل البوصورى
(بسملة)
الى متى انت بالذات مشغول * وانت عن كل ما قدمت مسئول

Last line of the *qaṣīda* (p. 146):

ما لاح ضوء صباح فاستسرّ به * من الكواكب قنديل فقنديل
تمت القصيدة المباركة بعون الله الملك الوهاب،

(12) pp. 146–147. *al-Kāf al-Arbaʿūn* by al-Shaykh Muḥyī al-Dīn al-Ğīlānī, three distichs in which a total of forty letters *kāf* are a used. The name of the author, which is mentioned on p. 147, may be a contamination of the names of Muḥyī al-Dīn Ibn al-ʿArabī and ʿAbd al-Qādir al-Ğīlānī.

هذا الكلام المبارك امّا الهي الهامي خطاب من الله تعالى لعبده الملهم اليه او لكل عبد راجع اليه
تعالى امّا بخصوصه كما هو مدلول اللفظ او لعمومه باعتبار الباء القريبة او مع البعيدة كما هو
عرف القرآن قال الله واذ نجيناكم من ال فرعون وقال تعالى واذ فرقنا بكم البحر وقال جلّ ذكره يا
بني اسرآئيل اذكروا نعمتي التي انعمت عليكم والى غير ذلك، || واما كلام الشيخ محيي الدين
الجيلاني قدس الله سره وافاض علينا من بركاته بالخطاب العام او بالمريدين خاصة او من باب
الالتفات مع صفة التجريد وهو الموفق لقوله الآتي كفاك الى آخره،
(بسملة)
كفاك ربك كم يكفيك واكفة * كف كافيا ككمين كان من كلكا
تكرّ كرّا ككرّ الكرّ في كبد * تحكي مشكشكة كلّت لك الكلكا
كفاك ما بي كفاك الكاف كربته * يا كوكبا كان تحكي كوكب الفلكا
تمت الكاف الاربعون

Here follows the printer's colophon, in which God's blessing is invoked for both the owner's of the printing presses and the calligrapher who wrote the texts:

هجرة ١٤٠١ جمادى الاولى ١عيسوي ١٩٨١مارچ ٨ دّ ترورغادي . سي. اچهـ. محمد آنرسنسر
عامر الاسلام لثو پور پرسل اد كيپدت. كان الله لمالي المطابع ولمن خطها في الدين والدنيا
والآخرة،

On p. 148 is a list of books published by this same publisher Muḥammad Ānrsansr of the ʾĀmir al-Islām Litho Power Press in Tirurangadi, Kerala (which is treated hereafter). The publisher's imprint is on the back cover (as in no. 2).

## OTHER PUBLICATIONS FROM THE SAME PUBLISHERS

On the final pages of two editions (nos 5 and 2) there are lists of publications by the same publishing house.

In 1981, the publisher, C.H. Muḥammad Ānrsans in Tirurangadi, Kerala, offers the following titles for sale (no. 5):

> Murshid al-Ṭullāb, Naḥw al-Kitāb, Kifāyat al-ʿAwāmm (Naẓm), Riyāḍ al-Badīʿa, Dhakhāʾir al-Ikhwān, Qaṣīdat al-Witriyya, Tuḥfat al-Ikhwān, Ēžkitāb, ʿAsharat Kutub, Fatḥ al-Muʿīn, ʿUmdat al-Sālik, Nafāʾis al-Artaḍiyya, Taṣrīḥ al-Manṭiq, Taʿlīm al-Mutaʿallim, Qaṣīdat al-Hamziyya, Irshād al-ʿIbād, Tafsīr al-Ǧalālayn (ačadīl).

Two years later, In 1983, the publisher, C.H. Muḥammad Ānrsans, Āmir al-Islam Power Press in Tirurangadi, Kerala, offers the following titles for sale (no. 2):

> Tafsīr al-Ǧalālayn, ʿUmdat al-Sālik wa-ʿUddat al-Nāsik, Irshād al-ʿIbād, al-Qaṣīda fil-Suʾāl wal-Ǧawāb, Mukhammas al-Witriyya, al-Qaṣīdāt (bīt kitāb), Taʿlīm al-Mutaʿallim, Alfiyyat Ibn Mālik, Tuḥfat al-Ikhwān, Nafāʾis al-Artaḍiyya, Fatḥ al-Muʿīn bi-Sharḥ Qurrat al-ʿAyn, Riyāḍ al-Badīʿ maʿa Safīnat al-Ṣalāt, Murshid al-Ṭullāb, Manḥūmat ʿAqīdat al-Anām, Qaṣīdat al-Witriyya, Zīnat al-Qārī, Kitāb al-Naḥw, Kitāb al-Samarqandī, Taṣrīḥ al-Manṭiq, Risālat al-Mārdīn.

## CONCLUSION

The present descriptions of the thirty-five Arabic school texts from Kerala give a first impression of some of the material available. It is a first attempt to describe and characterize this material, of which we may assume that much greater quantities and varieties exist. The textbooks from this remote corner of the Islamic world, which, however, has a long standing Islamic tradition, are not or nearly not bibliographically known, let alone described. That in itself is a sufficient reason to describe them. Within the wider framework of the study of peripheral Islamic scholarship in which I am engaged they form an interesting corpus produced in a typical style of their own, not comparable to any sort of schoolbooks in other regions on the periphery, and apparently unaffected by the streams of books pouring from the great book producing centres of the Islamic world.

## A TITLE INDEX OF THE TEXTS DESCRIBED ABOVE

*Ağnās al-Kubrā* 1 (3)
*al-Alfiyya* 3
*Arkān al-Īmān* 2 (2)
*ʿAwāmil* 1 (5)
*ʿAyn al-Hudā bi-Sharḥ Qaṭr al-Nadā wal-Sharḥ lil-ʿĀlim al-ʿAllāma al-Shaykh ʿUthmān* 1 (9)
*Badʾ al-Amālī* 5 (6)
*Faṣl fī Ağnās al-Afʿāl* 1 (2)
*Fatḥ al-Raḥmān fil-Islām wal-Īmān* 2 (5)
*Iḥyānrūṣawm* 2 (7)
*ʿIshrūn Ṣifa* 2 (3)
*al-Kāf al-Arbaʿūn* 5 (12)
*Kifāyat al-ʿAwāmm* 5 (7)
*Kitāb al-Sanūsī* 2 (4)
*al-Minhāğ* 2 (1)
*Mīzān* 1 (1)
*Mukhtaṣar Arkān al-Nikāḥ* 2 (6)
*Mukhtaṣar al-Minhāğ* 2 (1)
*Nafāʾis al-Durar fī Tawḥīd al-Malik al-Muqtadar wa-Madḥ Sayyidinā Muḥammad Khayr al-Bashar* 5 (8)
*Qaṣīdat al-Adhkiyāʾ* 5 (3)
*Qaṣīdat al-Burda* 5 (10)
*Qaṣīdat Dhakhr al-Maʿād* 5 (11)
*Qaṣīdat Kaʿb b. Zuhayr al-Sulamī* 5 (10)
*Qaṣīdat Kifāyat al-ʿAwāmm* 5 (7)
*al-Qaṣīda al-Lāmiyya fil-Tawḥīd* 5 (6)
*Qaṣīda Razzāna* 5 (4)
*Qaṣidat Ṣalāḥ al-Dīn* 5 (5)
*Qaṣīdat Shams al-Īmān fī Tawḥīd al-Raḥmān wa-ʿAqīdat Ahl al-Ḥaqq wal-Itqān* 5 (1)
*Qaṣīda Ukhra wa-hiya Mushtamila ʿalā al-Masāʾil al-Iʿtiqādiyya al-Ḍarūriyya* 5 (2)
*Qaṣīdat yaqūl al-ʿAbd* 5 (6)
*Qaṭr al-Nadā wa-Ball al-Ṣadā* 1 (9), 1 (10)
*Qayd al-Jāmiʿ* 2 (6)
*Ṣafwat al-Zubad* 5 (9)
*Sharḥ Āmantu billāh* 2 (2)
*Sharḥ al-Khulāṣa al-Alfiyya* 3
*Sharḥ Qaṭr al-Nadā lil-ʿĀlim al-ʿAllāma al-Shaykh ʿUthmān* 1 (9)
*Shawāhid al-Alfiyya* 3
*Shawāhid al-Qaṭr* 1 (10)
*Shawāhid al-Tuḥfa al-Wardiyya* 1 (8)
*Taqwīm al-Lisān* 1 (6)
*al-Tuḥfa al-Wardiyya wa-Sharḥ hādhihi al-Tuḥfa al-Wardiyya* 1 (7)
*ʿUmdat al-Sālik wa-ʿUddat al-Nāsik* 4
*Umm al-Barāhīn* 2 (3)
*Zanğān* 1 (4)
*Zubad* 5 (9)